"*Suffragette City* provides many surprises. These lively essays document women's activist coalitions aimed at reforming housing and the built environment in several national contexts. Highly recommended for readers interested in the history of feminism, architecture, and city life."

– *Dolores Hayden, author of The Grand Domestic Revolution: A History of Feminist Designs for American Homes, Neighborhoods, and Cities, Professor Emerita, Yale University*

"*Suffragette City: Gender, Politics and the Built Environment* is a wonderful book—a remarkable, timely achievement. Clearly written with verve and with conviction, and using little-known and important examples, the authors share stories of women in architecture and their work to build a better, more just, more equitable world. It is indispensable reading for architects, activists, historians, and women everywhere."

– *Marta Gutman, The City College of New York and the CUNY Graduate Center*

"In the spirit of Emmeline Pankhurst, this valuable collection of histories emphasizes "deeds, not words": *Suffragette City* describes a metaphorical place where women design and preserve their cities, transform the professions that marginalized them, and reinvent their homes and architecture in ways previously unimagined by men. It is also, in the end, a call for new deeds to achieve equal rights to the city and to the professions that shape the built environment."

– *Peter L. Laurence, author of Becoming Jane Jacobs*

I0802326

SUFFRAGETTE CITY

Suffragette City brings together a collection of illustrated essays dedicated to exploring and analysing cases in which women have resourcefully leveraged or defied the politics of gender to form and reform architecture and urbanism. Throughout much of modern history, women have been assigned to the margins and expected to play passive social roles. *Suffragette City* draws on nineteenth- and twentieth-century architectural case studies from the English-speaking world, including the USA, South Africa, Scotland, India and England, to examine places and moments when women stepped into the centre of public life and claimed opportunities to shape the fabrics of their communities. Their engagements with the built environment consistently transcended architecture to achieve the level of urbanism, as whole networks of relationships came into their purview, transforming the architecture of socio-political connection as well as confronting the physical divisions that have historically lain along racial, economic and gendered lines. Academics, researchers and students engaged in architectural history, theory, urbanism, gender studies and social and cultural history will be interested in this fascinating, politically-charged text.

Elizabeth Darling is Reader in Architectural History in the School of History, Philosophy and Culture, Oxford Brookes University, UK.

Nathaniel Robert Walker is an Assistant Professor of Architectural History at the College of Charleston, South Carolina, USA.

SUFFRAGETTE CITY

Women, Politics and the Built Environment

Edited by Elizabeth Darling and Nathaniel Robert Walker

Routledge
Taylor & Francis Group
LONDON AND NEW YORK

First published 2020
by Routledge
2 Park Square, Milton Park, Abingdon, Oxon OX14 4RN

and by Routledge
52 Vanderbilt Avenue, New York, NY 10017

Routledge is an imprint of the Taylor & Francis Group, an informa business

British Library Cataloguing-in-Publication Data
A catalogue record for this book is available from the British Library

Library of Congress Cataloging-in-Publication Data
Names: Darling, Elizabeth, editor. | Walker, Nathaniel Robert, editor.
Title: Suffragette city : gender, politics and the built environment / edited by Elizabeth Darling and Nathaniel Robert Walker.
Identifiers: LCCN 2019024824 (print) | LCCN 2019024825 (ebook) | ISBN 9781138571631 (hardback) | ISBN 9781138571648 (paperback) | ISBN 9780203702628 (ebook)
Subjects: LCSH: Architecture and women. | Space (Architecture)–Social aspects.
Classification: LCC NA2543.W65 S84 2020 (print) | LCC NA2543.W65 (ebook) | DDC 720.82–dc23
LC record available at https://lccn.loc.gov/2019024824
LC ebook record available at https://lccn.loc.gov/2019024825

ISBN: 978-1-138-57163-1 (hbk)
ISBN: 978-1-138-57164-8 (pbk)
ISBN: 978-0-203-70262-8 (ebk)

Typeset in Bembo
by Swales & Willis, Exeter, Devon, UK

CONTENTS

CONTRIBUTORS

Ann Marie Borys is an architect and Associate Professor of Architecture at the University of Washington. Previous publications include *Vincenzo Scamozzi and the Chorography of Early Modern Architecture* (Ashgate 2014) and contributions to *Architecture as a Performing Art* (Ashgate, 2013) and *Modernism and American Mid-20th Century Sacred Architecture* (Routledge, 2018).

Elizabeth Darling is Reader in Architectural History at Oxford Brookes University, UK. Her research focuses on inter-war modernism, the environments of social welfare reform, and gender. Her publications include *Re-forming Britain: Narratives of Modernity before Reconstruction* (Routledge, 2007), *Women and the Making of Built Space in England, 1870–1940* (Ashgate, 2007) co-edited with Lesley Whitworth, *Wells Coates* (RIBA Publications, 2012) as well as numerous articles for journals including the *Journal of British Studies* and *Gender and History*. Most recently, with Lynne Walker, she co-curated the exhibition, 'AA XX 100: AA Women in Architecture 1917–2017', which commemorated the centenary of women's entry to the Architectural Association School of Architecture, and co-edited the accompanying book, *AA Women in Architecture 1917–2017* (AA Publications, 2017). She serves as adviser to the *Oxford Dictionary of National Biography* on widening the coverage of women architects, and is currently writing a history of the material and spatial culture of broadcasting in inter-war England, with a focus on the design of BBC Broadcasting House and the wireless sets of the pioneering manufacturer ECKO Ltd.

Erin McKellar is Assistant Curator, Exhibitions at Sir John Soane's Museum in London. Her research centres on the role of women and children in the design cultures of the 1930s and 1940s. She recently published 'Designing the Child's World: Ernö Goldfinger and the Role of the Architect, 1933–1946' in the

Journal of Design History (2019). Her current book project, 'From Aircraft to Housecraft: Exhibiting the Family Home in the U.S. and Britain, 1940–1950', investigates how the rhetoric and display strategies of housing exhibitions in the two nations revealed the Allied Forces' political goals while creating an audience for modern architecture. She has previously been a Fellow of the Paul Mellon Centre for Studies in British Art in London and the Clarence S. Stein Institute for Urban and Landscape Studies at Cornell University in New York.

Aparna Parikh is a feminist urban geographer and currently an Andrew W. Mellon Postdoctoral Fellow at Dartmouth College. Her research focuses on gendered dimensions of globalisation, environmental change, and labour dynamics in relation to urbanisation in South Asia. She examines how women navigate and negotiate urban belonging within capitalist heteropatriarchal systems. Her work has been published in *Gender, Place & Culture*, and is forthcoming in *ACME: An International Journal for Critical Geographies.*

Jacqueline Taylor received her PhD in art and architectural history from the University of Virginia in 2014. With a focus on race, gender, and sexuality, her research spans the urban environment and art of ninteenth- and twentieth-century United States. She has published on early twentieth-century architecture, urbanism, and art history in edited volumes and anthologies, including with the University of Virginia Press, Oxford University Press, and Routledge.

Katie Lloyd Thomas is Professor of Theory and History of Architecture at Newcastle University where she co-directs the Architecture Research Collaborative (ARC). Publications include *Material Matters* (Routledge, 2007) and with Tilo Amhoff and Nick Beech, *Industries of Architecture* (Routledge, 2015). Her research often examines intersections between gender, architecture, and technology.

Sharóne L. Tomer is an Assistant Professor in the School of Architecture + Design at Virginia Polytechnic Institute and State University (Virginia Tech), where she teaches architectural design and urbanism courses. She holds a PhD in Architecture from the University of California, Berkeley, and has worked in architectural practice designing innovative community housing. Her research and writing focus on architectural responses to urban inequality, with attention to issues of race, gender, and class. She is currently writing a monograph about architectural dimensions of apartheid's end in Cape Town, South Africa.

Nathaniel Robert Walker is Assistant Professor of Architectural History at the College of Charleston. He earned his PhD at Brown University, and studies the relationships between architecture, public space, and the socio-political power networks that seek to drive their forms and uses. He is also concerned with quests for the 'good life' – with dreams of the past and the future, and how these affect our actions in and perceptions of the present. Much of his research has focused on visions of paradise and on the utopian dreams of modernity that have proliferated in modern literature, film, advertising, and other media.

Catherine W. Zipf is an award-winning architectural historian and author with expertise in historic preservation. Her research examines women's participation in American architectural and decorative arts history during the nineteenth and twentieth centuries. She earned an AB from Harvard University and a MaH and PhD from the University of Virginia. Her book, *Professional Pursuits: Women and the American Arts and Crafts Movement* (University of Tennessee Press) was named Outstanding Academic Book by *Choice* Magazine.

Zipf writes frequently for a range of publications, including *The Providence Journal* and the *National Trust for Historic Preservation's Leadership Forum Blog*, and for organisations such as Docomomo and Architexx.com. She is a contributing author to the anthologies *Monuments to the Lost Cause* (University of Tennessee Press, 2003), *A Gendered Profession* (RIBA Publishing, 2016), and *Peanuts and American Culture* (McFarland, 2019). She has also written scholarly articles for *Buildings and Landscapes, American Periodicals, The Journal of City, Culture, and Architecture*, and *Radical Teacher.* Her research has been supported by The National Trust for Historic Preservation, The Massachusetts Institute of Technology, and The Beverly Willis Architecture Foundation. She is currently writing her second book, *Making a Home of Her Own: Newport's Architectural Patronesses, 1850–1940*, while serving as the Executive Director of the Bristol Historical and Preservation Society.

ACKNOWLEDGEMENTS

Suffragette City: Women, Politics and the Built Environment has its origins in a conference with a nearly identical title held in 2016 at the College of Charleston, South Carolina. We would like to thank all of the people and institutions who made that conference so rewarding, including Gayle Goudy, who helped to organise it, and Marta Gutman, who served as its keynote speaker.

As editors we must acknowledge the help and support of a great number of people.

Elizabeth Darling would like to acknowledge the support of the Research Fund of the School of History, Philosophy and Culture, Oxford Brookes University, in the preparation of this book, and thank her colleagues in the School for the creation of an atmosphere conducive to balancing teaching and research. Nathaniel Robert Walker is grateful to the Art and Architectural History Department, the Historic Preservation and Community Planning Program and the School of the Arts at the College of Charleston for their unfailing professional support and camaraderie. He is also grateful to the leadership and staff of the Preservation Society of Charleston and to Harlan Greene of the Special Collections Department of the College of Charleston for their kind and knowledgeable research assistance. Finally, he is very thankful to his wife, Sally Caithness, for her perpetual kindness, wise counsel and exemplary skills as a historian and graphic designer.

We are grateful to Grace Harrison and Aoife McGrath at Routledge for their help, support, and guidance in bringing this manuscript to fruition. We are also thankful to the blind peer reviewers who evaluated this book, both as a whole and as individual chapters. In every case, their insightful criticisms and suggestions were extremely valuable, helping our project reach its fullest potential. To our contributors we owe a great debt of thanks for their spirits of collaboration, the richness of their writing, the depth of their research, and the power of their ideas.

ABOUT THE COVER

The photograph used on the front and back covers of this book features the German actress Hedwig Reicher, dressed as Columbia, a personification of America, as she helped lead a 'Suffrage Parade' on March 3, 1913. During this event, women, young girls, and their supporters flooded the streets and occupied the public spaces of Washington, DC – in the case of this photograph, the steps of the Treasury Building – as part of the nationwide struggle to claim the right to vote.

The photo was originally taken by Bain News Service and is now in the collection of the Library of Congress (call number LC-B2- 2501-14). Courtesy of the Library of Congress.

INTRODUCTION

Elizabeth Darling and Nathaniel Robert Walker

In the final chapter of this book, Aparna Parikh opens her discussion with an apparent throwaway remark from 'Anushi', one of the Mumbai call-center workers on whose break-time behavior Parikh's research focuses. It was Anushi's habit – and that of many of her fellow (female) workers – to use the brief respites between answering English-language enquiries from around the world to step outside, into the night-time city, to claim a piece of the ground and a bit of the open air for herself and her friends, smoke a cigarette, and perhaps enjoy a mug of *chai*. She was puzzled that Parikh was fascinated by what seemed like a private act – a way to alleviate the personal strain of talking to disgruntled customers of global corporations, whose demands she could never quite satisfy. Why, she asked, was her smoking anyone's business but her own? Yet, as Parikh and this book seek to show, it is everyone's business.

Anushi's decision to step out in the dead of night into the urban public space of a globalizing city such as Mumbai to smoke a cigarette, is, in its disruption and transgression of contemporary Indian gender norms, a small but significant twenty-first century episode in the politics of women and space that this book charts. We are interested in the ways that women, both historically and today, have taken up the making, appropriation, and remaking of the built environment, both to satisfy their own personal desires and as portions of larger struggles of great social significance. Time and again, we have found that despite – or perhaps because of – the longstanding practice of precluding or marginalizing female architects, women have, just like Anushi, transcended the traditional gendered boundaries of their societies and the traditional disciplinary boundaries of architecture to reform their environments and make space in bold new ways. When tradition asserted, for example, that women should constrain themselves to the role of housekeeper, they stormed into the streets, declared that the whole city was a common house shared by all, and claimed their right to keep it as they saw fit. Indeed, it is the contention of this book that many became pioneering examples of what we would today call urbanists, which is to say they came to think and operate beyond discreet spaces and buildings, reaching the scale of streets, neighborhoods, districts, and whole settlements, and they did so long before the academic discipline of urban studies existed and leaders such as Jane Jacobs and Edmund Bacon emerged, and well before most professional architects recognized that such a complex role could and should be played by anyone, let alone by women. Some of the women studied in this book were architects; most of them were not. In the process of their work, some of them gained considerable power, while others chose to remain anonymous. Whichever their status in their own times and places, today most have been forgotten or are deeply underappreciated, which is a disservice both to them and to us, and another reason we have chosen to create this book.

In our concern to construct a mode of historical writing that includes rather than excludes women's praxis, we find ourselves at an exciting time to study the history of women in architecture. Both past achievements and future prospects make clear the richness of feminist approaches to architectural history and design. Studies that were ground breaking in their time, such as Dolores Hayden's *The Grand Domestic Revolution* of 1981 and Alice Friedman's *Women and the Making of the Modern House* of 1998, have by now become canonical works, laying firm foundations that have supported many additional layers of more inclusive history and more enlightened criticism and practice.[1] In 2017, Britain's Architectural Association School of Architecture celebrated its first hundred years of including women with a major exhibition and book entitled *AA Women in Architecture 1917–2017*.[2] As Chapters 5 and 6 of this volume reveal, the first decades of women's participation in this key institution were not clear sailing, but it is nonetheless indisputable that a century's worth of increasingly liberated practise has made architecture a richer and more just discipline, and the recent exhibition offered vivid documentation of these hard-won improvements. Meanwhile, other scholars, critics, and practitioners are turning their eyes to the emerging horizon. The recent edited volume *Architecture and Feminisms*, for example, worked to identify ways that the past, present, and future of feminist practice might help inform broad efforts to pull the world back from the brink of social and ecological collapse, reforming architecture to make it less complicit with the short-sighted systems of exploitation that are killing our planet.[3]

Suffragette City is situated, in some ways, between these two recent milestones, hoping to achieve something akin to the global, even as it stays rooted in the local. The chapters herein work to trace concrete, detailed historical connections between gendered political struggle and the built environment, touching upon interconnected discourses in politics and design that have emerged across time and space in different contexts and communities that shared the English language and, to varied extents, a common history of imperial oppression and resistance. Our contributors work to unite and compare urban reform efforts tied, for example, to the provision of working-class public kindergartens in both Edinburgh and Michigan, slum remediation in London and in New York, grassroots feminine resistance against political and spatial marginalization in the racist and misogynist environments of Petersburg, Virginia and the South African cities of Durban and Cape Town, and debates about the proper presence of female agency in the squares and streets of Rhode Island and Mumbai. Similarly, the chapters of this book show how women have creatively constructed spaces to support themselves and their agendas both within existing environments – sometimes by preserving and/or modifying them, as was the case in London and Charleston, South Carolina – and sometimes through the formation of new forms of design practice both without and within architecture, as happened in early twentieth-century Rochester in upstate New York, interwar London, and wartime Britain and the US. In all of these spaces and places, struggles by women to achieve greater autonomy and power in the political sphere were accompanied by changes in the physical fabric of communities, including both private and public realms. Across a period of nearly two hundred years women in these interconnected cities and nations looked abroad and looked within, engaging with shifting notions and systems of tradition, modernity, gender, and politics as they agitated and voted, worked and played, bought and sold, praised or shamed, empowered or opposed; in response, the streets trembled and buildings rose and fell. Women have been, are, and will remain city-makers.

The method of this book is persistently and primarily historical, but it is intended that the knowledge of the past thus gained will shine critical light on the possibilities for future reform, particularly in our urban places. Of particular value for future practitioners is the power of the women studied in this book to conceptualize and engage with incredibly complex, nuanced systems of relationships – between people of different backgrounds, between people and buildings, between the private and public realms, between economics and art, between different cultural values, and other such nodes of social, political, and spatial construction. Everywhere that they encountered the limitations of simplistic thinking in both politics and architecture – including complacency with injustice and misery, as well as prejudice against the capacities of women – they responded with defiant complexity. Their work designing, appropriating, and reforming built environments, whether cast in stone or greensward, whether framed by historical interpretation or social media, was accordingly rich.

Divided into three parts, the chapters that make up *Suffragette City* offer focused case studies that document, often for the first time, the activities of women, working both individually and, more often, collectively and collaboratively to create environments that better fitted their needs and values. A common theme in the chapters that comprise Part I, 'Reconfiguring communities,' is one of creating spatial refuges from oppressive systems or powers, and thereby providing stages for personal resistance and community realization. Both Elizabeth Darling's discussion of the coming together of women of all classes in Edinburgh to make redemptive spaces in urban slums and Jaqueline Taylor's analysis of Amaza Lee Meredith's design for a house for her and her partner, Edna Colson, show how domestic (or quasi-domestic) spaces can offer, as bell hooks puts it, 'homeplace,' shelters from the dehumanizing tendencies of exploitative social and political systems, whether these are raw capitalism or violent racism.[4] Nathaniel Robert Walker's focus on the rise of the historic preservation movement in Charleston, South Carolina, is also a tale of community resistance. It has long been known that some of the first public calls to understand and honor historic architecture were issued by women, but it has not yet been appreciated how often these calls were joined to radiantly modern hopes for social reform fueling urban vitality, and how many women realized that all of the above could only be achieved if the shallow materialist values of capitalism were mitigated by education and virtue, both private and public.

If these first three chapters gave rise to specific and tangible (if not always permanent) marks on the built environment, those in Part II, 'Pathfinding in the professions,' show how women developed new or alternative modes of spatial practice in the face of professional hegemonies which resisted, deliberately or otherwise, women's participation. Ann Marie Borys traces the diverse career of Caroline Bartlett Crane from Unitarian minister to 'Minister of Municipalities,' creating hybrid ecclesiastical-domestic spaces in the churches that she commissioned in Michigan, before creating a new career for herself as a sanitation and urban reform consultant and ultimately an expert in modern domestic space. Katie Lloyd Thomas complicates our understanding of women's agency and the gender of architecture within the interwar architectural profession in Britain through her focus on the Building Centre. This admixture of retail space and industrial display office provided expert advice on proprietary building products to architects, thus turning them into shoppers – a 'feminine' activity. Erin McKellar makes similar links between the technologies available to architects but in her instance shows how female architects such as Hilde Reiss and Jane Drew, excluded from the war work available to male colleagues, recast themselves as expert advisers in both the interior planning and equipment of wartime housing and in anticipation of reconstruction after the war. Pushed to the margins, they ended up impacting the daily lives of thousands, and, through a skillful command of print media and display space, worked to sustain vibrant public discourses on the ideal methods and materials of modern design.

If many of the chapters thus far move between the scale of the domestic to the public and back again, the final part of the book, 'Staking claims to urban space,' focuses more directly on the open, shared public spaces of the city. Catherine Zipf explores how very quickly class and gender became a contentious issue when a project to redesign a public square in Newport, Rhode Island, was initiated. The nearly mythological legacy of a bygone lady preservationist was pitted against the threatening modernity of a usurper female architect, and the ideal role of women in the shaping of city life was ultimately put to tumultuous public trial. The intersections of class, race, and sexism are also the focus in Sharóne L. Tomer's chapter. Her focus on how these tensions played out in South Africa both during and after apartheid emphasizes how women there have been disempowered by multiple layers of prejudice and exclusion, but also how, through canny and subtle strategies, they have worked collectively to subvert and overcome those restrictions, often choosing urban sites as their battlegrounds. Returning to Aparna Parikh's chapter, which is the final contribution to *Suffragette City*, we find a reiteration of many of the book's themes. She situates Anushi's decision to smoke outside within wider movements for social change in India, exploring how social media has been adopted by activist women to reframe public spaces and build social solidarity. In the process, she shows how small, seemingly innocent activities can, in fact, be read as signs of a gathering undercurrent.

Today, and we hope in the future, too, women continue to push from the edges to the center and make profound social, political, and architectural changes with every single step. There are many obstacles, now as in the past. Even as women march around the globe in defiance of ongoing patterns of exploitation, and even as the #MeToo movement has fostered a sense of solidarity, casting off the isolation and disempowerment that follow in the wake of abuse, it seems that the fearful and the cruel are always prepared to leverage every tool at their disposal to keep women in the shadows. We hope that the architectural and urban histories contained in this volume help to amplify the irrepressible light that creative and resourceful women have shone upon the fabrics of our communities. Their legacies, both as architectural reformers and as political leaders, promise to make our world better and brighter still.

Notes

1 Dolores Hayden, *The Grand Domestic Revolution: A History of Feminist Design for American Homes, Neighbourhoods and Cities* (Cambridge, MA & London: The MIT Press, 1981), and Alice Friedman, *Women and the Making of the Modern House: A Social and Architectural History* (New York: Harry Abrams, 1998).

2 'AA XX 100: AA Women and Architecture 1917–2017', was held at the Architectural Association, London between October and December 2017. Its accompanying book, *AA Women in Architecture 1917–2017*, edited by Elizabeth Darling and Lynne Walker, was published in October 2017 by AA Publications.

3 Hélène Frichot, Catharina Gabrielsson, Helen Runting, eds. *Architecture and Feminisms. Ecologies, Economies, Technologies* (London: Routledge, 2018).

4 bell hooks, 'Homeplace: A Site of Resistance,' in *Yearning: Race, Gender and Cultural Politics* (Boston, MA: South End Press, 1990), 47.

PART I

Reconfiguring communities

1

AN URBAN EXPERIMENT IN SPIRITUAL MOTHERHOOD

Gender, class and reform in Edwardian Edinburgh

Elizabeth Darling

The photograph shows an urban scene: a street lined with tenement buildings; washing hangs from windows; groups of women cluster around shop doorways; a lone figure, a woman, walks towards where the photographer must be standing; a small boy claps his hands excitedly, perhaps at something he has seen in the shop window (Figure 1.1). His delight translates into the movement that forever blurs his place in the historical record.

Another photograph (Figure 1.2): this time showing a domestic interior, almost certainly in one of the tenements seen in Figure 1.1. A woman sits on a bed holding a baby; a chair can just been seen on the right hand side of the frame. We infer that this might be all the furniture contained in a room that is otherwise dominated by the large fireplace. Housing the range, with ornaments and a gas lamp on its mantelpiece, it is as much a source for bodily warmth as it is for cooking.

A second domestic interior, a bedroom and this time a description only:

> it was big and full of strange objects, scents, and other mysteries. There was an electric ozone machine to purify the air. There were spirit lamps for midnight meals ... Celtic crosses, scarabs and drawings from Egypt, several Buddhas of dubious sex, eaux de Cologne and lavenders galore.[1]

These scenes – photographed or written – have been chosen as shorthands for the themes that this chapter explores. All are Scottish and depict environments that were formed in Edwardian Edinburgh. The two images were probably taken around 1908, and show life in the Canongate, the steep street that forms part of the Royal Mile, the spine of Edinburgh's Old Town, which runs from Holyrood Palace up to its famous Castle. The description takes us to the New Town, and is a recollection of the bedroom of Jane Whyte who lived at

FIGURE 1.1 View of the south side of the Canongate, Edinburgh, ca. 1908
Source: Reproduced by kind permission of the Episcopal Church of Old St Paul's, Edinburgh

number 7 Charlotte Square, part of a terrace that formed one side of arguably the grandest set piece of the city's neo-classical development, designed by Robert Adam. While at first glimpse these sites might appear to have nothing in common, as will be shown, the historical connections were strong and between them they serve to disrupt and redirect understandings of how urban environments are made, or re-made, and shed light on who has agency and who does not in this process. Gender is central to this story.

This chapter proceeds from the observation that despite decades of feminist revisionism, there remains an ongoing failure to think of urban sites generally, and, in this instance, early twentieth-century Edinburgh in particular, in terms of their female population. Equally, there is a failure to consider that women might have played some sort of active role in the spatial and material formation of the environments in which they dwelt or worked.[2] Yet, as these examples show, these were feminine landscapes; in each instance, female protagonists dominate. This chapter seeks therefore to show how we might understand such sites as the products of the ideas and labors of women, and thus foreground women's activities and concerns in our analysis of them. This will allow us to understand the historical relationship between the sites introduced above, and to comprehend the significance of that relationship, which wove the city together on a large scale, both physically and politically. In so doing, the aim is to articulate and posit a recalibration of hierarchies of significance and importance in histories of the built environment.

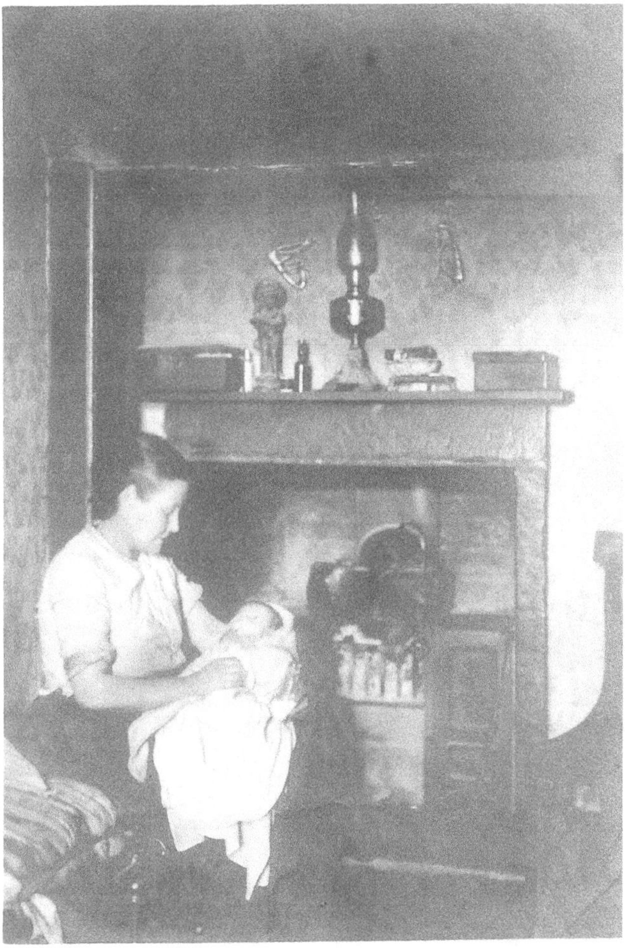

FIGURE 1.2 Tenement room interior, taken from a fundraising pamphlet, *The Life History of a Slum Child*, produced to raise funds for the St Saviour's Child Garden, Edinburgh, c. 1908

Source: Reproduced by kind permission of the Episcopal Church of Old St Paul's, Edinburgh

The photographs and description also signal a further, and often overlooked, dimension to this disruptive process of recalibration, that of class. The Edwardian Canongate was a slum. Once the locus of Edinburgh's civic and commercial life, the development of the New Town from the late eighteenth century had seen the fine stone courts and tenements of the Old Town transformed into overcrowded dwellings by waves of migrants from the Highlands and Ireland. They sought work in the industries which remained on that side of the city: gasworks, breweries and piecework conducted at home for shoe manufacturers and publishers. By the end of the nineteenth century, the majority of the figures we see in Figure 1.1, whose garb – shawls, no shoes – marks them as members of the urban working class, were the objects of much social anxiety. This, in turn, led to a wave of reform activity, which ranged from slum clearance and social work to new forms of education, and which was very often instigated and devised by women.

It was the combination of anxiety and reform that allowed figures such as that lone woman to establish a presence in this classed landscape. The confidence in her demeanor, and her clothing – matching jacket and skirt, hat, the small bag she carries – suggest someone of more certain means. She is, perhaps, a social worker or a lady rent collector; the only certitude is that she is not in this slum area because poverty has rooted her there. We do not know her name or her particular history but she was probably on this street as an agent of her own volition. A key concern in this chapter, then, is to consider how gender and class intersected to enable women such as she to lead a professional, or quasi-professional, life, as a dispenser of urban and social reform. Similarly, it seeks to ascertain the extent to which Jane Whyte's status as an upper-middle class lady enabled her to play, as we shall see, the not inconsiderable role she did in reforms enacted in the Canongate, but also limited her spatial freedom to her home in Charlotte Square. A preoccupation too is to ask how such women interacted with the working-class women at whom their activities were aimed. Did the politics of gender unite them, as Figure 1.1 seems to suggest, in a cross-class mutual endeavor to transform urban and domestic environments, or were more complex negotiations conducted across the class divide?

Such considerations matter because when historians – academic and popular alike – talk about urban reform in Edinburgh, the usual referents are the metropolitan clearance and improvement programs of the city council (much influenced by its medical officer of health, H.D. Littlejohn) and the Conservative Surgery approach developed by Patrick Geddes. These were the work (we are told) of middle- and upper-middle-class professional men doing heroic, highly visible things, such as ordering buildings to be knocked down (histories rarely mention the working-class men who carried out this work). Geddes, in particular, by virtue of the gigantic publicity machine that he built up around himself, and today for the heritage value he attracts in a city increasingly dependent on tourism, is particularly over-emphasized in our understanding of urban reform activity in the Old Town. Most will be aware of his decision in 1887 to move himself and his new wife to live at James Court, a tenement in the Old Town's Lawnmarket. From this base he went on to initiate projects such as the Outlook Tower and develop his theories of planning and conservation.[3] This was, of course, not insignificant work, but it is only a small fraction of the larger story.

To challenge the obstinate narratives that place the careers of men at the center and fixate upon fame and valor, let us take a lead from the women who lived and reformed in and around the Canongate and view our history differently. Rather than think about urban reform and transformation as residing solely in individual heroic acts, demolition and new building, and enacted through legislative and formal mechanisms, our focus could shift. We can look instead at the often *ad hoc*, cumulative, small changes that were effected collaboratively through networks of people working over time, and understand that all genders have agency. We then might see the Canongate less as a landscape "saved" by the grand vision of the heroic Geddes, and more as one re-imagined and re-worked through the labor of the women of all classes who lived there, worked there and sought to make it a more habitable place.

In the main body of this chapter, therefore, the focus will be on how class, gender and site intersected in Edwardian Edinburgh. Through a discussion of three protagonists and the places they occupied, we will see how their activities demonstrated contemporary ideas about women's and children's rights and their consequent impact on the built environment; how class could be both a liberating device and an inhibiting one; and how much women's gender affects our ability to tell their history.

7 Charlotte Square

To start with a discussion of Jane Whyte (1857–1944) is useful because she was very much part of what, for now, will still be called the circle *around* Patrick Geddes. The accounts which have been written about her have tended to discuss her in these terms, or in relation to male family members. To trace Whyte's agency and activity as an autonomous individual will, however, sketch in a more substantial sense of her work and life, and move towards shifting Geddes's place in that circle. It will also go some way to explaining why he has for so long been seen as the center from which things radiated.

Until very recently, what has been known about Jane Whyte has been gleaned from studies of her husband, the Reverend Alexander Whyte (1836–1921), who was a minister of the Free Church (Presbyterian) of Scotland, theologian and the principal of New College, Edinburgh University (1909–1918). This status warrants him an entry in the *Oxford Dictionary of National Biography*, one in which the sole reference to Whyte is to describe her as "a cultivated person who shared his intellectual interests" before noting the number of children the couple produced (seven). No more is said.[4]

A cultivated woman, then, but how so? Her husband's biographer relates that as the daughter of a wealthy entrepreneur father, she was not deemed worthy of a formal education, unlike her brothers. It was, however, one of them, Robert Barbour (a distinguished graduate of the University of Edinburgh's medical school), who instead chose to study with her daily: one summer's reading was "the *Niebelungen Lied*, part of the *Divina Commedia*, the *Odyssey*, and sections of the *AEneid*."[5] Jane Whyte also attended university extension classes in literature and philosophy.[6] Such determined self-education suggests someone not content to settle for life as a lady of the leisured classes. Her subsequent activities confirm this.

More recent scholarship by feminist historians and those informed by them has embarked on the long process of documenting the generations of Scottish women active historically in politics, reform and public life. This has situated

Whyte more precisely in the context which enabled her to realize her ambitions and break out of gendered confines.[7] Married to Alexander in 1881, and settled permanently in Edinburgh's New Town (initially in a house in Melville Street and then in Charlotte Square), at the same time as she executed her duties as the wife of a leading member of the city's religious community, she very quickly became part of a wider network of progressive elite women, all of whom were resident in the New Town. From the early 1880s, they turned their attention to the amelioration of the lives of the city's urban poor, especially those who lived in the Old Town. This activity, as Robert Morris has noted, emerged from a web of influences, including new philanthropic ideas being developed in London (primarily by Octavia Hill and her networks) and changing evangelical ambitions within the Free Church of Scotland to which many belonged. This was all underpinned by the wealth and prestige of their place within a growing professional and financial class.[8]

A concomitant and equally significant influence were developments within the contemporary women's movement, in particular the notion of "Spiritual Motherhood" (or Womanliness), which emphasized, in Karen Offen's analysis, "women's rights *as women* (defined principally by their childbearing and/or nurturing capacities in relation to men). It insisted on *women's* distinctive contributions in these roles to the broader society."[9] This was a pan-European movement and one that had parallels with progressive era municipal housekeeping in the US, whose advocates, as Marlene Stein Wortman has noted, sought to "domesticate the city," and make it conform to the demands of an "ideal home environment."[10] Such emphases meant that what Offen calls "relational feminism" formed something of a counterpoint to "individualist feminism," which was more concerned with women's access to the professions and (increasingly) to suffrage (she also acknowledges that the two could often overlap). That the stress on women's caring nature served to legitimize (or was a handy pretext for) upper- and middle-class women's entry into public life should be noted. It also meant that female engagement with reform was often framed by the desire to improve the lives of fellow women whose economic handicaps prevented them from attaining full "Womanliness."

For a wealthy upper-middle-class lady like Whyte, the concept of Spiritual Motherhood allowed her to exercise her concern for matters in the public realm but to do this from a domestic context which befitted her status as wife (and mother). This might be her own home (especially the inner sanctum of her bedroom), but equally it could be the homes of other women. Domestic environments were thereby transformed into crucibles for public engagement. Thus we find her, in the early stages of her ventures into philanthropy, a member of the secular positivist group, which met in the nearby home of James (an advocate for women's education) and Edith Oliphant for philosophical discussion. Among its members was Patrick Geddes (who would marry Edith's sister Anna Morton in 1887). It was from this group that what would become a significant force for social welfare reform in the city, the Edinburgh Social Union (ESU), was formed in 1885, with Whyte one of the founders.[11] This sought "to bring together all those who feel that the misery of the poor arises in a large measure from the want of sympathy and fellowship between different classes."[12]

The ESU has invariably been associated with Patrick Geddes, however, close study of its activities shows that he played little role in the day-to-day management of the Union and that it was female agency on which the Union was modeled, and women who developed and enacted its methods of work.[13] A key influence was the activities of Octavia and Miranda Hill in England, with which Anna Morton was familiar.[14] From the mid-1860s, Octavia Hill had developed a method of housing reform that favored the rehabilitation of existing slum properties and the building of relationships with tenants through the weekly collection of rent by a lady collector. Hill's aim was to facilitate a sense of self-responsibility and self-reliance among tenants and foster a sense of community; the latter achieved by the provision of amenities such as meeting rooms, open spaces or playgrounds nearby and excursions for tenants' children. Miranda Hill's Kyrle Society, founded in 1876, built on this latter work by her sister and provided a focus for the encouragement of creating gardens in slum areas and morally instructive decorative work in clubrooms and schoolrooms.[15] In emulation, the ESU developed activities in the Old Town which ranged from making interventions to its built environment through new gardens and murals and, from very early on, the rehabilitation and management of housing on the Hill model. Given this, might Geddes be better placed on the circumference of "his" circle?

Geddes's role in the ESU and its predecessor is important, but for another reason: the Scottish inflection it brought to Spiritual Motherhood and the model of the relationship between men and women (and in Whyte's instance married men and women) which informed how many of the subjects under discussion in this chapter behaved, and consequently, their historical legacy. Throughout the 1880s Geddes was developing his ideas of the complementarity of the sexes, deriving from his interest in the role biology played in the determination of gender; concepts that had significant overlaps with Spiritual Motherhood's emphasis on the distinctiveness of women's nature and thus their agency. For Geddes, as Helen Meller notes, these ideas would become core to his evolving theories of urban planning. Hence:

> Men were the creators, the actors, who engaged vigorously with the public sphere; women were the best helpmates who attended to the private sphere, the home and, in their communities, brought their nurturing skills to place and people, thus contributing much to bringing men's plans to fruition.[16]

Here Whyte's son's description of her Charlotte Square bedroom might be recalled, and the quotation completed:

> it was big and full of strange objects, scents, and other mysteries. There was an electric ozone machine to purify the air. There were spirit lamps

> for midnight meals … Celtic crosses, scarabs and drawings from Egypt, several Buddhas of dubious sex, eaux de Cologne and lavenders galore … mother sitting up in bed writing letters to extraordinary men all over the world: men with dreams to convert mankind … to new and better religions and more wonderful ways of living. She did not need to save money, so she gave it away, I imagine, to geniuses and cranks. Patrick Geddes I remember, the cranks are forgotten.[17]

His description suggests that Jane Whyte understood herself as fulfilling the traditional female role of helpmate to men like Geddes and to her husband, and perhaps did not see herself as a direct agent worthy of an independent historical legacy. At the same time, and despite this, her self-fashioning as a patron with informed opinions and considerable means and her role as a hub of discourse gave her significant power and it is this, and the ends to which she exerted this power, which make her, and other women like her, so important to analyze. Without her money, how much could Geddes and "his" Social Union (and other ventures) have achieved? This was a circle but one with no center. It is better understood as a collective linking of equal hands.

Whyte's behind-the-scenes agency, and its impact on the built environment, is clear from the earliest days of her involvement with the ESU. The later 1860s had seen Edinburgh's city council undertake a substantial program of slum clearance in the Old Town but one that focused primarily on opening up densely packed sites and the widening or creation of new streets. Substandard dwellings were removed (a third of the area's stock) but provision for new housing for those displaced was minimal (and at higher rents) and the Canongate became ever more overcrowded and insanitary.[18] In this context, further systematic clearance was unwelcome – and, indeed, unforthcoming – and it was into this gap that the ESU stepped. Through its Housing Guild it sought to purchase tenements and rehabilitate them on the Hill model, focusing primarily on the provision of better drainage systems and the installation of water closets, and, once this work was complete, placing them under the careful management of a lady rent collector.[19]

In 1887, it was Whyte and another of her brothers, Doctor Alexander Barbour, who enabled the Union to instigate one of its first schemes. All the tenement properties in White Horse Close, near the foot of the Canongate, had been identified as unfit for inhabitation. They bought them and commissioned an architect to effect repairs and improvements to the site and then placed the rehabilitated blocks under the management of the ESU.[20] Such interventions were nowhere near as dramatic as clearance and new building but they were effected quickly, and without the trauma of demolition. Moreover, while a road widening or building demolition was indiscriminate in its impacts on local residents – for better or for worse – the specific improvements that were undertaken in the ESU's re-modeling had uniquely powerful impacts on the lives of women tenants, reducing some of their daily drudgery and thus enabling them, perhaps, to embark on the process of becoming more "womanly." The preference for rehabilitation, as Morris notes, also had the consequence of conserving the historic architecture of the Canongate, and retaining a sense of place and community that new buildings (often in a rather faux sub-Baronial style) could not achieve.[21]

Whyte's indirect interventions to the built environment of the Old Town continued. There was a second phase of rehabilitation around Whitehorse Close, but, as the 1890s wore on, new interests emerged. Chief among these was child welfare, and a new idea to address the desperate circumstances in which working-class children were raised. Central to these efforts was the new tool of the Free Kindergarten, an adaptation of Friedrich Froebel's original concept that is often known as revisionist Froebelianism. This sought to bestow upon the slum Froebel's progressive pedagogical methods of learning through play, self-realization and the formation of community.[22] This interest on Whyte's part was a logical development given her familiarity with slum conditions in the Canongate. It perhaps also reflects a realization that by focusing on children, before they became hardened by slum conditions, societal change was more likely to be permanent. For, in these settlements for children, a new generation of urban citizens might be formed.

The Free Kindergarten movement had emerged in Germany in the 1880s at Pestalozzi-Froebel House in Berlin, and soon had advocates across Europe and North America.[23] It should be understood as another manifestation of Spiritual Motherhood in its emphasis on kindergarten as an appropriate area of work for women; one which drew on their "inherent" ability to nurture. The British movement began in London in the 1890s, and it was there that Whyte encountered some of its advocates on one of what seem to have been quite frequent visits to the city. In 1899, a group of these advocates founded the Sesame House for Home-Life Training in London, which followed the curriculum developed in Berlin, and sought "to fit girls and women more fully for the woman's life, [and] as its secondary purpose the preparing of girls who need to earn their livelihood as certificated lady nurses to children, as kindergarten teachers, and as nursery governesses."[24] Whyte became a member of its Advisory Council.

Among the first to enroll at Sesame House was a young woman called Lileen Hardy (1872–1947). Then aged 27, she would have been somewhat older than her fellow students. It was perhaps her comparative seniority that drew her to Whyte's attention; a contemporary article reported that many ladies bespoke (reserved) students before they had finished their studies.[25] Certainly, by 1901, Hardy, her Froebel Certificate achieved, had moved to Edinburgh to take up the post of governess to the younger children of the Whyte family.

Whether, at this point, either knew of the other's commitment to the political principles of Free Kindergarten, or that Whyte recognized a good teacher and Hardy simply needed a job, is not clear. Nevertheless, the reform work that they would go on to achieve together offers further evidence of the way women effected spatial and material change in the Old Town's environments and, importantly, how what each was able to do personally was inflected by their class position. As an elite married woman, Whyte's ability to personally step into and engage with the streets was limited. Spatially, she was confined to her bedroom-cum-powerhouse in Charlotte Square and visits and tours with her husband (which were frequent if his biography is to be relied upon) throughout her home nation and to England. Her chief power lay in gathering and sharing ideas and then using her financial resources to deploy others as her proxies. This she did for Geddes, whose gender and class gave him free access to Old and New Town alike, and would do, in time, for Hardy (and many others, as her son's recollection suggests).

Hardy was obviously subject to the same Edwardian social concepts of women's roles as Whyte but her class status – she was a lower-middle class single woman, her father a pharmacist who ran a shop in Salisbury, Wiltshire – required her either to marry or to earn a living for herself. She embraced the latter, which meant that she would never be locked into a domestic interior. Her espousal of the discourse of Womanliness meant this led her to train as a kindergarten teacher. The job also allowed her to save the money to achieve what she later described as "the great desire of my heart:" to open a Free Kindergarten.[26] Her re-location to Edinburgh meant this would be in the Old Town's slums, while her middle-class and unmarried status allowed her to work and live among the poor in a way that Whyte simply could not. How these dynamics played out on the ground in the Canongate is the focus of the next part of this chapter.

St Saviour's Child Garden, Brown's Close 1906–1908; Chessel's Court 1908–1977, the Canongate

By accident or design, Hardy found herself in a milieu of progressive Edinburgh women and it was likely because of Whyte's connections that she was able to form the networks through which she achieved her "heart's desire." Evidence of precisely how she went about this is scant, but by 1905 she was involved in the first Free Kindergarten to be established in Edinburgh, at Reid's Court on the Canongate. A 1906 report shows that she served on its governing committee and that Jane Whyte was among those "expressing approval" of the work being undertaken.[27] Close by the kindergarten was St Saviour's, the mission hall of the Episcopalian church of Old St Paul's (OSP), which had, since the 1890s, embarked on an ambitious program of missionary and social work in the slums that formed the hinterland of its mother church. The church itself stood further up the Royal Mile on Jeffrey Street, overlooking the city's main railway station, Waverley. In the early 1900s, this missionary activity was stepped up under the direction of its charismatic rector, Canon Albert Laurie. As was the case with Geddes and the ESU, Laurie relied on a predominantly female workforce to enact "his" vision, and he was particularly keen to expand this work to focus on the youngest inhabitants of the Canongate. It seems that knowing this, Hardy, who had been saving consistently since she arrived in Edinburgh, approached him with the proposal that she open her own kindergarten under the church's auspices.[28]

Thus it was that the St Saviour's Child Garden (SSCG) opened in the mission hall at Brown's Close, Canongate in November 1906. It was to be an exemplar of Free Kindergarten principles: located within the slum area from which its children were drawn and with its main worker (Hardy) also resident in the community. This working within an existing landscape is important to emphasize because it had particular material and spatial, as well as social, implications. At the SSCG, as at Whitehorse Close, new environments were formed from existing buildings. They thus generated what seems to have been a characteristic form of women's design practice in the period, the creation of transitory, temporary or cumulatively re-worked spaces (interior and exterior). This policy of adaptive re-use had, of course, economic advantages. In this instance this was an important factor given that Hardy's capital was the main source of funding for St Saviour's, but there was a more profound rationale beneath this practice. Retaining the existing urban fabric would have broadcast a public message that care was being taken to improve and serve the existing neighborhood rather than simply erase it, especially in an area that had recently undergone dramatic slum clearance which had deprived many people of their homes. It did not disrupt unduly either the existing building or the community around it. It was also done quickly. Such schemes' impact – and the example they embodied – did not take long to be normalized, because little, at least on the outside, had changed, and thus, it was hoped, they would be easily accepted by those who would use or inhabit these spaces.[29] Similarly, the fact that Hardy moved to live in the Old Town (initially in St Saviour's Hostel, a tenement refurbished by Old St Paul's to house its missionary workers) meant that, like the woman we see in Figure 1.1, she became integrated into the landscape, a familiar, if better-dressed, part of the scenery.

The SSCG in fact represented a form of double re-use. The mission hall in which it was housed had itself been formed within two rooms of what was originally a pair of three-story cottages which, as can be seen in Figure 1.3, stood at the end of one of the Canongate's closes. These were narrow lanes that interspersed the street frontage of tenement blocks and led into further ranges of buildings behind them (we see such an entry in Figure 1.1). The oasthouse just behind the access staircase is a reminder of the close juxtaposition of home and industry in this part of the city. The result was that the children navigated a familiar passage as they made their way from their homes to their kindergarten.

The hall's primary use was for church services, which meant that Hardy had to set up and dismantle the kindergarten on a weekly basis. Hardy described what happened once inside, writing:

> To visit the kindergarten you enter by a narrow little door under a stair, which looks as if it led into a coal cellar ... but inside when the children are there it looks quite nice. It is a mission hall and if you saw it set out

FIGURE 1.3 Brown's Close, off the Canongate, Edinburgh, looking towards the cottages that housed for St Saviour's Mission Hall, taken from *The Life History of a Slum Child*

Source: Reproduced by kind permission of the Episcopal Church of Old St Paul's, Edinburgh

> for church on Friday evenings you would think it would never do for a kindergarten. But Monday morning there is a great transformation. I have made a big Liberty curtain to draw right across the room in front of the altar, and all the forms, chairs, kneeling mats etc go out of sight. Then little tables and chairs come out, dolls and cradles, washing up bowls, cans etc. canaries, doves, plants, brushes, dusters etc, and it looks quite homely.[30]

Hardy's use of the term "transformation" suggests she well understood the metaphorical nature of the material changes she effected on a weekly basis. On the one hand, the children found themselves in a place which had many echoes of their own homes: a one-room space within a somewhat dilapidated dwelling (Figure 1.4). Indeed, they assumed this was Hardy's home because of this. On the other hand, the improvised classroom was cleaner, lighter and undoubtedly warmer than their homes, which is to say, it was a better version of what they were accustomed to. The refurbishment of the building's fabric and interiors – making the existing anew – embodied, therefore, the transformation that the children would themselves undergo as they experienced kindergarten. This almost magical process was reiterated by the smocks each child put on as they entered the hall: a visible symbol of the overlaying of the old with new values.

In seeking to complicate how we understand agency in the making of environments, it is also worth noting how often such transformations were funded by

Photograph by Francis C. Inglis, Calton Hill, Edinburgh.

EARLY DAYS

FIGURE 1.4 Interior of the St Saviour's Child Garden in the St Saviour's Mission Hall at Brown's Close, Edinburgh, ca. 1908

Source: Reproduced by kind permission of the Episcopal Church of Old St Paul's, Edinburgh

women. Hardy's capital, which supported the kindergarten for its first three years, was supplemented by donations from women (annual reports show a predominantly female list of donors) either financial or in kind. Countless New Town women provided smocks, handkerchiefs, toys and other gifts for the children, and the women of the ESU also expanded the kindergarten's message of renewal and wellbeing architecturally by improving the environs of the adjacent property which it owned and managed. Ever behind the scenes, Jane Whyte proved the conduit to benefactors with larger pockets or more practical skills. The latter is particularly evident on the occasions she intervened when Hardy was seeking to develop a key part of the kindergarten: the garden in which children could play freely and also learn to nurture plants and pets as they were being nurtured themselves.

The garden would not be ready – nor the season sufficiently clement – for the first months of St Saviour's existence. By spring 1907, however, work was underway on making a green space from a piece of wasteland attached to the Mission Hall that Hardy had been able to acquire on a peppercorn rent. In this venture she was assisted by Patrick Geddes, to whom she wrote in October 1906 with a list of the "delightful things" she would like her garden to include if funds sufficed. She mentions a "swing, see saw, sand-heap, bank to roll down, … pigeon house and fowl run," among other requirements, although it is unclear how many of these made the final cut.[31] Certainly Geddes seems to have advised on less expensive matters such as planting and layout, as his sketch in Figure 1.5 shows (though the toboggan run was perhaps an ambition too far). Surviving photographs suggest at least some of his design was enacted (Figure 1.6).

In 1908, expanding numbers meant that the kindergarten had to move premises to a suite of rooms on the first floor of Chessel's Court on the opposite side of the Canongate. This was a much grander, if still rather rundown, building and had the advantage not just of more space which could be converted permanently, but a private garden to the rear. Initially rented, in 1912 the lease was bought for the church by a Miss Playfair, at which point a series of projects was undertaken. A Miss Brebner paid for a new tool house, a Miss Bucknell was behind the provision of "very necessary drain-pipes," while Whyte recruited a regular visitor to her house, Prince Nicholas Galitzin, a Russian much interested in matters of social welfare, to pay for the construction of a garden shelter so that the children could take lessons outside.[32] The earlier connections in 1906 with Geddes, now working through the Open Spaces Committee of his Outlook Tower (a new headquarters for his planning activities) subsequently led to a commission to his daughter, Norah Geddes, to produce plans for a public garden to occupy the space behind the street frontage and the main elevation of Chessel's Court.

Norah Geddes had first sketched the site in July 1909, showing what Lileen Hardy described as "a disused and neglected builder's yard."[33] Like her father, from whose networks she benefited in gaining early commissions, Geddes shared a concern for combining gardening with social improvement, but it

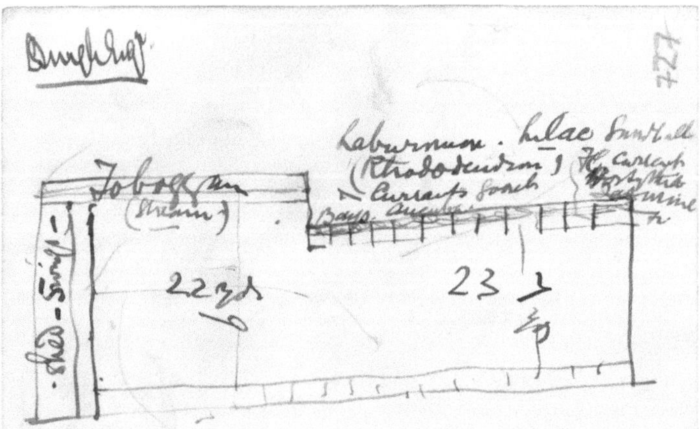

FIGURE 1.5 Patrick Geddes's sketch plan for the garden of St Saviour's Child Garden at Brown's Close, Edinburgh, with his annotations for planting and amenities, winter 1906

Source: Archives and Special Collections, University of Strathclyde Library

FIGURE 1.6 Lileen Hardy, Canon Albert Laurie and kindergarten children in the garden at St Saviour's Child Garden, Brown's Close, Edinburgh, ca. 1907

Source: Reproduced by kind permission of the Episcopal Church of Old St Paul's, Edinburgh

would take two years negotiation with the brewery that owned the land before the lease was secured and work could begin. This was a substantial site and was intended, as Deborah Reid notes, as the "*piece de resistance*" of the Open Space Committee's program. Geddes's was a particularly sensitive design that re-ordered the space and opened up its visibility to surrounding buildings by removing the old palings (Figure 1.7).[34] Hardy noted, "the dignity which the large open space gives to the really fine old houses is very striking."[35] This statement is important, revealing that her investment in the Old Town was animated by a nuanced appreciation for both historicity and modern improvements, and a desire to see them mutually reinforcing one another as the neighborhood was brought to new health.

The garden at Chessel's Court, and the kindergarten that faced it, formed part of a patchwork of interventions up and down the Royal Mile by both the ESU and the Open Spaces Committee. There were more gardens (Norah Geddes worked on many of these, lamenting the hard work of planting bulbs under the watch of mischievous Old Town lads),[36] three further Free Kindergartens and a considerable number of properties rehabilitated and managed by the ESU – all of which were effected by groups of women reformers (and their female backers). Now mostly gone, they represented not just transformations to the built environment but also to the lives of the

FIGURE 1.7 Sketch, 1909, by Norah Geddes of the derelict builder's yard at Chessel's Court, Edinburgh, and proposal for its re-design into a public garden, 1910

Source: Archives and Special Collections, University of Strathclyde Library

women who enacted them. Like the woman who walks so confidently in Figure 1.1, it gave them a career and some considerable personal, and cross-class, freedom. Hardy, as noted, was able to set up home in the Canongate when the SSCG opened, moving later to separate quarters at Chessel's Court in 1908. Furthermore, central to the kindergarten method was close association with the children's families, especially mothers. Hardy wrote:

> Every church ought to have a kindergarten for the sake of both generations. It is much the most easy and natural method of getting a welcome in the homes. "She who takes a child by the hand takes the mother by the heart".[37]

She worked hard to build a rapport with the mothers through regular meetings and invitations to tea, augmented by her daily presence up and down the Canongate. That this was personally and emotionally, as well as professionally, liberating is clear from a 1907 reflection following an afternoon's work with parents on the garden at Brown's Close: "There is a delightful naturalness in our personal relations all working together. To exchange tools with a man and take a turn at his job gives a pleasant intimacy which nothing else brings."[38]

The intimacy that Hardy describes here was made possible, and legitimated, by her status as a professional woman. It was the intimacy of common endeavor, in which she and local parents, especially mothers, built a new social foundation and a new urban fabric for a better tomorrow. Her professional status also allowed her to use such experiences as evidence of the effecting, and effectiveness of, her reform work in the promotional writings she produced about the SSCG. It is from these that we are able to gain some sense of how those who were the subjects of her activity responded to this work, and what agency, if any, they were able to exert over the environments in which they lived and worked.

Unknown tenement, Canongate, ca. 1909

Hardy's use of image and text in promoting the cause of the SSCG (and free kindergartens more widely) is exemplified in the photograph of the interior shown in Figure 1.2. It was one of a series of photographs Hardy used in a 14-page pamphlet entitled *The Life History of a Slum Child*, which she produced to raise funds for the SSCG in late 1909.[39] This followed the move to Chessel's Court in September 1908, and the exhaustion a year later of the money she had used to support the venture. The photograph is the first we see. The last is the scene reproduced in Figure 1.4. In between there are several pages showing the dangers of the street to which this "nameless lassie" (the slum child of the title) will be exposed, unless the future of the kindergarten can be assured. The scene of the children around the table, in the "homely" atmosphere of Brown's Close with its vases of flowers and reproduction paintings – the *Madonna and Child* that personifies Spiritual Motherhood – is a loaded juxtaposition, a visual criticism of the poverty of that first interior. An inevitable, and undoubtedly intended, further contrast would have been noted between the poor home and the domestic interiors of those at whom the pamphlet was aimed, and who were invited to a meeting to support the SSCG in the home of another benefactor, Lady Marjory Mackenzie, in the New Town's Heriot Row.

Hardy's use of (multiple) contrast was by this date a standard device in charity literature. It was underscored by a text alongside each image and in the alarmist tone of the pamphlet's preface which reads thus (it was written in stanza form):

> To those
> Who love the nation
> Who wish Scottish grit and fibre to last
> Who "think of the generations to come",
> Who are lovers of little children.
>
> Those Human Documents
> gathered on the spot – without arrangement
> – haphazard – as the chance came, on an
> ordinary day in the Canongate of Edin-
> burgh, are presented for consideration
> (yes! and for humbling and shame!)
> in the hope that an experiment, not
> made with chemicals in bottles, but
> with the bodies and souls of posterity,
> may be furthered and if the mercy of
> God permit, fulfilled.

Hardy's tone here is, in fact, untypical of her writing more generally. In the 1912 book, *Diary of a Free Kindergarten*, and the manuscript diary on which it was based, an initial tendency to objectify and criticize those she sought to reform soon gives way to an abiding quasi-parental pride and affection for her charges, and a deepening sympathy for their parents, especially the mothers and the impossibility of their achieving Womanliness in the conditions in which they lived, worked and had to bring up multiple children. Nevertheless, for the serious and urgent purpose of fundraising, dramatic abjection was a device to encourage sympathy and donations and it inflected, perhaps subconsciously, how photographs were taken. This means they are difficult sources for the historian to analyze but they remain rare evidence of everyday life in the Canongate and, especially, of a slum interior. These, and other SSCG photographs and texts, can tell us something of home- and place-making by those at whom the Free Kindergarten was aimed.

The interior, the text notes, shows the home of the mother of the lassie's father (who was then in prison). The room is "not untypical" and contained

> a chair-bed with old coats for covering, a chair, a box for a second seat, a table, a lamp, a pot and kettle, a strip of old worn-out carpet, a few dishes and odd (indeed odd!) ornaments (sic). And literally nothing else.[40]

For Hardy, the lack of things was a sign of fecklessness, poverty both absolute and of aspiration, while the choice of ornaments signaled dubious taste. The whole constituted the lack of homeliness that pushed inhabitants into the dangerous street. A more dispassionate reading might see a woman, who is not identified and is now unidentifiable, trying hard to make a home of a no-doubt damp and cold single room in a run-down tenement. The furniture is sparse but sufficient to allow eating meals at a table, while the ornaments' very existence, though the symmetry of their arrangement implies the photographer's hand, suggests an attempt at personal expression and attachment to things despite the exigencies of her circumstances. If it is not too much of an extrapolation, might we see such attempts at decoration as, in fact, rather typical of Canongate women: fashioning homes from the most limited of materials and as acts of defiance against the numbing, dehumanizing tendencies of poverty.

While evidence to support this extrapolation is not profuse, that such women were as perfectly capable of being sensitive to environments as their wealthier sisters, even if their ability to express this sensitivity on a significant scale was limited by their poverty, comes across in a conversation Hardy recorded with a mother who came to see the new quarters at Chessel's Court. Viewing Hardy's room, she admired its simplicity and commented, "If ye put onything mair in it ye would spile it."[41] This chat took place after the mother had taken part in one of the many working parties that Hardy organized to assist her in making good the fabric of first Brown's Close and then Chessel's Court. Not just mothers but older brothers and fathers collaborated with her, and it was they who did the hard work of clearing the wasteland next to Brown's Close, painting and decorating interiors and building walkways for the garden at Chessel's Court.

Such voluntary work suggests how the parents felt that it was in their interests to support the kindergarten as they saw the long-term benefits this might offer to their children. Without this active cooperation and intelligent agency, the reform efforts of the ladies of the New Town would have improved the closes and the courts, but little else. In this way working men, women and children made their mark on the landscape of the Canongate. Their cooperation with Hardy also shows that one of the broader aims of the Free Kindergarten movement was achieved, that of making a community of the kindergartners, the children and their families; a new form of social relations. There are other examples: in June 1908 the mothers invited Hardy and other kindergarten workers to a picnic in the seaside village of Cramond. Subsequently they created a Mother's Guild with the aim of cooperation between the SSCG and home, and clubbed together to gift a new offertory table to the kindergarten (Canon Laurie visited weekly to conduct prayers). Perhaps most symbolically, parents and New Town benefactors alike attended the annual performances the children put on for those whose donations – monetary or in kind – made possible the SSCG's continued existence. In such uses of and adaptations of space – that experiment in the bodies and souls of posterity that Hardy described – we see, perhaps, a microcosm of a different form of society: one of mutual cross-class endeavor with the goal of liberating children to be their best selves and go on to create a better Scotland.

Conclusion

This account of women's socio-spatial reform activity in Edinburgh's Canongate has sought to reflect on the intersections of gender, class and environment and, in so doing, to complicate understandings of how that particular landscape was re-shaped at the beginning of the twentieth century. This chapter has refused the idea that one or two men were the lone, heroic architects of its transformation, and has insisted, instead, that a whole host of people, and especially a host of women, were equal partners in this process. This chapter has also suggested that the evolution of Edinburgh's urban fabric was achieved in ways that are easily overlooked when one thinks only in terms of valiant architects and not in terms of social systems: adaptive re-use of historic fabric including both permanent and temporary changes, such as the weekly construction of the SSCG in its early days, as well as the population of old and new structures with new purposes, social interactions and the complex webs of financial transactions and coordinated labor that enabled these transformations. The re-forming of the Canongate was, then, like its Edwardian self, a busy affair. A mesh of people – elite progressive women, working-class mothers and fathers, middle-class social workers and kindergartners and small children – united by a desire to make the Canongate a more habitable place, worked both in partnership and individually, to achieve this goal through changes to spaces private, public and somewhere in between.

Why, then, has their legacy been so easy to ignore? This question can be answered in large part by the nuance of their methods: the architectural and urban components of the sort of work that they did were designed to have light footprints, and to blend harmoniously into the pre-existing fabric of Edinburgh's Old Town. Their success was, by very definition, visually quiet. At the same time, the sort of work that they did very often left no permanent trace. Once the SSCG closed in 1977, so too did its physical presence disappear. Similarly, the types of reform activity concomitant with the kindergarten, resided in forms of personal exchange – medical welfare, lady visitors, rehabilitated housing – which, very often, left no official or permanent record. Moreover, the fact that in the period when such records might have been saved, methodological prejudices favored an historical narrative that focused on the state as the agent of urban reform and thus viewed voluntary activity with suspicion (not least because it was very female) has meant many records have not survived.

Whyte, operating within the discourse of Womanliness, understood herself as a helpmate to her husband and to the people (men primarily, but not solely) whom she supported financially, but her elite status tied her to the New Town and thus she worked through others. Hardy was perhaps a helpmate to her cause, that of the Free Kindergarten, but her lower-middle-class status enabled her to move more freely than Whyte could and become something of a warrior on behalf of her children. These circumstances mean that Whyte's presence in the archive remains, as yet, highly elusive. While some records have been located that allow a more detailed examination of her work and life, for the moment she remains knowable primarily through her husband. Hardy, because of the assorted publications she created to promote the SSCG, is a more frequent presence in the archive. From this it is possible to gain some sense of her as a person and to re-construct her motivations. Neither, however, unlike Geddes, considered themselves sufficiently important as an individual to leave a legacy of both personal and professional papers. Nevertheless, for both these women we have their names and know where they lived and worked. Their engagement in the public realm through social reform activities allows, at least, the possibility of locating other archival and contemporary material in which they might be mentioned and, thus, the possibility of situating them quite precisely in their historical context and of re-constructing with some confidence their historical agency.

For the nameless grandmother of the nameless lassie, the task is more difficult, perhaps impossible. As noted above, she and her granddaughter are known only through their inflection in the reformist narratives produced by Hardy. The same is true for the parents and children mentioned by name in her writings; Hardy's tendency is not to reflect on why they might have worked with her. Nor has a comprehensive list of pupils survived and only a few of the names and addresses that might allow research into census returns and thus at least the basis for some interpretation of the sorts of families who sent their children to kindergarten.

Yet, however difficult it is to do so, and it is not impossible, we would do well to work to reconstruct and remember. This chapter began with an image of life in the Canongate and has shown how everything in that photograph is connected: the child, the street, the buildings and the women, prosperous and poor. These connections – to each other and to the people and places of the New Town – have much to teach us today. It is important to create a more representative mode of history which seeks to include all those who have shaped the world we now live in. Furthermore, while there is much that can be seen as patronizing about what Hardy and her contemporaries did and said, we might also admire their willingness to extend their monies and their bodies beyond the safety and comfort of their

FIGURE 1.8 Children of the St Saviour's Child Garden at play in the private garden at Chessel's Court, Edinburgh

Source: Edinburgh Museum of Childhood

middle-class homes to work with poor communities and hear what they had to say. At the same time, the realms of urban planning and design can learn from the progressive complexity of their architectural strategies, which saw them respond to the scorched-earth demolition policies of city governments with much more productive, human-scaled, historically sensitive adaptations of problematic but nonetheless valuable urban fabric. Finally, as we look down the contemporary Canongate, subject, as it is today, to substantial and often unsympathetic re-development, we should remember the men and women of the Edwardian Canongate, and the women of the Edwardian New Town, who demonstrated the transformative power of collaboration as they refurbished, re-built, re-planted and revivified the courts and closes, and that, once upon a time, these places rang to the voices of small children who rose above the poverty of their environment and simply lived for the day (Figure 1.8).[42]

Notes

1 Lancelot Law Whyte, *Focus and Diversions* (London: The Cresset Press, 1963), p. 7.

2 There is some work that considers women's agency in the Scottish public realm. See for example, Megan K. Smitley, *Feminine Public Sphere: Middle Class Women in Civic Life in Scotland, ca 1870–1914* (Manchester: Manchester University Press, 2009) and Esther Breitenbach, Linda Fleming, S. Karly Kehoe and Lesley Orr, eds, *Scottish Women: A Documentary History, 1780–1914* (Edinburgh: Edinburgh University Press, 2013). Much work remains firmly male-focused.

3 See Jim Johnson and Lou Rosenburg, *Renewing Old Edinburgh: The Enduring Legacy of Patrick Geddes* (Edinburgh: Argyll Publishing, 2010), for an insightful analysis of Geddes.

4 A.B. Macaulay, Whyte, Alexander (1836–1921), *Oxford Dictionary of National Biography*, accessed May 14, 2018: https://doiorg.oxfordbrookes.idm.oclc.org/10.1093/ref:odnb/36886
5 G.F. Barbour, *The Life of Alexander Whyte DD* (London: Hodder and Stoughton, 1925), p. 228. Robert Morris notes that the family money came from land, cotton spinning and latterly from major shareholdings in banks and railways, see his "White Horse Close: Philanthropy, Scottish Historical Imagination and the Rebuilding of Edinburgh in the later Nineteenth Century," *Journal of Scottish Historical Studies*, 33.1 (2013), p. 114.
6 Barbour, *Life of Alexander Whyte*, p. 227.
7 See Smitley, *Feminine Public Sphere*, and Breitenbach, et al., *Scottish Women*, and also Walter Stephen, ed., *Learning from the Lassies: Women of the Patrick Geddes Circle* (Edinburgh: Luath Press Ltd, 2014), especially the essay by Veronica Burbridge, "Sympathy, Synthesis and Synergy: Patrick Geddes and the Edinburgh Social Union," pp. 73–93.
8 Morris, "White Horse Close," p. 102.
9 Karen Offen, "Defining Feminism: A Comparative Historical Approach," *Signs*, 14.1 (Autumn 1988), p. 136 (emphasis in original).
10 Marlene Stein Wortmann, "Domesticating the Nineteenth-century American City," *Prospects*, 3 (October 1978), pp. 532–33.
11 For an account see Burbridge, "Sympathy, Synthesis and Synergy."
12 Edinburgh Social Union, *Annual Report*, 1904 (not paginated), held in the Edinburgh Room, Edinburgh Central Library.
13 See Burbridge, "Sympathy, Synthesis and Synergy."
14 Rosenburg and Johnson, *Renewing Old Edinburgh*, pp. 64–5.
15 On Octavia Hill, see Elizabeth Baigent and Ben Cowell, eds, *"Nobler Imaginings and Mightier Struggles": Octavia Hill, Social Activism and the Remaking of British Society* (London: The Institute of Historical Research, 2016), and on the sisters, see Anne Anderson and Elizabeth Darling, "The Hill Sisters: Cultural Philanthropy and the Embellishment of Lives in Nineteenth-Century England," in Elizabeth Darling and Lesley Whitworth, eds, *Women and the Making of Built Space in England, 1870–1940* (Aldershot: Ashgate, 2007), pp. 33–50.
16 Helen Meller, "Gender, Citizenship and the Making of the Modern Environment," in Darling and Whitworth, eds, *Women and the Making of Built Space in England*, p. 13.
17 Whyte, *Focus and Diversions*, p. 7.
18 See Chapter 3 of Johnson and Rosenburg, *Renewing Old Edinburgh*.
19 See Burbridge, "Sympathy, Synthesis and Synergy."
20 I rely here on Morris, "White Horse Close." It is interesting to note that throughout he discusses Whyte entirely in terms of her brother.
21 In 1893, Edinburgh's council resumed a slum clearance program but this time, clearly influenced by the ESU's work, took a more piecemeal approach. Geddes was appointed to develop two sites in the Lawnmarket and here he pursued the Hill-inspired Conservative Surgery approach for which he achieved renown. Instead of complete demolition, this combined partial demolition (usually behind the street line) to reduce density and introduce space and air, with rehabilitation of the original architecture. See Johnson and Rosenburg, *Renewing Old Edinburgh*, pp. 114–37.
22 On this see, for example, Kevin J. Brehony, "English Revisionist Froebelians and the Schooling of the Urban Poor," in Mary Hilton and Pam Hirsch, eds, *Practical Visionaries: Women, Education and Social Progress 1790–1930* (Harlow: Longman, 2000), pp. 183–200.
23 See Michael Steven Shapiro, *Child's Garden, The Kindergarten Movement from Froebel to Dewey* (University Park: Pennsylvania State University Press, 1983) and Marta Gutman, *A City for Children: Women, Architecture and the Charitable Landscape of Oakland, 1830–1950* (Chicago: University of Chicago Press, 2014).

24 Mrs Hirst Alexander, "The Sesame Club in London," *The Strand Magazine* (September 1900), p. 3.
25 "Report of the First Year's Work at Sesame House," *Child Life*, 2 (1900), p. 253.
26 I draw here on the manuscript *Diary of a Free Kindergarten* (held privately), compiled from letters Hardy circulated to supporters in the first three years of her kindergarten's – known as St Saviour's Child Garden – existence and referred to henceforth as DoFK MS. The quotation here comes from an entry for July 1908 (not paginated). This was later published as a book (with numerous amendments) in 1912 by Gay and Hancock. There was also an American edition published in 1913 by Houghton, Mifflin and Company.
27 Anonymous, "Free Kindergartens in Great Britain," *Child Life*, 5 (1905), pp. 94–100; Report of the Free Kindergarten for City Children (September 1906), Patrick Geddes Papers (PGP), University of Strathclyde Archives, T-Ged 12/2/181.
28 DoFK MS, July 1908.
29 Marta Gutman's 2014 study of child welfare in Oakland, California (see note 23 above) shows how this principle applied equally in the US context.
30 DoFK MS, April 1907.
31 Hardy-Geddes, 29 October 1906, PGP, T-Ged 9/727.
32 OSP Church Magazine, March 1912, p. 6. The description of Galitzin is taken from Barbour, *Life of Alexander Whyte*, pp. 403–4.
33 Lileen Hardy, *Diary of a Free Kindergarten* (Boston and New York: Houghton, Mifflin and Co., 1913), p. 169.
34 Deborah Reid, "Unsung Heroines of Horticulture: Scottish Gardening Women, 1800–1939" (Unpublished PhD Thesis, Edinburgh College of Art, 2015), p. 244.
35 Hardy, *Diary of a Free Kindergarten*, p. 169.
36 Patrick Geddes Papers, National Library of Scotland, MS 10501: Letters of Norah Geddes-Patrick. 10501/8 Norah to Patrick, 19 October 1910, and 10501/10 Norah to Patrick, 21 November 1910.
37 DoFK MS, July 1908.
38 DoFK MS, March 1907.
39 The copy consulted is held privately; there also a copy in the Edinburgh Room of Edinburgh Central Library. Quotations are taken from this until signaled otherwise.
40 The "sic" is in the original. A contemporary report on 1400 school children in the area (the school that many SSCG children would have gone on to attend, and therefore a good benchmark) and their homes, calculated that approximately 20 per cent of the children lived in what it calls "one-room houses," and almost 55 per cent in two-roomed; so Hardy is somewhat overstating what was typical. See City of Edinburgh Charity Organisation Society, *Report on the Physical Condition of Fourteen Hundred Children in the City Together with Some Account of their Homes and Surroundings* (London: P.S. King & Son, 1906), pp. 3–4.
41 DoFK MS, November 1908. Hardy always transliterated the voices of the children and their parents.
42 I am indebted to Peder Aspen, archivist of the Episcopal church of Old St Paul's for his assistance in my research. I am also grateful to the previous rector, Canon Ian Paton and the current rector, Father Tony Bryer, for help with permissions to reproduce images of the SSCG.

2

AMAZA'S AZUREST

Modern architecture and the 'New Negro' woman

Jacqueline Taylor

On the edge of the grounds of Virginia State College in Petersburg, Virginia, a white stuccoed house nestles in a dip in the landscape behind a screen of symmetrically planted trees. Although modest in size, the single-story, flat-roofed dwelling commands attention (Figure 2.1). Its cube-like form, with rounded corners punctuated by bands of glass bricks, emphasizes the horizontal. Picture windows along the building's smooth planar surface pull the outside in, creating a dialogic relationship between interior and exterior. The small, textured glass bricks puncturing the rounded ends of the building's façade suggest a cocoon of intimacy and desire for privacy; nevertheless, a roof terrace, framed by curved metal coping and accessed by means of a steel ship's ladder, opens the building to the sky and claims the right to visibility. This unique assemblage of avant-garde architectural forms and materials represents a personal, creative expression of the innovative trends in modern architecture occurring in progressive pockets of the United States and across the Atlantic. Seen alongside the red brick and white trim of the Colonial Revival structures of the neighboring historically black college campus, the building presents a sharp contrast.

This boldly modernist house, designed in 1938 and completed in 1939, was home to two African-American women who taught at the neighboring Virginia State College and lived unabashedly as a couple (Figures 2.2 and 2.3). Amaza Lee Meredith (1895–1984) designed the white stucco house to share with her companion Edna Colson (1888–1985) and their unique modern dwelling inscribed a new mark on the local landscape. The land had once been agricultural, serving as Ettrick Banks and Matoaca Plantations, and later industrial, as John C. Griffin's Fleets Mill and Manufacturing. In 1836, the property transferred to Boisseau and Smith, and supported a foundry where iron, steel, brass, and other metals were manufactured. The adjacent city of Petersburg, remarkable for its status as a center of industry in the antebellum South, grew partly as

FIGURE 2.1 Azurest, a modernist house on the edge of Virginia State College, designed by Amaza Lee Meredith, 1938

Source: Photograph by the author, 2009

FIGURE 2.2 Amaza Lee Meredith, photograph ca. 1922

Source: Series VII, Amaza Lee Meredith Papers, 1912, 1930–1938, Accession #198220, Special Collections Department, Johnson Memorial Library, Virginia State University, Petersburg, VA

FIGURE 2.3 Edna Meade Colson, photograph ca. 1915

Source: Series VII, Amaza Lee Meredith Papers, 1912, 1930–1938, Accession #198220, Special Collections Department, Johnson Memorial Library, Virginia State University, Petersburg, VA

a result of their success. These past uses of the land have long been enshrined on signage and maps, where the names of previous owners, mostly white and elite, claim their place in American history, asserting their role in a well-known progressive story that evolves through the agrarian past to industrial, urban modernity. Yet those who worked in the plantations, or dedicated their lives to the industries sustaining the city, are all-too-often publicly invisible. They have ghostly traces, visible only to those who personally know their individual or family histories.

The modern dwelling, by contrast, asserts itself as highly visible, demanding that we account for its presence. This chapter is dedicated to that task. The story of this house reveals a neglected layer of social and cultural enterprise, in which struggles to escape the confines of racist and misogynist bigotry motivated and shaped the lives and work of the building's designer and her partner. Situating Meredith's architectural achievement in her personal history reveals her deep desire to claim a place in the modern world that connected her life and work, and through them the lives of her community, to national and international progressive trends, politically and aesthetically. On one level, the house and its relationship to the nearby college represent her longing to mount a national stage of aspirational black social and political leadership—specifically, to join the class of the African-American professional elite identified by W.E.B. Du Bois as the Talented Tenth. On another level, the house cries out for the recognition of a woman's right to craft her own identity and live on her own terms, including choosing the nature of her intimate relationships. By designing her own house, Meredith demonstrated how new possibilities for women's lives might arise in a non-patriarchal society. Moreover, her enthusiastic use of modern aesthetics represented her claim on historical agency and her efforts to embrace an emerging cosmopolitan future of openness, in contrast to the old, restricting patterns of intolerance that have long haunted America. By showcasing her modernism in a landscape dominated by the architectural style of Colonial Revival, Meredith dared to defy expectation even for a member of the educated, professional elite, and determinedly pushed against the boundaries of Petersburg's provincialism, where the oppression of her race and gender was typically accommodated as a means to appease tense race relations. In short, this house is a physical manifestation of aspiration. A study of its history illuminates a rich and informative intersection of early-twentieth century American struggles, both personal and political, for women's rights, racial liberation, and the building of progressive communities through broad education and bold leadership.

Too much mixing for us

Amaza Lee Meredith was born in 1895, in Lynchburg, Virginia. She was the youngest of four children born to Emma Pink Kenney (1871–1941), an African-American woman, and Samuel P. Meredith (1862–1915), a white man. At the time, it was illegal in Virginia for white and black people to couple. Meredith's birth certificate identifies her simply as a daughter born to Kenney, and the father's name remains blank. Forced to reside at different addresses, Meredith was nonetheless committed to supporting Kenney and their four children, building them a large, wood-frame Victorian home with fashionable trimmings and a wrap-around porch (Figure 2.4). Meredith was a master craftsman, a carpenter whose family had owned property and lived by the trade for generations.[1] He taught his youngest daughter how to draw blueprints, build cardboard models, and turn a perfectly curved stair newel. Eventually, as Amaza Lee turned fifteen, Samuel and Emma were married, probably in Washington D.C., and he moved into the house he had built, despite the dangers of his doing so.

Emma Kenney, for her part, was educated to an atypical standard for the period, in that she could read and write. For a time, she earned a living as a seamstress, but as she began bearing children it appears Samuel, the father of her four children, supported her financially as she is listed in census records as a head of household, meaning she was self-sufficient. Emma Kenney had purchased land alongside plots owned by her future husband, and eventually the two combined them in order to construct their home. Emma Kenney also built a local network of support at Lynchburg's Eighth Street Baptist Church, which represented the crucible of female political and social empowerment typical of prominent Baptist

FIGURE 2.4 The house that Samuel Meredith built for his family on Monroe Street in Lynchburg, Virginia

Source: Series VII, Amaza Lee Meredith Papers, 1912, 1930–1938, Accession #198220, Special Collections Department, Johnson Memorial Library, Virginia State University, Petersburg, VA

churches in many communities, as Evelyn Brooks Higginbotham has discussed. Kenney was also close to and respected by local educators, including influential white women.[2] Asserting the semblance of a middle-class social existence and valuing education as key to transcending the pejorative public image of African-American character, Kenney actively nurtured her children's schooling and supported their entry as young adults into the teaching profession through sending them off to college as they came of age. By all appearances, Emma Kenney and Samuel Meredith had successfully defied a racist system to carve out a life together and achieve the comfort and stability of respectability. Tragically, however, in 1915, some time after Samuel Meredith moved into the home with his wife and their remaining daughter, he found life increasingly difficult: his work as a carpenter dried up, he was in debt and deeply depressed. Early one morning shortly after Amaza Lee's twentieth birthday, Samuel Meredith put a revolver to his head and killed himself.[3]

In her letters, Amaza Lee Meredith never mentions her father, but in a series of biographical notes she documents his influence. Despite his early instruction in drawing, Samuel Meredith dissuaded his daughter from pursuing her dream of becoming an architect, most likely because he understood that as a woman, and particularly as a black woman, such a career choice was closed to her. Meredith's mother had, however, instilled a faith in education and personal achievement in her daughter. The young Amaza Lee attended Lynchburg's Jackson Street High School, which had been first established to serve liberated slaves as a Freedmen's Methodist Episcopal School. It had an all-white faculty and a curriculum rooted in classical humanities with supplemental manual arts instruction.[4] Schools such as these were explicitly designed to fashion future leaders, and advocates of African-American success expected great things of them.[5] In 1912, at the age of seventeen, Meredith graduated top of her class, receiving a three-year diploma. She wanted to become a teacher, but found she lacked the credentials newly determined by the Negro Organization Society, an authority recently formed to raise the pedagogical standards established in 1907 to administer and promote universal improvements in education, increase school attendance, develop high schools, build better elementary school facilities, and create improved conditions for teachers, including higher pay.[6]

In the summer of 1915, seeking to comply with the new rules for teaching, Meredith attended Virginia Normal and Industrial Institute in Petersburg, Virginia. She took classes in grammar, mathematics, geography, and European history to prepare for a primary school teaching certificate. It was at this time that Meredith fell for one of her teachers: Edna Colson, a woman only a few years older but already established as a college-level instructor. Colson was strongly independent with a keen intellect and sense of purpose. A political activist, she was among the first black women to vote in Virginia in 1920 and established the elite Delta Omega Chapter of the Alpha Kappa Alpha Sorority in 1921. This was the female equivalent to a black fraternity known for producing leaders dedicated to the mission of providing community services including education, healthcare, economic empowerment, improved family relations, political action, and support for the arts. Together with other members of her family, Colson dedicated her life to increasing her own academic credentials in order to improve educational opportunities for other African Americans. Colson was indicative of African-American women of a certain social standing who were trained to serve their communities and to do so in a number of ways, from teaching in classrooms to instructing field workers in simple health and hygiene.[7] Colson was an enthusiastic participant in the politics and practice of racial uplift, and she had a deep influence on Meredith's career trajectory, guiding her and supporting her with pedagogical literature and advice.

National discourses on race, women, and political progress were beginning to shift in important ways in the years that Meredith and Colson joined them. African-American women had fought for their rights as equal citizens from the earliest days of the female suffrage movement, demanding to be considered a critical component of political progress. It was at the National Women's Rights Convention of 1851 in Akron, Ohio, that Sojourner Truth delivered her famous speech, 'Ain't I a Woman?'[8] But even though African-American women continued to demand recognition throughout the second half of nineteenth century, racism meant, as Firor Scott has noted, that '[b]lack women and white women followed parallel but quite separate tracks' in the struggle for suffrage and other rights.[9] Particularly in the South, a handful of religious groups were the only associations that attempted to fuse the efforts of white and black women. This began to change in the 1920s in the wake of national victory for female suffrage, thanks to the pioneering efforts of the League of Women Voters, 'which in a few southern towns … began to examine its own community situations.'[10] Amaza Lee Meredith and Edna Colson thus both came of age at a key moment when female solidarity was very slowly beginning to grow across racial boundaries, primarily in cities. Central Virginia must have seemed far away from the most progressive developments taking place in the country, but the fact that progress was being made anywhere was enough to fuel hope for change everywhere.

The Virginia Normal and Industrial Institute also experienced profound change at precisely the time that Meredith and Colson found their lives intertwined there, making substantive advances as an agent of black empowerment after many years of attack and repression by Virginia's racist white elite. Considering the evolution of the school in context with the larger history of African-American education sheds light on the vision for continued change that Meredith encapsulated in her unusual modern house. The drive for state-sponsored African-American education began in the first days after the Civil War ended in 1865 and the door opened to Reconstruction, a brief period of optimism and progress in which African Americans attained and exercised many of the rights and responsibilities of citizenship. At this time, the federal government's Bureau of Refugees, Freedmen, and Abandoned Lands (later known as the Freedmen's Bureau), Northern missionary societies, and African Americans themselves took responsibility for educating the almost 90-percent illiterate black adults who had been prohibited from learning to read and write by state law.[11] Federal aid to education, land redistribution, and civil rights were all critical areas regarded as necessary to the political and economic rehabilitation of the South.[12] For newly freed African-American men and women, 'universal schooling was a necessary function of a free society,' and stood as the '"token and pledge" of emancipation.'[13]

Certain enclaves in the South received greater attention than others: Lynchburg, Virginia, established a stable and relatively strong middle school system, while Petersburg, a few miles away, became a center of higher education. Even before the Civil War, the latter city had, in fact, been known as place where free black people could expect to receive at least a semblance of respect relative to most southern cities and certainly compared to rural areas.[14] In 1882, State Delegate Alfred A. Harris, a black attorney and resident of Dinwiddie County, Virginia, presented a bill proposing an institution of higher education with a college and teacher training program specifically for African Americans. He stipulated that this institution be presided over by black teaching faculty and a black president. The founding papers declared this 'the first time a colored man has been placed in entire control over his own destiny.'[15] Significantly, Harris also supported establishing a vocational training school for low-income rural African Americans, suggesting an existing class differentiation within the black community that required a two-tier pedagogical system with one curriculum founded on academic liberal arts principles, and another dedicated to mechanical arts and industrial training. On the fourth day of July in 1883, with support from the Grand Lodge of Colored Masons, the foundation bricks for the Virginia Normal and Collegiate Institute were laid with great pomp and ceremony on the outskirts of Petersburg.[16] In 1886, graduation ceremonies conferred the first baccalaureate degrees. Members of Edna Colson's family were among those graduates, becoming major players in the education of the South and in the case of Colson's father, James M. Colson, became one its first teachers.

The reassertion of white supremacy, however, brought Reconstruction to an end in the 1890s, and African Americans entered a whole new period of violent discrimination and segregation. It was into this period that Meredith and Colson were born. The political situation in the southern states grew increasingly complex and turbulent as northerners concerned with the slow pace of economic improvement allied themselves with white southerners in an attempt to create greater national unity, and in doing so, turned their backs on African Americans. Black gains in economic and social status had been resented and feared by southern whites, and the removal of northern oversight permitted a slew of restrictive laws and covenants, known as Jim Crow segregation laws, intended to keep the races apart and African Americans in a subordinate position. These social shifts had profound personal and political impacts on Meredith, contributing to the demise of her father and undermining black education across the board. African-American schools and colleges were no longer heralded as key to a new era.[17] The consequences for the Virginia Normal and Collegiate Institute were profound, as the outspoken and dynamic African-American president, John Mercer, and the interracial Board of Trustees were replaced with a new president and an all-white board. The new chair of the all-white Board of Trustees insisted that the school introduce cooking, sewing, and other 'industrial courses' into the curriculum.[18] Funds originally intended for the Institute's college curriculum were used to pay for new industrial training equipment and instructors. The word 'college,' and the academic curriculum it represented, was erased from the school's name. Soon, manual training for men and domestic science for women formed the basis of study.[19]

In July 1902, the Virginia Normal and Collegiate Institute was downgraded to become the Virginia Normal and Industrial Institute, with a set of courses that the Board had decided would 'fit our graduates to be better teachers.' The school received a new African-American president, James Hugo Johnson, but he was profoundly restricted in his power to resist state-mandated erosions. He protested vocally but mildly, wary of seeing the school defunded or shut down completely. He also, however, fought hard to maintain the teacher training that would later shape Amaza Lee Meredith, and attempted to leverage the language of Jim Crow to cling to his black teachers, writing,

> There is no danger of the white and colored schools ever being mixed, that is beyond the bounds of probability, is antagonistic to the wishes of both races … We are so much opposed to it that white teachers for colored schools is too much mixing for us.[20]

Those black teachers and their students resisted in other ways. While the official curriculum of Virginia Normal and Industrial Institute appeared to focus on teacher training and limit other students to the basics of industrial jobs, subjects such as fine art and art appreciation were subversively introduced in the form of school clubs. These were precisely the subjects that Meredith would later choose to take up as a teacher, and to practice as a scholar and designer in her own right. Meanwhile, in order to gain her first teaching credentials, Edna Colson went south to attend Fisk University in Nashville, established in 1867, and fast becoming an elite institution with such eminent graduate scholars as W.E.B. Du Bois. As she took up her post in Petersburg, however, the Virginia Normal and Industrial Institute received a new president, John Gandy. Gandy, also a Fisk graduate, had been hired as a teacher of Greek and Latin but was converted to a general teaching instructor when the school was downgraded in 1902. Partly due to his determination and resourcefulness, and partly due to a slightly softening state climate, he managed to elevate the Institute back to a higher position over the next decade, as Colson and Meredith taught and attended the school. He oversaw the conversion of the school into a 'land-grant college' for black Virginians in 1920, gaining considerable long-term resources through the acquisition of state-donated real estate, and he reclaimed the upper-level college department in 1923 after its two-decade absence. These were considerable achievements, offering tangible demonstration of positive social and political change that valorized education as both the means and at least some of the ends of racial struggle. When Amaza Lee Meredith entered the Virginia Normal and Industrial Institute, she was a young woman empowered by a newly gained right to vote, in an institution that had reclaimed its mandate to forge intellectual leaders.

To measure her powers

Meredith fell in love with learning and with her instructor. Colson made it clear that she reciprocated her student's romantic feelings, and they began a sporadic but long-term love affair. Much of this was conducted long-distance at first, for after securing her teaching credentials, Meredith began a journey through what could be described as the entire African-American education system, taking up teaching roles at every level open to her, from the most meager rural, one-room school, through urban elementary and high schools, and culminating in the college system.[21] During her time working through the system, Meredith spent many years away from Colson, but Petersburg remained her intellectual and emotional center, and she kept in touch through regular and intense correspondence. Even when their relationship was still new and undefined, Meredith wrote:

> My dear Miss Colson, I was lying on the divan in the sitting-room, all alone. I was thinking of you, Miss Colson, thinking so tenderly of you. Have you ever thought of anyone until your emotion was so intense that your heart frightened you by its beating?[22]

Subsequent messages speak of love and commitment to true friendship, and excitement over anticipated visits. The spirit of those reunions sustained through subsequent years of absence, was kept alive through frequent letter exchanges over a period of thirty-five years. As Colson made clear in a letter to her mother, it was unlikely that she would marry as her commitment to the teaching profession, and the service to community it demanded, was prohibitive to the point of personal sacrifice, and the duties of housewife and mother could scarcely be accommodated within the schedule of one dedicated to developing the pedagogical field.[23]

Meredith's first full-time, permanent teaching job consisted of two years in an elementary school in Botetourt County, deep in the western Virginia mountains. Her experiences reveal the devastating condition of education for rural folk as well as the extent to which young women of a more affluent and educated social status were expected to sacrifice themselves. Meredith wrote to Colson sharing the hardships stemming from the fact that her meager schoolhouse was no match for the mountainous climate: 'Cold! Cold! Cold! That isn't the word. And the wind—The temperature has been flirting around zero for a week, I could not hold school yesterday.' Two weeks later, weather conditions were still preventing students from attending class. Meredith confided her frustration:

> I can readily assure you, it is a mess. I used to think that it would develop a teacher to have experience in a country school … of course the 'experience' is good, but there are so many disadvantages that the ideal school is too far removed … No method and management in the world can bring a country school up to par. They are rotten from the beginning to end; they're a disgrace to the State. It makes me fighting mad every time I think of it and that is just what I'm doing, Fighting![24]

After completing two years' teaching experience in these dreadful conditions, Meredith responded eagerly to encouragement by Colson and members of her family with connections to the leadership of the influential National Association for the Advancement of Colored People to go north and expand her professional credentials. In 1926, she joined her older sister, Maude, in her recently established home in a large brownstone apartment at 416 West 146th Street, a neighborhood on the north side of Harlem. Harlem, New York, was what Howard University philosophy professor and cultural critic Alain Locke identified in 1925 as the birthplace of *The New Negro*. It was here he argued that the offspring of a 'new era' resulting from the coalescing of social, psychological, and cultural change was occurring. Moreover, for Locke, Harlem was nothing less than a modern 'race capital' where African Americans were beginning to dispel old, negative stereotypes, and simultaneously reinforce black centrality to American democratic life. Disillusioned with the lack of political progress and the denial of civil rights owed to African Americans, Locke pushed for the use of art and culture to force a 'revaluation by white and black alike of the Negro in terms of his artistic endowments and cultural contributions, past and prospective.' It was through the arts, he declared, that African Americans could secure this re-evaluation and find entry into the 'main stream' of American culture, a euphemism for equal rights and assimilation.[25]

Accordingly, Meredith enrolled at Columbia University Teacher's College in 1926 to specialize in fine art and art appreciation. These areas of expertise would qualify her as a member of what prominent black intellectual W.E.B. Du Bois had defined as the Talented Tenth, an elite group distinguishable from the black masses by their high level of education, moral authority, and cultural knowledge.[26] They would lead the black community, acting as a buffer between the black underclass and white society, and overcoming America's relentless racism. Although women, desperate to move beyond the limits of domestic service, had already begun entering the ranks of leadership as educators, it seems Du Bois and many of his followers had men in mind for the Talented Tenth.[27] As historian Kevin Gaines has noted, this was one of the problems of 'racial uplift' ideology. Internal divisions along gender, class, and other fault lines led to 'intensive soul-searching, ambivalence, and dissension on the objectives of black leadership and on the meaning of black progress.' There were those who, quite simply, did not agree with patriarchal authority and had their own ideas about progress.[28] Thus, even while Meredith fell in line with certain aspects of the Talented Tenth ideology, her doing so as an independent, self-sufficient, active woman represented a bold adaptation of the strategy. By obtaining her education from the elite, urban, northern Columbia University, she not only gained the level of qualification necessary to join the Talented Tenth, she was also exposed to New York's modern cultural scene, which would prove extremely influential.

In the 1920s, *New York Times* travel writer Miriam Beard called the city a 'Wild Urban Jungle,' describing it with imagery of the untamed, the raw, the feared, and yet anachronistically modern and implicitly sophisticated urban.[29] Historian Ann Douglas argued:

> A good part of New York's cultural preeminence and power in the 1920s came from the simple fact that New York was chief Mecca to the

> hundreds of thousands of Negroes emigrating South to North in the Great War years and bringing their 'gift of story and song' with them.[30]

This is not to say that New York was a racial utopia—even the vibrancy that African Americans brought to the city was subject to attack and ridicule. Critics of racial mixing called New York a 'mongrel city,' and it was usually in reference to African-American cultural production that images of the untamed temperament were summoned, as in the new black dances brought to the city bearing animalistic names such as the Turkey Trot, the Fox Trot, and the Monkey Glide. Crowning all of this was the increasing notoriety of the most famous black female dancer, Josephine Baker, whose stardom blossomed as an expatriate in Paris, commanding entire nightclubs and hobnobbing with, among others, early modernist architects.[31] Yet, even if many whites simultaneously derided and delighted at the growing international profile of jazz culture, the public liberation of figures such as Baker were suggestive of broader possibilities for African Americans. By contrast, Elise Johnson McDougald, writing in Locke's *New Negro* anthology, defined less-sensational opportunities, singling out Harlem as a 'modern city in the world's metropolis,' where achievement and refinement were accessible to black educated women. It was in this new homeplace where the 'Negro woman is free from the cruder handicaps of primitive household hardships and the grosser forms of sex and race subjugation. Here she has considerable opportunity to measure her powers in the intellectual and industrial fields of the great city.'[32]

In New York, from her arrival in 1926 until 1930, when she received her Bachelor's degree at the age of thirty-two, Meredith grew into the 'New Negro' ideation. As an educated, modern individual, she presented a vision of womanhood which strongly denied the persistence of black female stereotypes lingering in the American imagination. She pursued her intellectual growth with great discipline and perseverance. Despite the sexual longing she expressed in letters to Colson, Meredith declared a distaste for the city's libertine night life and a preference for the quieter, more refined recreational and commercial outlets.[33] She delighted in learning and found tremendous fulfillment in the turn she had taken towards the arts, writing,

> This education is my whole life … I've 'found' myself, thank God, through my love for you and … Now I'm trying to loose [sic] myself in my work … Think of my majoring in Fine Art after wanting to all these years! Are you glad, Edna? Do you think it a wise step?'[34]

Meredith's studies followed the guiding principles set out by Arthur Wesley Dow in the Fine Art curriculum for Columbia Teacher's College, particularly in a course on Home Decoration and Interior Design, which included 'Lectures, discussion, experiments, and studio work—trips to shops, museums, civic buildings and centers.'[35] Design elements would be explored through a focus on 'line, tone, color, and the use of these elements through the great historic periods of interior decoration to the present.' A modern approach to designing domestic space, 'including the plan of the house and the use of hand and machine processes in furnishing and decoration,' was 'to be developed in conjunction with trips to shops, and museums.' Meredith was in the right city to immerse herself in modern design. In June 1927, the trade press praised Macy's department store for presenting modernism to the general public: 'Macy's has finally commercialized this modern art, but based upon the soundest of foundations: the demand of the consumer.'[36] Later in 1927, Wannamaker's department store also established a permanent department devoted to modernist furniture and decorative objects. In 1928, Lord & Taylor's followed suit and Abraham & Strauss hired architectural designer Paul T. Frankl to 'transform its "livable house," an area dedicated to furnishings, from an American Colonial cottage into a sophisticated Modernist Villa.'[37] Not to be outdone by the commercial venues, in 1926 and 1929 the Metropolitan Museum held exhibitions showcasing furniture by Jacques-Emile Ruhlman, purchased at the Paris Exposition des Arts Decoratifs et Industriels Modernes, exposing the American public to the new modernist mode in home furnishings. In 1928, the Metropolitan Museum hosted the *Architect and the Industrial Arts: An Exhibition of Contemporary American Design*, noted for its lavishness. These were part of a series of exhibits stemming from an initiative to further the 'application of the arts to manufacture and practical life.'[38] An Architectural League exhibition organized by Raymond Hood showed the work of architects and interior designers side by side for the first time. Meredith visited this show and on returning to teach art and architecture at Virginia Normal and Industrial Institute, she used the catalogue in her syllabus for Principles of Architecture. Coming from an institution that trained teachers and students in industrial arts, Meredith would surely have been satisfied to see the application of such knowledge being promoted in the most upscale of venues such as the museums and sophisticated department stores in the nation's economic and cultural capital.

Meredith's tenure in the 'racial capital' of Harlem, in the 'wild urban jungle' of New York, provided her with a new perspective on life and the credentials to teach at Virginia Normal and Industrial Institute. She returned to Petersburg as a 'New Negro' as well as a new woman, and she discovered that things were continuing to evolve there, too. In 1930, President John Gandy led the change in the institution's name from VNII to Virginia State College for Negroes, reflecting greater ambitions for its pedagogical mission and prestige. As the curriculum became increasingly rigorous, more was demanded of the teachers, and Meredith once again found herself in need of burnishing her credentials. No sooner had she returned home to Colson than she returned to Columbia Teacher's College for a master's degree, which she completed from 1930–1935. During her second plunge into New York's cultural scene, Meredith attended exhibitions put on by the American Union of Decorative Artists and Craftsmen (AUDAC) at the Brooklyn Museum in 1931, and the Museum of Modern Art's influential *Modern Architecture: International Exhibition* of 1932. Again, Meredith kept the catalogues from these exhibits to use in her course syllabi back in Virginia. She would also use them to design her home. Meredith's thesis, 'An Orientation Course in Art Appreciation for College Students,' expressed her desire to see 'art function vitally' in society, both to nourish employment and to help develop 'a more worthy citizenship.' She hoped to teach art appreciation so that it 'might function in all phases of the student's life, both in college and out.' She was careful to identify a socially dynamic engagement with art as something more than 'this pseudo art appreciation that has as its criterion a glib though limited parlor conversational ability to discuss what is termed "Kultur."' No, she wrote, 'it is a dynamic art appreciation that will function in the student's whole life.'[39]

At home in Azurest

With her master's degree firmly in hand, Meredith returned to Virginia State College in 1935 and immediately initiated the Art Department, which she would lead for the rest of her career. She aimed to attract students away from domestic science courses and into the arts where they could learn graphic design, fine art, and the principles of architecture, and then enter new professions in those fields. She also worked hard to take her design principles into the community at large, serving as 'an advisor of interior decoration' on the local Better Homes Committee, part of a nationwide movement known as Better Homes of America. Discussed in Chapter 4 of this book, the movement was dedicated to increasing American home ownership and improving the efficiencies and healthiness of domestic life. Meredith's affiliation with this group was a considerable achievement, indicating that she was being recognized as a voice of authority in design. The full flowering of her professional life was interwoven with the fulfilment of her romantic desires when, after years of sporadic long-distant relations with Edna Colson, throughout which both women lived as boarders or took up residence at college dormitories, the two women entered into a permanent relationship.[40] Meredith built an independent home for herself and her partner, naming it Azurest. This poetic word, also her invention, suggests a place where the deep blue sky of hope meets the safe space of comfort. It was a place Meredith and Colson could finally call home together.

Feminist and race theorist, bell hooks, has argued that the construction of a homeplace, 'however fragile, and tenuous; the hut, the wooden shack,' has historically had a radical political dimension for African Americans. Because, she argues, 'in a world of racial apartheid, of domination, one's "homeplace" was the site where one could freely confront the issue of humanization, where one could resist.' Moreover, it was in making safe and ennobling homes that black women resisted the all-encompassing, seemingly inescapable systems of racial oppression.[41] It is also worth revisiting the notion that homeownership itself was seen at the time as a key component of racial liberation, if also an elusive one. Census statistics covering the decade between 1920 and 1930 indicate that fewer than 50 percent of all Americans owned their own home, but fewer than 23 percent of African Americans were homeowners. Reliance on the property of others meant that African Americans were exposed to discrimination, abuse, and neglect, including uncontrolled rent rises, poor property maintenance and relegation to neighborhoods at the margins of urban environments. Campaigns by white and black groups alike—including the Better Homes Committee of which Meredith was a part—encouraged property ownership and the development of homes worthy of American citizens. Such homes were tastefully decorated, well maintained, and model spaces of Christian virtue. Most of these followed local vernacular and traditional aesthetics such as Colonial Revival, reinforcing a nostalgic connection to a romanticized past.[42]

Meredith was not enamored with the past. Azurest may have been hopeful and restful, with a quiet site and modest scale, but it was bold for a black woman to build and own her own home, and this boldness was made manifest in the house's style. Declaring its presence in the avant-garde language of architectural revolution, Azurest reflects the radical European modernist work she encountered studying in New York, particularly the architecture of Le Corbusier, which was featured prominently in the International Style exhibition Meredith attended. Azurest also fits the contextual narrative of other progressive homes that women were building in the early twentieth century. These worked to demonstrably modify behavior through the provision of new kinds of spaces, visibly transforming perceptions both of what women wanted and what they had the capacity to achieve. The architectural plan around which Meredith organized her domestic realm focused on a central living space (Figure 2.5), cushioned by the more functional spaces of daily activity. Serving both a private and a public role, the living room was a quiet sanctuary in which to relax unexposed to scrutiny, and a place of entertainment for those given permission to enter. To the south, within the rounded ends of the dwelling, Meredith placed two large bedrooms of equal size, suggestive of a balanced partnership built on equality. Utilitarian spaces were placed on the periphery to the north including a small kitchen, located with direct access to the rear entrance and connected to a utility room and a garage. A studio space also located on the periphery of the dwelling indicated the importance of work as integral to life and reinforced the living room's overlaps of the private with the public.

The inclusion of a studio space on the north façade can be understood as representing what Alice T. Friedman has called a 'hybrid domestic type,' in which the home was redefined in new terms signaling changes in the compositions of and relations within families. Moreover, Friedman has argued, the heterosexual 'norm' reflected in the spatial composition of traditional domestic buildings no longer applied in the modern world of the early twentieth century, as female couples or unrelated groups began to reconfigure the spaces in which their relationships were played out. Friedman has recognized the significance of women as forces of social and architectural change in the history of modern design, arguing that the newly independent women of the early twentieth century,

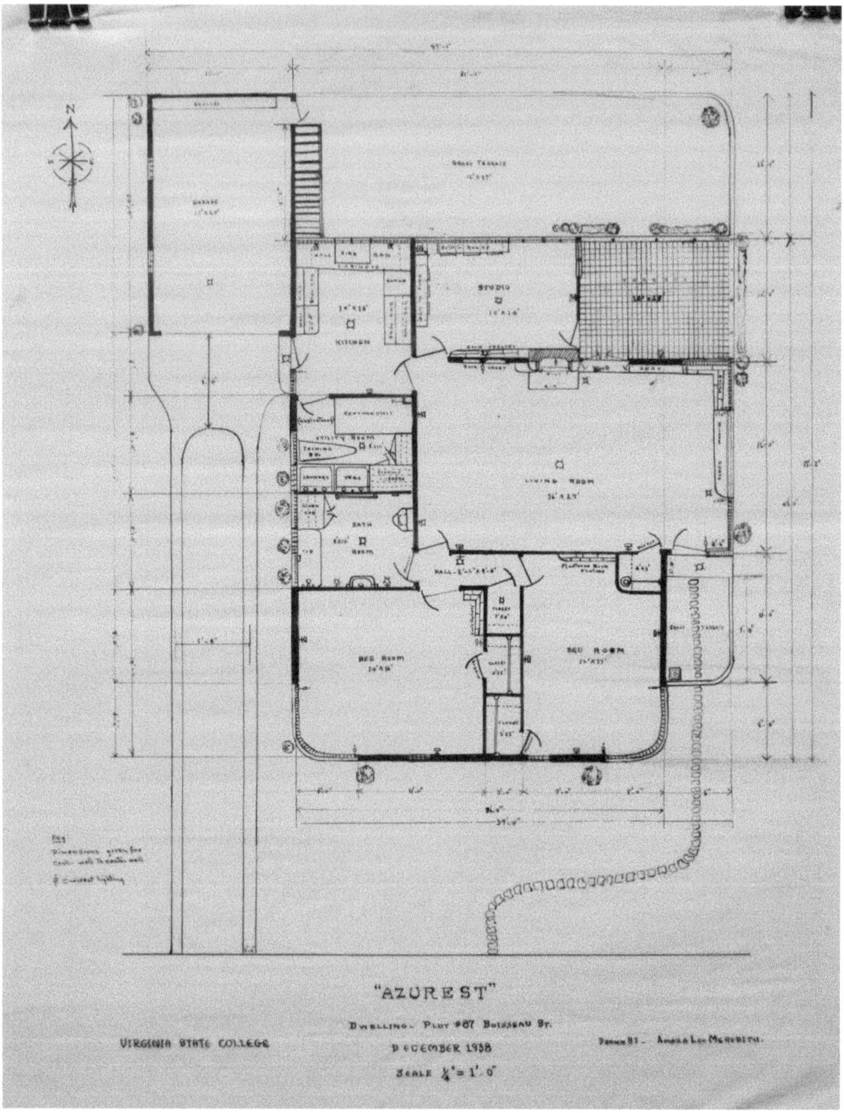

FIGURE 2.5 The floor plan of Azurest, Amaza Lee Meredith, 1938

Source: Architectural Drawings, Series IX, Box 18, Amaza Lee Meredith Papers, 1912, 1930–1938, Accession #198220, Special Collections Dept. Johnson Memorial Library, Virginia State University, Petersburg, VA

commonly referred to in contemporary literature and in scholarship as the 'New Woman.' Serving as 'catalysts for innovation in domestic projects,' they came together to discuss their values and visions for change, and redefined the fundamentals of domesticity in spatial and physical terms. 'Given the opportunity to act as clients in their own right,' Friedman explained, '[they] would seek out new architectural solutions to accommodate unconventional ways of living.'[43]

Meredith's carefully designed house seems custom-tailored to serve as a showpiece of art appreciation and modern design, celebrating her and Colson's status as exemplary scholars of value to their community. Her drawings are intricately detailed with clearly defined built-in shelving and cabinetry, window seats, and even exterior landscape features suggesting a strong interest in the interactive functioning of space (Figure 2.6). As a student, Meredith's aesthetic was most importantly influenced by the proto-modernist Arthur Wesley Dow, whose concept was to teach the value of art through applying a formula based on structural form. This method focused on the harmonic design combination of line, tone, and color, which had the effect of essentializing and universalizing artistic composition, dissolving the distinctions, real or perceived, of historical, national, racial, and ethnic boundaries. Line was critical as it permitted the artist or designer to sketch out a composition through the division of space within a square. This design method translated into architecture as horizontal and vertical lines intersecting at 90-degree angles to divide wall planes into sections.[44] Meredith's drawings reveal a commitment to the use of such lines to create overall forms and interior details.

Meredith also photographed her home interior, using it as laboratory for design and living, preserving her design method and providing a model for home ownership (Figures 2.7 and 2.8). They capture the sheen of modern materials as well as other trappings of modern living: a couple of armchairs nestled before a streamlined, art moderne fireplace, a large radio, framed photos, a small wooden statue and other *objets d'art* on the mantle, newspapers piled on a side table. Her photographs are *tableaux* staged to reveal the inhabitants' shared identity, which was built on sophisticated knowledge of current trends in design, the most up-to-date fashions, and, most importantly, avant-garde ideas about modern living.

One entrance to the house faced the community, but the other opened onto the carport and garage of the house, which, like many other modern houses, gave precedence to the automobile. Such a conscious embrace of the car further articulated Meredith's and Colson's independence as modern women (Figure 2.9). While men tended to play the role of automobile owners and operators in advertising literature, women were depicted as passive passengers. At Azurest, a house without men seized the automobile and made the most of the safety and independence it offered female motorists. A fuller understanding of the significance of women becoming their own 'drivers'—in both a literal and metaphorical sense—is aided by the definition some scholars have given to the 'New Woman': she is a denizen of the liberating, jazz-age cosmopolitan city, where she is 'mediated and mediatized by emerging industries, pulp fiction, advertising, and cinema,' and where she is 'pictured as "going places" … at the wheel of an automobile, at the helm of a speedboat, in the cockpit of an airplane.'[45] Meredith was now a long way from New York, but she had clearly

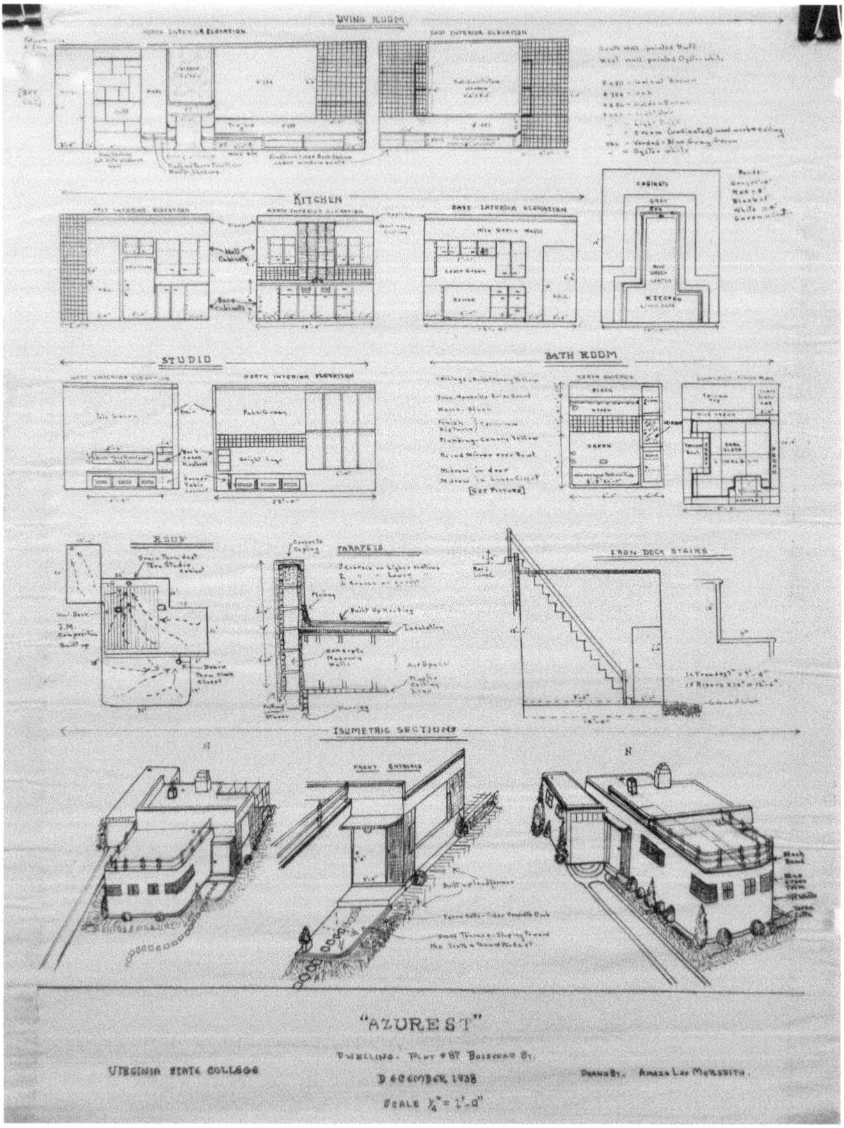

FIGURE 2.6 Perspective and detail drawings for Azurest, Amaza Lee Meredith, 1938

Source: Architectural Drawings, Series IX, Box 18, Amaza Lee Meredith Papers, 1912, 1930–1938, Accession #198220, Special Collections Dept. Johnson Memorial Library, Virginia State University, Petersburg, VA

brought some of the spirit and independence of that city with her when she returned to the more provincial environs of Petersburg. Her modernist house asserted as much, and the roar of her automobile amplified it. She would take that car around her city and occasionally up north, to Long Island, New York,

FIGURE 2.7 Interiors

Source: Architectural Drawings, Series IX, Box 18, Amaza Lee Meredith Papers, 1912, 1930–1938, Accession #198220, Special Collections Dept. Johnson Memorial Library, Virginia State University, Petersburg, VA

where her design career continued to unfold. That part of her life falls outside the purview of this chapter, but it should be noted, at least, that she continued to develop the architectural themes and principles established at Azurest.

Amaza Lee Meredith was a member of the Talented Tenth, an ambassador of the arts, and a harbinger of modernity. The importance of modernity in the architecture of Azurest cannot be seen merely as an expression of personal taste or commitment to the patterns of her education, although these were also certainly in play. The promises offered by modern progress were drawn in highly political, racial, and gendered terms by the traditional conditions of Virginia for black women. These conditions had visited personal tragedy upon Meredith in her Victorian childhood home, and they had long undermined black life in the communities and schools where she worked. Recently, some hard-won gains had been achieved in women's rights and black education, but such gains had been stolen by white supremacists before, and much more progress would be necessary before full liberation could be achieved and secured. Wielding her education—itself a political triumph—Meredith designed a home that could serve as a haven for herself and her companion, and one that spoke to the aesthetics and values of a woman who was cosmopolitan, progressive, and sophisticated. She was not just entering the future on her terms, she was helping to build it.

Prominent housing critic Catherine Bauer noted in a *New York Times* article of 1928 that it was the French who led the vanguard in envisioning new ways of living, specifically in the way they 'looked to the house as a machine,' but that:

FIGURE 2.8 Interiors

Source: Architectural Drawings, Series IX, Box 18, Amaza Lee Meredith Papers, 1912, 1930–1938, Accession #198220, Special Collections Dept. Johnson Memorial Library, Virginia State University, Petersburg, VA

FIGURE 2.9 Amaza Lee Meredith driving an automobile, ca. 1943

Source: Architectural Drawings, Series IX, Box 18, Amaza Lee Meredith Papers, 1912, 1930–1938, Accession #198220, Special Collections Dept. Johnson Memorial Library, Virginia State University, Petersburg, VA

'Americans were still living in their Colonial Revival homes, surrounded by the bric-a-brac of a bygone age.'[46] Here, however, only a decade later, in a small Virginian community far from any major metropolis, was a house answering Bauer's call for 'a complete break with architectural tradition.'[47] Azurest was an architectural intervention in a landscape dominated by a provincial, conservative, segregated society's values and constraints. The house designed to claim and assert the interests of independent and self-determined women, for the benefit of the entire community who depended upon Virginia State College for their education and who called Petersburg home. Today the feat that Meredith achieved is listed on the National Register of Historic Places, significant for its unique contribution to modernist architecture. Continuing to draw attention, the house testifies to the possibilities of a homeplace in which black women could resist, relax, be themselves, and teach others that they need not be contained by old and stifling systems of exclusion.

Notes

1 Land records indicate Henry H. Meredith, Samuel's great grandfather, purchased property in 1806, 1810, 1814, and 1816. Succeeding generations are also listed as purchasing property. Index to Real Estate Conveyances, Circuit Court, Records and Archives, Lynchburg, Virginia; see also United States Department of Census Records for 1850, 1860, 1870, 1880, and Directories of the City of Lynchburg for 1887–1900.

2 Evelyn Brooks Higginbotham, *Righteous Discontent: The Women's Movement in the Black Baptist Church, 1880–1920* (Cambridge, MA: Harvard University Press, 1993), p. 13. Evidence of friendship between Kenney and local white educators is visible in, for example, the letter from Anna LeGrande, principal of Jackson Street School, to Emma Kenney Meredith, July 28, 1936, Amaza Lee Meredith Papers, 1912, 1930–1938, Accession #1982–20, Series II, Box-Folder 1:2, Special Collections Dept., Johnson Memorial Library, Virginia State University, Petersburg, VA.

3 Newspaper articles indicate that at 2:00am, Emma Kenney Meredith called for the police after hearing a shot and finding her husband dead, *Lynchburg News,* "Killed Himself: Samuel Meredith Killed Himself by his Own Hand Yesterday," August 6, 1915.

4 Kelly Miller and Joseph R. Gay, *Progress and Achievements of the Colored People* (Washington, DC: Austin Jenkins Co., 1917), pp. 227–233; See also "Struggle, Sacrifice, and Scholarship—Black Education in Central Virginia, 1800–1922," Legacy Museum, Lynchburg, Virginia, online exhibition: https://legacymuseum.org/exhibits/struggle-sacrifice-scholarship (accessed March 24, 2011).

5 Annual Report of the Hampton Negro Conference, vol. 11–16 (Hampton, VA: Hampton Normal and Agricultural Institute, 1907), p. 72. Lynchburg is singled out along with Norfolk as a place in which a good education was assured.

6 *Ibid.*, p. 66.

7 For a comprehensive discussion of the commitment expected of young African-American women whose families could afford to support their daughter's education and the role they then played in uplifting the less-able members of the race, see Stephanie J. Shaw, *What a Woman Ought to Be and to Do* (Chicago, IL: Chicago University Press, 1996), specifically pp. 211–214.

8 Sojourner Truth, *Speech to the Women's Rights Convention in Akron, Ohio, 1851*, printed in *Anti-Slavery Bugle* of Salem, Ohio, June 21, 1851.

9 Anne Firor Scott, *Natural Allies: Women's Associations in American History* (Urbana and Chicago, IL: University of Illinois Press, 1991), p. 180.

10 *Ibid.*, p. 181.

11 James Anderson, *The Education of Blacks in the South, 1860–1935* (Chapel Hill, NC: University of North Carolina Press, 1988), p. 18.

12 Edward L. Ayers, *The Promise of the New South: Life After Reconstruction* (Oxford: Oxford University Press, 207), p. 8.

13 Anderson, *The Education of Blacks in the South: 1860–1935*, p. 18.

14 Luther Porter Jackson, *Free Negro Labor and Property-Holding* (New York: D. Appleton-Century Co., 1942), pp. 146–148.

15 R.F. Walker, *Thirteenth Annual Report of the State of Virginia Superintendent of Public Instruction, Year ending July 1883* (Richmond, VA: Superintendent of Public Printing, 1883), Virginia State University Digital Archives Collection, HBCU Library Alliance: A Digital Collection Celebrating the Founding of the Historically Black College and University online: https://hbcudigitallibrary.auctr.edu/digital/collection/VSUD (accessed May 3, 2012).

16 Anderson, *The Education of Blacks in the South: 1860–1935*, pp. 110–148.

17 Raymond Wolters, *The New Negro on Campus: Black College Rebellions of the 1920s* (Princeton, NJ: Princeton University Press, 1975), p. 7; Adam Fairclough, *Better Day Coming: Blacks and Equality, 1890–2000* (New York: Penguin, 2001), p. 3.

18 Adam Fairclough, *A Class of Their Own: Black Teachers in the Segregated South* (Cambridge, MA: Belknap Press, 2007), p. 168.

19 See Julian B. Roebuck and Komanduri S. Murty, *Historically Black Colleges and Universities: Their Place in Higher Education* (Westport, CT: Praeger, 1993), p. 93.

20 "Virginia Normal and Industrial Institute Gazette," July 1902, Virginia State University Digital Archives Collection, HBCU Library Alliance: A Digital Collection Celebrating the Founding of the Historically Black College and University online: https://hbcudigitallibrary.auctr.edu/digital/collection/VSUD (accessed March 2, 2009).

21 Biographical Notes, Amaza Lee Meredith Papers, 1912, 1930–1938, Accession #1982–20, Series II, Box-folder 5:52A, Special Collections Dept., Johnson Memorial Library, Virginia State University, Petersburg, VA. It is not known what Amaza did in the two years between graduating high school and attending summer school at VNII, but in order to teach in the rural elementary schools the qualification she needed was a Southern Board of Education Teaching Certificate. From this point on she studied sporadically at VNII and at Columbia Teacher's College to gain her teaching credentials.

22 Amaza Lee Meredith to Edna Colson, Lynchburg, Virginia, September 9, 1916, The Colson-Hill Family Papers, Accession #1965–13, Series IV: Box-folder 29:1, Special Collections and Archives, Johnston Memorial Library, Virginia State University, Petersburg, VA.

23 Edna Colson to her mother, Kate Hill, April 10, 1924, The Colson-Hill Family Papers, Accession #1965–13, Series IV: Box-folder 24:10, Special Collections and Archives, Johnston Memorial Library, Virginia State University, Petersburg, VA.

24 Amaza Lee Meredith to Edna Colson, Indian Rock, January 6, 1917, The Colson-Hill Family Papers, Accession #1965–13, Series IV: Box-folder 29:1, Special Collections and Archives, Johnston Memorial Library, Virginia State University, Petersburg, VA.

25 Alain Locke, *The New Negro* (New York: Touchstone, 1997, reprinted from Albert & Charles Boni, 1925), pp. 15, 157. For an interpretation of Locke's *The New Negro*, see Arnold Rampersand, "The Book that Launched the Harlem Renaissance," *The Journal of Blacks in Higher Education*, no. 38 (Winter, 2002–3), pp. 87–91.

26 Henry Louis Gates, Jr. and Terri Hume Oliver, eds, W.E.B. Du Bois, *The Souls of Black Folk* (New York: W.W. Norton, 1997), pp. 39–41.

27 Shaw, *What a Woman Ought to Be and to Do*, p. 90.

28 Kevin Gaines, *Uplifting the Race* (Chapel Hill, NC: University of North Carolina Press, 1996), p. 78.

29 Miriam Beard, "Wild Urban Jungle Has No Terrors for Man," *New York Times*, March 14, 1926, p. 2. http://proxy01.its.virginia.edu/login?url=https://search-proquest com.proxy01.its.virginia.edu/docview/103757253?accountid=14678 (accessed August 5, 2012).

30 Ann Douglas, *Terrible Honesty: Mongrel Manhattan in the 1920s* (New York: Noonday Press, 1995), p. 52.

31 *Ibid.*, pp 72–90.

32 Elsie Johnson McDougald, "The Task of Negro Womanhood," in Alain Locke, ed., *The New Negro*, p. 375.

33 See Meredith and Colson's correspondence: Amaza Lee Meredith to Edna Colson, NYC August 8, 1927; Amaza Lee Meredith to Edna Colson, Lynchburg, February 19, 1928; Amaza Lee Meredith to Edna Colson, New York City, January 13, 1928; Amaza Lee Meredith to Edna Colson, NYC January 27, 1929, The Colson-Hill Family Papers, Accession #1965–13, Series IV: Box-folder 29:3, 29:4, Special Collections and Archives, Johnston Memorial Library, Virginia State University, Petersburg, VA. Much has been written about the licentiousness of Harlem nightlife both at the time and since the Harlem Renaissance. See for example Steven Watson, *The Harlem Renaissance: Hub of African American Culture, 1920–1930* (New York: Pantheon, 1995), pp. 136–137.

34 Amaza Lee Meredith to Edna Colson, October 7, 1928, New York City. The Colson-Hill Family Papers, Accession #1965–13, Series IV: Box-folder 29:3, Special Collections and Archives, Johnston Memorial Library, Virginia State University, Petersburg, VA.

35 Arthur Wesley Dow, "Methods of Using the Museum," *The Metropolitan Museum of Art Bulletin*, vol. 11, no. 9 (September, 1916), p. 195.

36 "Modern Art in a Furniture Store," *Good Furniture*, 30 (January, 1928), cited in Robert A. M. Stern, Gregory Gilmartin, Thomas Mellins (eds) *New York 1930: Architecture and Urbanism Between Two World Wars* (New York: Rizzoli, 1987), p. 336.

37 Robert A. M. Stern, Gregory Gilmartin, and Thomas Mellins, eds, *New York 1930: Architecture and Urbanism Between Two World Wars* (New York: Rizzoli, 1987), pp. 337–338.
38 *Ibid.*
39 Amaza Lee Meredith, "An Orientation Course in Art Appreciation for College Students," Master's Thesis (New York: Columbia University Teachers College, 1935).
40 Biographical Notes, Amaza Lee Meredith Papers, 1912, 1930–1938, Accession #1982–20, Series II, Box-folder 5:52A, Special Collections Dept., Johnson Memorial Library, Virginia State University, Petersburg, VA; Amaza Lee Meredith to Edna Colson, December 14, 1935, The Colson-Hill Family Papers, Accession #1965–13, Series IV: Box-folder 28:20, Special Collections and Archives, Johnston Memorial Library, Virginia State University, Petersburg, VA.
41 bell hooks, "Homeplace: A Site of Resistance," in bell hooks, *Yearning: Race, Gender and Cultural Politics* (Boston, MA: South End Press, 1990), p. 47.
42 "Wm. Cooper Heads Va. Homes Drive," *The Chicago Defender*, Dec. 14, 1935.
43 Alice T. Friedman, *Women and the Making of the Modern House* (New Haven, CT: Yale University Press, 2007), pp. 16, 24. Friedman discusses Eileen Gray, Edith Farnsworth, Eleanor Raymond, and Edith Kingsbury, and as a footnote she includes Amaza Lee Meredith.
44 Walter Sargent, Book Review of *Theory and Practice of Teaching Art* by Arthur Wesley Dow, *The Elementary School Teacher*, vol. 13, no. 9 (May, 1913), pp. 455–456; Nanyoung Kim, "A History of Design Theory in Art Education," *Journal of Aesthetic Education*, vol. 40, no. 2 (Summer 2006), p. 12.
45 Whitney Chadwick and Tirza True Latimer, *The Modern Woman Revisited: Paris Between the Wars* (London: Rutgers, 2003), p. 3; see also Laura Doan, ed., *Sapphic Modernities* (New York: Palgrave McMillan, 2006). In African-American literature of the 1920s, 'New Negro' women are often depicted in cosmopolitan cities, exposed to new ideas. Meredith and Colson are very concerned with the way they dress and write frequently of the new fashions they have seen in New York. Meredith experiments with wearing trousers and in later life is typically pictured in them rather than in a traditional skirt or dress. Doan argues that 'Women in the 1920s were given the opportunity to experiment with self-expression in their dress, later they may have identified themselves as lesbian but in 1920s they were testing the boundaries of sartorial expression.' See Laura Doan, *Fashioning Sapphism: The Origins of a Modernist English Lesbian Culture* (New York: Columbia University Press, 2001), p. xxi.
46 Catherine Bauer, "Machine-Age Mansions or Ultra Moderns: French Builders Apply Ideals of the Steel and Concrete Era in Domestic Architecture," *New York Times Magazine*, April 15, 1928, pp. 10, 22.
47 Calder Loth, Mary Harding Sadler, James Hill, Azurest South, Statement of Significance, National Register of Historic Places, Department of the Interior (October 20, 1993), p. 5.

3

LIFE AND BREATH TO THE CITY

Women, urbanism, and the birth of the historic preservation movement

Nathaniel Robert Walker

By the start of the twenty-first century, the preservation of historic buildings had become a cause of global significance, inspiring passionate, if not always successful, work in communities from Boston to Beirut, from Buenos Aires to Bangkok.[1] While the origins of the movement cannot be traced to any single source, there are a handful of early advocates in a few special places who have been celebrated as prophets of preservation.[2] One of these is Susan Pringle Frost (1873–1960) of the beautiful, old, coastal city of Charleston, South Carolina. Her leadership led to the creation and adoption in 1931 of the world's first zoning ordinance explicitly dedicated to historic preservation, and she has consequently been the subject of a number of studies, few of which fail to point out the remarkable fact that she achieved powerful influence over the destiny of a conservative southern city despite her status as a working, unmarried woman.[3] There have been no systematic attempts, however, to discover and analyze meaningful connections between her gender, her architectural interests, and her political accomplishments. This chapter asserts that such connections exist, and it argues that when they are critically considered, they push to the fore an often-neglected but important dimension to Frost's values and goals: namely, that in addition to her concern with saving old buildings as historic relics, she was also passionate about protecting and enhancing urbanism. She considered it her womanly obligation and privilege to cherish and support the social and political fabric that was made possible and ennobled by densely built, elegant, long-lived city streets and neighborhoods. Importantly, she was not alone in linking preservation with good urban placemaking in general; the decades that preceded Frost's work featured a number of important calls by politically engaged women, now mostly forgotten, for improvements to American cities, and their visions were also interwoven with early declarations of appreciation for historic architecture. This chapter seeks to shed new light on the roots of the modern historic preservation movement, first by recalling early voices that linked active, politicized feminine virtue to the protection of old buildings and the sustenance of urban fabric, and then by taking another look at Susan Pringle Frost, whose accomplishments appear differently in the light of her neglected forbears. These early voices set the terms of the success that Frost enjoyed in Charleston, where her energy and resourcefulness combined with fortuitous political and economic circumstances to transform a city that was itself, strangely but advantageously, understood poetically as a woman.

For spacious public squares

One of the earliest calls for both historic preservation and American urban rejuvenation came from the pen of Mary Griffith (1772–1846). Little of her life is known. She was a resident of New Jersey who used the money she inherited upon the death of her husband to develop herself as a natural scientist and author, pursuing both arenas with an eye towards improving the conditions of American life. In the past, scholars of literature have glossed over her work, or else condemned it as 'interesting rather than important,' perhaps because the press did the same in her day.[4] Griffith's political prescience and sheer inventiveness have, however, led to a more recent reappraisal in which she has been described as a 'trailblazing' pioneer who heralded 'nineteenth-century reformist views' on the politics of gender, and who thus deserves to be acknowledged as a forerunner of more famous Victorian feminists such as Margaret Fuller and Sarah Grimké.[5]

In 1836, Mary Griffith published *Camperdown; or, News from Our Neighborhood*, a collection of several works of short fiction.[6] The first story in the book, entitled 'Three Hundred Years Hence,' was a futuristic utopian narrative, and one of the first such works to be published in America. Griffith was perhaps drawing upon Louis-Sébastien Mercier's 1770 futuristic narrative about a radically transformed Paris, published in both Britain and the United States as *Memoirs of the Year 2500*, as her book has more in common with this work than it does any British or American utopias of the period. Like Mercier, she celebrated the possibilities of urban life, while British radicals like Robert Owen or American works such as *Equality, A Political Romance* (1802, published again in 1837) and *The Paradise Within Reach of All Men* (1833) consistently insisted cities should be destroyed and replaced with mechanized landscapes of pastoral bliss.[7] The reasons for Griffith's pro-urban inclinations were suggested right at the start of the book in its dedication to Louisa Davis Minot, an accomplished author and painter who was fortunate, Griffith wrote, 'to belong to Boston; a place, above all others, wherein a woman receives that high respect and consideration to which she is so justly entitled.'[8] This valorized one of the nation's largest and most dynamic cities as a worthy, even ideal, environment for an intelligent woman, at a time when most Americans lived in rural environments or small towns.

Griffith went on to suggest reasons why women might prefer urban centers in general. The story of 'Three Hundred Years Hence' begins in the present day, in the Pennsylvanian countryside near Philadelphia, where a wealthy young bachelor, flush with success from his career in business, is building a suburban villa and contemplating the potential ups and downs of marriage. In this character's musings about female behavior, he reveals that Griffith perceived a gendered division in ideal living environments:

> he feared that when his beloved twilight found him sitting under the noble porticos which he intended to build, his wife would drag him away to some far distant route in the city; or that she would, untimely, fill the house with visitors.[9]

These two dreaded possibilities are clearly related, as both represent a disturbance of the secluded suburban idyll by social activity. The man, who has retreated to his rural domain after becoming sated with the city as a busy professional, fears contending with his wife's unquenched thirst for company and conversation.

As she developed her story, Griffith returned to the thematic tension between male and female relationships with country and city. The protagonist gets married, has a son, and nearly completes his great mansion, but is then called away to business in New York. When he bids goodbye to his sensible and normally quite restrained young bride, she 'grieved as if the separation was to last for years instead of a fortnight,' and 'followed him with her eyes' until he disappeared from her sight.[10] This was partly a testament to her affections for him, but it also spoke to the loneliness she anticipated in her isolated home. For the male protagonist, the countryside offered respite from dynamic and demanding urban life, whence he was regularly called to join the fray. For his wife, however, constrained as she was to the rural domestic realm, there was only, in addition to her own hard work, endless waiting.

Her husband never makes it to his business appointments, however, because a strange accident sends him into a three-hundred-year underground slumber. Upon emerging, he is shocked to learn that his bucolic country estate had been almost completely absorbed by a beautiful new town.[11] Taken to Philadelphia, he sees that the city is bustling more than ever. While most of its fabric had been replaced by superior architecture, a few great and significant structures from the past were saved – these include early Victorian monumental Greek Revival masterworks such as Girard College and the United States Bank, and the colonial-era, 'small, brick building' where Pennsylvania's founder William Penn had lived. This, he learns, had been restored and transformed into a public museum by a 'lady of great wealth.' Upon seeing the shameful state of decay into which the house had fallen, she had 'purchased a number of the old houses adjoining' the small residence,

> and opened an area around it, putting the whole house in thorough repair. She collected all the relics that remained of this great man, and placed them as fixtures there, and she left ample funds for repairs, so that

> there is a hope that this venerable and venerated building will endure for many centuries to come.[12]

This is an extremely early proposal for American historic preservation, coming almost immediately after the earliest campaign to preserve Philadelphia's Old State House, and antedating the first efforts to preserve George Washington's Mount Vernon estate by seventeen years.[13] The visual strategy of isolating the Penn residence through *dégagement*, in which selective demolitions extract it from the surrounding fabric, exposing it to view from all sides and declaring its special cultural value, evokes the prophecy of Mercier in *Memoirs of the Year 2500* of the liberation of the Louvre by a similar process, when it would become 'a new building by sweeping away the ruins' that encased and obscured it.[14] This became real practice in early-nineteenth century Europe and gained popularity until it became a principle strategy of figures such as Georges-Eugène Haussmann and Eugène Viollet-le-Duc, who transformed Paris, among other places, in the decades after Griffith wrote her story.[15] 'Three Hundred Years Hence' was thus extremely prophetic in both its call for historic preservation and in the specific methods suggested for the curation of old buildings in urban contexts.

That it was a 'lady of great wealth' who led the initiative is also significant. First of all, this suggested that, in the future, women would enjoy the prerogative to hold and manage both capital and real estate on an urban level, purchasing, demolishing, and restoring properties as they saw fit, transforming whole streetscapes. It was not until three years after Griffith published her book that American states even began to pass laws recognizing the rights of females to hold property independently of their husbands. Second, Griffith's story suggested on a subtler level that ladies, given the opportunity, would be unique forces for good in public life. The ruined state of the Penn House indicates that Philadelphia's menfolk had failed to demonstrate filial piety, but the lady of means had perceived this failure and taken the initiative to rectify it for the sake of the public and posterity. This would become a recurring theme over the next century, when those attuned to the politics of gender would argue that men were blinded and made shallow by day-to-day mercantilism, and that women were America's best hope for achieving any cultural depth. The emerging issue of preservation fit naturally in discussions of women's cultural prerogative in part because it was compatible with the traditional female roles of maintaining the memory of ancestors – especially male ones – by flowering graves and educating children.[16] Patricia West has pointed out how the preservation of old houses in particular 'was appealing to conservative as well as activist women because it was consistent with women's private, domestic role,' offering traditional cover for what might otherwise be critically perceived as an uncouth entry of a women into public life.[17] Griffith's imaginary engagement with the Penn House was inextricable from public life, however, because of its urban site. The transformation of that house physically impacted the fabric at large, and thus the body politic. American women had left the isolated rural homestead to claim, and redeem, life in the city.

Testifying to her commitment to engage with the broader public realm, Mary Griffith imaginatively coupled her proposal to protect and publicize the political history of Philadelphia with modern urban improvements. Exploring the future city, her astonished male protagonist finds that the outdoor meat and produce markets are sparkling clean thanks to ingenious new mechanized buildings and a district-wide sanitation system. The chaotic array of shops that lined the old commercial streets had all been replaced by sanitary, glass-covered shopping arcades that laced through the interiors of city blocks – one such arcade had, in fact, opened in Philadelphia in 1827. Instead of smoky, hazardous steamships plying up and down the city's rivers, the protagonist is stunned to observe quiet, clean, and safe new high-tech vehicles. In short, Philadelphia had blossomed into a tidy, happy, healthier, more beautiful, but nonetheless large and lively, metropolis. Inquiring into the causes of all these changes, the protagonist is repeatedly told that the education, empowerment, and honoring of women was the primary source of most modern improvements, architectural and otherwise. The distinction between genders was still maintained in the twenty-second century, Griffith explained, but the belief in the inferiority of women was gone, freeing them to contribute to most human endeavors, and driving civilization forward with new speed. Surrounded by the blessings of feminine triumph, the Victorian man became 'quite ashamed of his own times.'[18] He 'rejoiced that women were now equal to men in all that they ever considered as their rights,' but he also felt deeply sorry that he could not return to the nineteenth century to liberate his own dear wife.[19] In the end, much to his joy, he discovers that his future adventure had all been a dream, and he is restored to his family upon waking. The book then ends, and the reader is left to wonder whether the protagonist will go on to honor the lessons of the future and move his family into a sociable and historic Philadelphia townhouse so that his wife might get an education in accounting and open her own business in the nearby arcade.

In the years after Griffith presented her vision of a great American city restored and improved by liberated women, there emerged a prominent popular discourse on the value of rural and suburban cottages as the ideal venues for female virtue and duty. As Dolores Hayden has explained in *Building Suburbia*, two authors in particular created powerful images of a dreamy suburban life: Andrew Jackson Downing and Catharine Beecher.[20] Downing was a landscape architect who published romantic engravings and descriptions of middle-class cottages surrounded by productive and delightful gardens, while Beecher was a popular author, critic, and amateur designer who drew up innovative plans for country homes designed to maximize the pleasure and efficiency of traditional female domestic duties such as cooking and cleaning. Both made clear their belief that a secluded life immersed in greenery was more conducive to health, virtue, and happiness than city life, which was competitive, loud, dirty, and dangerous. Urbanism was only inhabitable by men, and even for them it was risky. Downing and Beecher were, as Hayden explained, extremely 'tentative' in their confrontations with the loneliness that inevitably attended many women's lives in isolated homesteads, briefly suggesting potential remedies such as 'neighborhood laundries' or public parks.[21] The 'yard and the house' were the best venues for the development of the core domestic virtues of 'good taste and spirituality,' and loneliness was a small price to pay for women whose lives must be, in any case, homebound.

Victorian readers received the phrase 'good taste' with tremendous gravity. It was seen by many as the chief instrument though which women might act as cultural agents. As a civilizing virtue that sharpened minds, sensitized hearts, and added spiritual depth to daily life, 'good taste' was formed primarily in the home, but it had consequences far beyond, and thus provided a vehicle for female engagement with, among other things, public architecture and urbanism. In his influential 1848 pamphlet *The Sphere and Duties of Women*, George Burnhap (1802–1859) praised the deep value of good taste, and harshly chastised men for living under the delusion 'that life is to be spent in dull drudgery to acquire the means of living, without the least reflection how those means are to be used in procuring the greatest possible enjoyment.' Material prosperity, he asserted, 'can be enjoyed only in precise proportion to the enlargement of the mind, and the cultivation of the taste.'[22] By developing their critical faculties through invested engagements with religion and art, people of good taste could break free from the degrading chains of ignorance and the animalistic domination of base sensual pleasure to claim the full potential of their minds and spirits. It was women's unique power and duty to seek such intellectual development for themselves and their families. Men, Burnhap explained, should follow their lead.[23] This suggestion was not new, as assumptions about the 'finer internal powers' and more resilient moral character of women had earned them the role of 'arbiters of taste' at least since the eighteenth century.[24] It was not a tremendous leap to suggest the women might go beyond having an indirect role on the good taste of society, by proxy of the men they educated at home, and reach out to shape public life directly. Such was clearly evident in the role of Griffith's imaginary 'lady of great wealth,' who rose above shallow commercial interests to reclaim from ruin the history and culture of Philadelphia. For people such as Griffith and Burnhap, the end result of 'good taste' would go far beyond individual personal betterment to create a healthy social and political fabric. 'There must grow up here a large and splendid city,' Burnhap declared. 'Let it not be a vast, barbarian, unintelligent body, but animated by a great, a noble, a cultivated soul.'[25] This is the soul of a woman.

Soon thereafter, the popular children's author Louisa C. Tuthill (1798–1879) offered to the reading public the first comprehensive account of architectural history to be written in the United States. This work illuminated the means for building the kind of city that Burnhap longed to see, and the volume's dedication made it clear that Tuthill agreed this was a feminine calling: 'To the Ladies of the United States of America, the Acknowledged Arbiters of Taste, this Work is Respectfully Inscribed.'[26] The beautifully illustrated book opens with an engraving of Thomas U. Walter's (1833–1848) Girard College (Figure 3.1),

FIGURE 3.1 Girard College of Philadelphia

Source: Reproduced from the frontispiece of History of Architecture, from the Earliest Times, Luisa C. Tuthill, 1848. Public domain

the same complex that Griffith had proposed saving in future Philadelphia, with a veritable parade of men, women, and children strolling together along the nearby sidewalk. The book proceeds through a remarkably inclusive global survey of buildings, including North American Indian, Egyptian, Persian, Greek, Roman, Gothic, Islamic, Mayan, Hindu, and many other traditions. Tuthill explained that the 'study of ancient Architecture, is the study of history. It reveals the religion, government, social institutions, science and art of the mighty past. Its monuments have perpetuated the names and deeds of the great.'[27] Many, therefore, were the realms of human endeavor that a study of historical architecture would permit the ladies of America to more deeply comprehend. While Tuthill did not in any instance call for women to become architects, she made it clear that the 'principles of architecture' were to be studied by women so that they could help direct the field as critics.[28] She insisted that the appreciation of history be leveraged to inform innovation: 'With a due deference to the genius of the ancients … an American architect must possess the power to adopt what is suitable to our soil, climate, manner, civil institutions, and religion, without servile imitation.'[29] Thus, Tuthill called for American women to both understand and appreciate old buildings – a logical prerequisite for preservation – and serve as informed critics and advocates of the proper development of modern ones, which should together create a rich and meaningful fabric.

Concerning the latter, Tuthill echoed Griffith's calls for comprehensive urban reform leading to better cities. While she valorized greenery in most of her specific urban prescriptions, this did not come at the expense of the social life offered by dense urbanism; indeed, Tuthill was passionate about the power of shared, bustling urban public space to create stages for diverse social interactions of true substance, transcending the atomized isolation of domestic space and alleviating the emptiness of commercial life:

> Every city should make ample provision for spacious public squares … Here, beneath the shaded walks, the inhabitants might enjoy the sweet air, the children sport upon the fresh grass, and all be refreshed and cheered by the sight of beautiful natural objects. Here the young and old might meet to 'drive dull care away,' and lose for a few brief moments the calculating, money-making plans that almost constantly usurp American thought and feeling.[30]

Calling for all American communities to create such elegant and useful public spaces, Tuthill quoted an American traveler to Spain who fell in love with that country's evening promenades, in which

> public morals are beautified and refined by social intercourse, and by mutual observation; where families meet families, and friends meet friends … In these delightful associations, persons of every rank and every calling forget their exclusive pretensions, whilst the softer sex … banish indecorum, and shed a charm over the whole assemblage.[31]

This mixture of genders, ages, and classes would weave together a noble social fabric, each citizen refining the other, with the mere presence of women being sufficient to elevate everyone.

While neither Tuthill nor Griffith envisioned women actively designing the future of American cities, they both placed females' informed leadership in matters of history, culture and taste at the foundation of that future. Such participation would not be possible from the detached solitude of a cottage in the country to the suburbs, no matter how blessed it was with petunias and rhubarb, and no matter how pliant its menfolk might be. Female leadership in architecture, in part because they were non-professional, required regular access to the sights and social exchanges of dynamic, living public spaces in a 'large and splendid city.'

I love old places

The same year that brought the publication of Burnhap's and Tuthill's books saw the birth of the modern female suffrage movement in the United States, as a group of women gathered in Seneca Falls, New York, to write and publish a manifesto outlining a new movement 'against women's political, social, and economic inferiority in America.'[32] The suffragist movement had slowly evolved over the previous two decades as women dedicated to the antislavery movement confronted the evident truth that male politicians were incapable of ending the vile institution, and thus 'became unwilling to abide by the rules that limited their participation in public life.'[33] From the very start, the campaign to increase women's power in the United States was imbedded within a broader movement aimed at improving the whole of the nation's social fabric.

The American Civil War marked, in the words of Anne Firor Scott, 'a significant turning point, one that marked change in the life experience of many people,' expanding the social and political horizons of many women.[34] By the time the guns fell silent, chattel slavery had been abolished, but new systems of exploitation and new injustices seemed to rise on all fronts, most conspicuously in the industrializing cities. A growing number of upper- and middle-class women used their leisure time and expendable income to form societies dedicated to carrying the old moral politics of 'good taste and spirituality' forward into campaigns against the escalating crises of overcrowded, unsanitary, crime- and disease-ridden urban slums. These new public activities were often cast as a faithful expansion of traditional female social roles: 'municipal housekeeping,' which expanded domestic duties beyond 'the four walls of a home,' to engage with 'the neighborhood, the town, the city.'[35]

For guiding lights, American women had great British reformers such as Angela Burdett-Coutts and Octavia Hill, both of whose mid-nineteenth century efforts to ameliorate the conditions of the London poor were described and celebrated in U.S. publications. Hill became famous for her renovations of existing slum dwellings and for her work as an advocate for historic preservation, helping found the British National Trust in 1895.[36] The new model tenements and gardens developed by Burdett-Coutts were celebrated for their profound urban impacts, alleviating the 'gulf dividing the West from the East End of London,' which, in Dickens' words, was the border dividing 'wealth and luxury, flowers and perfumes' from 'an earthly hell' where 'women are perverted to be unwomanly, and the men … [possess] just enough humanity to make them more elaborate in brutishness.'[37] Americans applied the lessons of London with increasing scale and vigor, establishing relief and education centers such as Chicago's Hull House, set up by Jane Addams and her allies in 1889. Over the next four decades, as the U.S. struggle for female suffrage reached a fevered pitch, women leveraged the power of their societies and associations to achieve thousands of meaningful interventions in American cities. They commissioned new 'libraries, schools, colleges, kindergartens, museums, health clinics, houses of refuge … parks, playgrounds,' and other public amenities, and they opened up pre-existing ones to new, more efficient, and more inclusive uses.[38]

The importance of urban social life to American women was brought to the fore in the 1888 reform novel *Uncle Tom's Tenement*, by popular novelist Alice Wellington Rollins (1847–1897), the title of which clearly attempted to draw parallels between the old injustices of slavery and the modern ones of the city slum. Taking place in New York, the novel follows the lives of several independent men and especially women of conscience who attempt to alleviate the sufferings of the poor. One well-meaning but naïve middle-class female asks a widowed Irish tenement dweller, 'Why don't you move in to the country?' explaining, 'You could get a nice little home in the country very cheap, where you wouldn't be so crowded.' The widow forcefully answers: 'Naw; it's not to the counthry I'll be goin', w'ativer happens. I don' loike the counthry, that's so. It's lonely it is. Is it ter the counthry yer'd loike to be movin' out yerself, ma'am?'[39] As if to answer this question, the novel also tells the story of a middle-class widow who fights valiantly to retain her urban flat, despite privation and humiliation. Elsewhere in the story, a would-be male philanthropist despairs of attracting working-class women to a model country settlement, explaining that every one of them prefers 'the bit of gossip in her ugly old tenement with fifty or sixty exceedingly near neighbors,' to 'the meagre chance of any neighbors' dropping in if she had a whole house to herself.'[40] If the main female character in Griffith's older story had been privy to this statement, she would have doubtlessly nodded her head in agreement. While Rollins did tease her fictional slum dwellers for their stubborn attachment to dirt, she asserted that the solution to broken urban fabric was the creation of better urban fabric – which is to say, the construction of model tenements in or very near to the city, not far-flung cottages in the hinterlands.

The feminist reformer, suffragist, and writer Lucia True Ames Mead (1856–1936) added her voice to this conversation through a series of writings, most particularly the 1889 reform novel *Memoirs of a Millionaire*. This volume featured a female protagonist, Mildred Brewster, whose tastes and views clearly lined up with those of Mead herself, and whose love of cities and hatred of injustice leads her to commit to the design and construction of model tenements. At a time when most politically radical male writers in Britain and America, such as Henry George, Edward Bellamy, and William Morris, were still following the old utopian tradition of insisting that cities needed to be thinned out or abolished altogether, Mead resonated with Rollins and echoed the visions of Griffith and Tuthill by publishing calls for progressively reformed and historically rich urbanism.

Early in *Memoirs of a Millionaire*, Brewster declares her love for timeworn cities. She sits soaking in the view from her centrally located townhouse in Boston's Beacon Hill, 'in the broad, cushioned window-seat of my cosy attic room, looking far out over the mass of chimney-tops to the towers and spires beyond the hill and the Public Garden.'[41] She writes a letter declaring: 'I like old places. I like to be on the oldest spot in this old, historic town … I have not outgrown it in the least, in spite of all my modern radicalism about many things.' Mead reiterated this love of historic architecture it in at least two other short essays, both of which extolled the value of New England's historic buildings, and one of which criticized new buildings for failing to respect their neighbors. In 'Historic Boston,' an article from 1900, she revisited the urban vista her character Brewster had so loved, publishing an old photograph of it (Figure 3.2). The view

FIGURE 3.2 View of Boston over the Public Garden to Beacon Hill

Source: Published with Mead's 'Historic Boston,' 1900. Public domain

had been altered by modern intrusions in the decade since the publication of *Memoirs of a Millionaire*, and Mead attacked the towering new commercial buildings for failing to contribute to the urban whole, disfiguring 'the pleasant sky line' to 'belittle the stately Park Church spire, and the dome crowning the summit of Beacon hill.'[42] She praised, by contrast, the colonial landmarks of the Old State House, Faneuil Hall, the Old North Church, and the Old South Church. The last of these, she explained, had been 'preserved as a repository of historic treasures and is also an inspiring meeting place for the discussion of questions pertaining to American history and public duty.'[43] She was gratified to note that this had been made possible by 'the generous endowment of a noble woman, Mary Hemenway.' Indeed, a host of patriotic women, together with their male allies, had led the charge in the 1870s to save the Old South Church from demolition. In a remarkable fulfillment of Griffith's prophecy, Hemenway had proven a reliable 'lady of great wealth,' as her enormous contribution of $100,000 marked the turning point in their campaign.[44]

For Mead, the love of historic architecture, tied as it was to Boston's female political leadership and economic power, was compatible with her 'modern radicalism.' Her good taste led her to celebrate beautiful architecture that supported and ennobled public life, and to oppose the tendencies of selfish, thoughtless commercial enterprise to deface the city. Mead was not fearful of the new, for she also celebrated the 'notable modern buildings' that had risen around Boston's Copley Square in the last quarter of the nineteenth century, namely H.H. Richardson's Trinity Church and McKim, Mead, and White's Boston Public Library, with the democratic accessibility of the latter a special source of pride for her.[45] The key for Mead was that the new must not erode the old, and this was because the old provided important collective assets: common heritage and an aesthetically beneficial stage and background for public life.

Mead believed that the shared pleasures of good urbanism were of special value to the poor. Boston's Public Garden, she declared, was 'the resort in summer of the toiling thousands who possess not a foot of their own, but here rejoice in the common possession of all.'[46] Her proxy, Mildred Brewster, took up the implications this had on the ethics of urban design in *Memoirs of a Millionaire*. Urban houses should be

> more beautiful without than within, so that every line may be a positive delight to the many who can never look within its doors … A poor man has no money for a concert … he has no time for a visit to an art museum … but in sunlight and in moonlight, seven days in the week, as he looks from his window or passes to his work … the beauty wrought in stone is his.

Ugly architecture, she argued in *Memoirs of a Millionaire*, was an affront to the whole body politic because it forcefully imposed itself on the street:

> If a man writes a bad poem, I am not compelled to read it; if he paints a bad picture, I need not see it more than once, but if he erects an ugly building in my city he hurts me every time I walk the street, and I am helpless.[47]

Thus it was a broad public duty to keep good old buildings and build good new buildings, as both were required to create a beautiful and harmonious city that supported the happiness and wellbeing of every citizen, male and female, rich and poor.

In the world of *Memoirs of a Millionaire*, only a woman had the mind, heart, and good taste to steer urban life in such a wholesome direction. After Brewster inherits a vast fortune, she moves to the 'modern Babylon' of New York and forms an association, mostly of women, in order to leverage her newfound wealth to transcend the pecuniary narrowness of the city's predominantly male leadership and redeem the poor. Conversing with a dear friend while 'strolling through the park, after a morning [in the slums of] Cherry Street,' Brewster realizes the gravity of her task: 'tenement-house reform on a gigantic scale.'[48] Beginning by buying and improving old tenements, she then sets herself to personally designing and constructing 'the city home of the future': new kinds of urban flats that will accommodate density while offering excellent living conditions and relieving 'wives and mothers' of drudgery.[49] Brewster hires a contractor and an architect, and both were expected to submit to her innovative ideas.

Her architectural plans are described and shown in detail, including floor plans for one apartment unit (Figure 3.3). Instead of multi-floored row houses lined up 'side by side vertically, like so many bricks set up on end,' these

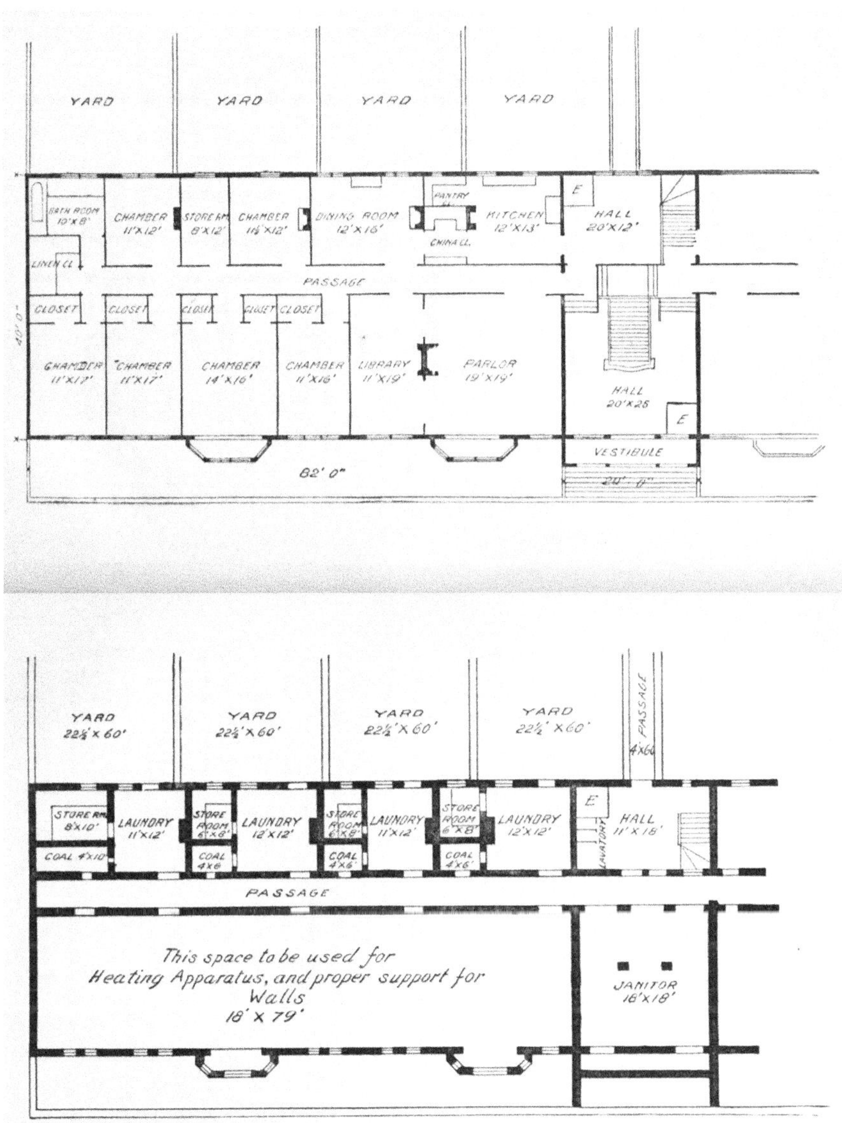

FIGURE 3.3 Half of a floorplan for a model tenement; the ground floor is shown in the lower register, a typical apartment is shown above

Source: Lucia True Ames [Mead], *Memoirs of A Millionaire*, 1889. Public domain

sizable six-bedroom apartments – each with high-tech heating systems, a modern kitchen, bathroom, ample storage, and a library – would be stacked on top of one another, with individual flats occupying one level. The shared building would be accessed by a single, grand entrance on the street, defined by beautiful yet sensible ornamentation, that leads to a common stairway and elevator. Circulation space in each unit would be minimalized so that living, cooking, and sleeping room could be maximized. All of the rooms in every flat would be 'directly lighted and ventilated from the outer air.' Every family would have access to a private garden space behind the building, and the tenement would also be crowned with a flat roof garden that is 'thoroughly guarded by a parapet or iron fence, thus affording a safe playground for children.'[50] Brewster also specified low, horizontal windows, which would maximize the amount of light in every room, and resist the 'ridiculous' tradition of blocking sunshine 'with lambrequins and two or three sets of curtains, all of which are never raised above the middle sash.'[51] In short, this model tenement was dedicated to the provision of light and air, with a modern circulatory system maximizing floor plan efficiency, a flat roof garden, and horizontal windows that would resist Victorian clutter. There is no evidence that Le Corbusier read *Memoirs of a Millionaire* before launching a career that would hit many of these same formal notes, but the similarities are striking.

While Mead seems to have anticipated certain elements of modernist apartment design by many years, she also heralded the emerging historic preservation movement, revealing a complex ability to celebrate the old while also embracing the new. Her goal was not to erase the American city, no matter how broken it might have been, but to make it 'great, not only in dimensions and numbers and wealth, but great in that kind of greatness which alone shall exalt a nation and give it memory.'[52] When Mead died in 1936, she was eulogized in newspapers across the United States as a 'woman's suffrage leader,' advocate for peace, and popular author.[53] These three threads – her faith in the capacity of women to help lead society, her longing for social justice, and her use of the written word to explore possibilities for change – came together in her visions for the future of American cities, where old and new architecture would be called to serve the public good through its cultural meaning, innovative usefulness, and immersive public beauty.

At the time that New Yorkers were turning the pages of Mead's novel, tenement reform was being pulled into a broader progressive movement including the integration of immigrants, the reduction of crime, temperance, and historic preservation.[54] The predominantly male-led American Scenic and Historic Preservation Society was launched shortly after the publication of *Memoirs of a Millionaire*, but it enjoyed decidedly mixed success. This was partly because its leaders marginalized women, who decided to strike out on their own as preservation 'auxiliaries.'[55] Such a dilution of energy is especially ironic considering the fact that so many of the earliest voices elucidating the value of historic architecture were those of women. Griffith, Tuthill, and

Mead all made explicit connections between the value of old buildings and the ideal future of American cities, where modern progress should be achieved, but only while supporting cultural memory and beautifying and vivifying the public realm. It was in Charleston, and because of another woman very much in the vein of these early public advocates, that historic preservation finally become a major cultural force.

Some of us do protest

The American historic preservation movement is often described as beginning with the Mount Vernon Ladies' Association, which was established to save the home of George Washington from decay and industrial development. Mount Vernon was in Virginia, but the campaign to save it was born in Charleston, with an 1853 letter by Ann Pamela Cunningham published in the *Charleston Mercury* to the 'Ladies of the South!'[56] In it, she decried modern American culture, where historical memory was overwhelmed by 'blackening smoke and deafening machinery, where money, money, only money ever enters the thought,' and accused the men in power of degeneracy and corruption. 'It is to *you*, mothers and daughters of the South,' she declared, 'that appeal can be made with a hopeful confidence. It is woman's office to be a vestal; and even the "fire of liberty" may need the care of her devotion, and the purity of her guardianship.' Thus evoking the sacred, feminine domestic duty of maintaining the hearth of filial memory, the Mount Vernon Ladies' Association called upon every woman in the region to deploy their good taste and redeem American honor by saving an old house. By 1859, they had raised all of the money they needed, with donations pouring in from all corners of the nation.

The Civil War interrupted their preservation work, as it did a simultaneous movement by the Ladies' Calhoun Monument Association to grace Charleston with a prominent sculpture celebrating the firebrand, white-supremacist South Carolina politician John C. Calhoun. By the close of the nineteenth century, however, Mount Vernon was permanently saved, and Calhoun's glowering visage dominated the city.[57] The women of Charleston had proven that they were capable of organizing large, sustained campaigns to raise money and care for public memory as crystallized in great works of architecture. Two important urban Charleston structures were saved in the decades that followed, in what would later be remembered as the 'beginning' of the preservation movement in the city.[58] The 'Sons of the Revolution' had petitioned the city to save the colonial gunpowder magazine in 1900, but it was the Colonial Dames of Charleston who, eighteen months later, succeeded in purchasing it to convert it 'into a meeting room and museum.'[59] They paid down the debt slowly, raising money through 'years of bridge parties.' In 1913, the Charleston chapter of the Daughters of the American Revolution (D.A.R.) saved the colonial Exchange Building from slow death by neglect, acquiring it without charge from the federal government and then patiently restoring it over many years. The assembly celebrating their success welcomed former governor and then-Senator Benjamin Tillman, who had supported the D.A. R.'s efforts to secure the building, and was so pleased by the outcome that he 'presented the chapter with a bronze bust of himself.'[60] Such was the cold, metallic face of paternalism, but male appropriation of female accomplishments would become more difficult in the era of vocal politics from the female suffragists. The chaos of the Civil War and the arrival of 'intellectual and material influences from the North' during the years of Reconstruction had irreparably torn the conservative social fabric of the South, and the 'legend of the southern lady,' with her flawless composure of demure devotion, now had to contend with the '"New Woman" of the New South.'[61] They furthered the nationwide women's voting rights movement by leveraging the tried and trusted technique of forming associations.

Leaders emerged in Charleston, most notably Susan Pringle Frost (1873–1960) (Figure 3.4). The place of her birth was prophetic and probably formative of her later passions for women's rights and preservation: the Miles Brewton house, a palatial Palladian mansion of ca. 1769 in the heart of downtown Charleston that survived wars, fires, and hurricanes to pass through the capable hands of five female inheritors in direct succession, so that by the time Frost inherited it from her dear aunt, it stood as a veritable fortress of womanly resilience.[62] As discussed by Sydney Bland in his biography of Frost, she grew up treasuring her life in the heart of Charleston, enjoying an unusual freedom of the city courtesy of her independent spirit and accommodating parents. She seized a once-in-a-lifetime opportunity to engage with architecture and planning during Charleston's 1901–1902 South Carolina Inter-State and West Indian Exposition, serving the fair's chief designer, Bradford Lee Gilbert, as his stenographer and secretary.[63] Frost recalled commuting by bicycle between her downtown home to the northern site of the fair, weaving her way through the cobblestone streets and among the subtropical parks and gardens of the densely built-up peninsula of Charleston. In many ways, this was also a journey through architectural history, from the past to the future and back again. None of it would have been possible had the Frost family home been located in a far-flung suburban or rural estate. City life provided these opportunities for the young Susan.

The Fair turned out to be an economic failure, dashing the hopes of many that a new era of prosperity, unseen since the Civil War, would dawn on Charleston. Only one portion of the exposition was a commercial success: the Woman's Building. This managed to turn such a significant profit that it offset the event's losses.[64] Importantly, it was also the only building not to be constructed especially for the exposition, as it was the 1786 Lowndes Grove plantation house (Figure 3.5). The choice of this old home for the Woman's Building played into a number of longstanding female stereotypes, including homebound domesticity and the 'vestal' duty of maintaining the flames of family traditions. While the women of the exposition reinforced such associations by operating a restaurant and childcare center in the building, they also offered exhibits on female inventors and scientists, and made proposals for future industries, including silk culture, which Frost personally supported.[65] The group of ladies running and

FIGURE 3.4 Susan Pringle Frost (1873–1960), taken when she was president of the Charleston League for Equal Suffrage, ca. 1918

Source: Courtesy of the Preservation Society of Charleston

speaking in the building also included leaders of the National Woman's Suffrage Association. Frost thus had many opportunities to gain new and challenging experiences at the exposition, as she watched the exuberant rise and despairing fall of a huge architectural ensemble representing male ambition, partly redeemed by

FIGURE 3.5 Lowndes Grove plantation house, ca. 1786, while it served as the Women's Building, 1901–1902. Public domain

female leadership in a historic structure given new meaning by simultaneous celebrations of old traditions and modern aspirations.

After the fair folded, Frost continued her stenography career in the law courts. As she travelled the state with circuit judges, she witnessed first-hand much of the suffering attending the poverty that haunted South Carolina. She never married or had any children of her own, but she took child abuse cases personally. The ethos of Municipal Housekeeping began to speak to her.[66] Tentatively at first, she became a supporter of female suffrage, finally committing herself fully to the cause after discovering that male stenographers made more money than she did for no other reason other than their gender. She joined local, state-wide, and national organizations, rising to president of the Charleston League for Equal Suffrage.[67] At the same time, she began to supplement her stenography income by using her uniquely deep knowledge of her historic downtown neighborhood to broker real estate, investing her personal savings in run-down structures, paying for their rehabilitation, and then selling them to new residents. To facilitate this work, she became one of the first women in the state to own and drive an automobile. After national victory for women's suffrage finally arrived in 1919, she turned to real estate full time, and carried over her energy, thirst for justice, and leadership skills to launch a new movement:

historic preservation. Like Griffith, Tuthill, Rollins, and Mead, she was a complex, nuanced thinker, perceiving new opportunities in the modern world for society at large and women in particular, as well as perceiving value in the shared public life of an old city. Claiming all of the above would require a fight.

While Frost certainly valued architectural details such as ironwork and loved elegant domestic interiors, she was more concerned with the larger urban fabric of which individual houses were merely one part. She saw urbanism as the infrastructure of human relationships, connecting them to one another and to their forbears. As one of her chief male allies later recalled, Frost fought to preserve the city center, 'not only for its buildings, and streets, and vistas, but also for those men and women she had known, or of whom she had been told,' so that the ancient architecture would continue to 'shelter the people who, living and working in harmony together, gave life and breath to the city.'[68] From the very start, she focused upon saving and restoring whole blocks, intersections, and alleys. She defended old flagstone pavements and characterful place names like Zig-Zag Alley. Even her methods relied on a social network, as she leveraged her real estate connections and personal charisma to establish a network of local craftspeople and laborers who would secretly report to her anytime they heard a beautiful balcony or mantelpiece was going to be sold or destroyed, so she could act.[69] She was, in short, an urbanist – one of the first American built-environment professionals to operate on the scale of a city. She may not have fully realized it, but Frost joined a tradition of American aspiration that had been decades in the making. The female urban advocates of the preceding century would have been amazed by the political and economic independence that allowed her to claim such a career, but they would have recognized her values.

As the 1920s brought economic growth and the pace of demolition quickened in her beloved city, Frost leveraged her old political skills to organize the Society for the Preservation of Old Dwellings and serve as its first president. Her rousing lectures and press releases rang with the zeal of the suffragist cause. She accused the people of Charleston of choosing short-sighted, shallow commercialism, as well as a senseless worship of newness and modernity, over the duty to cherish the cultural treasures handed down to them by their ancestors. 'Now is the time,' she asserted, 'for outside critics to be made to realize that some of us do protest.'[70] The Society quickly gained several key male allies in government and in the press, not least because the steadily increasing traffic from northern tourists promised to introduce a whole new economic lifeline into Charleston. For Frost, this new money offered an opportunity to open the eyes of blind businessmen who were in the process of wrecking the city, and she fought them on their own terms, in their own language.[71]

The average businessman was slow to open his eyes, however, and over the following years several of them publicly attacked the preservation movement as irrational and too constraining for commercial interests.[72] She and her allies were saving many structures, but as Frost watched others be reduced to rubble in order to serve automobiles, she became angry and disheartened. In 1926, the newspaper ran a letter in which she described in visceral language how she had

> struggled for years in what appears at times to be a losing game against the destructive forces of so-called modern progress and development … [and] witnessed the terrible vandalism going on all about us in the total destruction of these magnificent residences that represent the heart and soul and spirit and act of a generation.[73]

She hoped that the young people of the city might learn to appreciate the beauty of their community, but in the meantime, she believed that only a zoning law would protect the future of Charleston. Luckily for her personal and professional ambitions, the beauty of Charleston was then attracting many new residents from other locales, and downtown nourished an arts scene later known as the Charleston Renaissance.[74] Together with many progressive native-born Charlestonians, male and female, these newcomers joined Frost's efforts, and in 1931, Charleston passed the first historic district protection zoning ordinance in the world.[75] It was, in short, a government act designed to serve the common good by protecting what Frost knew and valued as the public realm. Specifically, it was drawn up to preserve the harmony of the old urban fabric by prohibiting the alteration of historic building exteriors and the development of new buildings in the Old and Historic District without prior approval from a new Board of Architectural Review. That board was all male, but Frost always had its ear, and it was often staffed by her allies.

The ordinance was a major victory and represented such an original strategy that other American cities that followed suit – from New Orleans to Santa Barbara, from Santa Fe to Boston – frequently referred to their own historic zoning initiatives as examples of the 'Charleston Plan' or 'Charleston ordinances.'[76] It might also have been fairly described as the 'Frost Plan,' and Frost and her allies wasted no time in working to strengthen and expand it. Importantly, those in favor of preserving downtown often used heavily gendered language in their rhetoric, following a very old local tradition that anthropomorphized the city of Charleston as a woman: 'An empress, brave and loyal,' a 'warrior Queen of Ocean' with a 'loving breast' and 'beauteous form.'[77] Frost appealed to the public to honor and protect the body of the city, suggesting that it could suffer: 'There is something so human about an old house,' she wrote to the newspaper in the early 1940s, 'that it is hard to believe anyone would be cruel to, or neglectful of, one.'[78] The personification of Charleston also seems to have encouraged conceptions of the city as an urbanistic whole, rather than a collection of discreet, individual structures. One of Frost's cousins and supporters, Eleanor Pringle Hart, explained:

> Charleston is like a woman of many moods! Like such a woman she is swayed by the views of every passing critic. If she is not to fly apart, she

> must soon decide where it is she wants to go? What it is she wants to be? She cannot be all things to all men, and remain a whole city.[79]

'She' was courted by many suitors indeed. A visitor from New York announced in 1940: 'Charleston is the aristocrat of all American cities … Some have fancifully called it a sleeping beauty which never grew up and never lost its charm.'[80] A writer known only as E.T.H.S. protested demolitions, writing:

> Is there no means by which the older Charleston that America loves can be saved – from Charlestonians? Must the city commit a new crime, eat itself up – be guilty of civic cannibalism? … Charm in a city is as precious and should be as jealously guarded as virtue in a fair woman.[81]

In 1933, the artist Charles W. Smith published a beautiful book of woodcut engravings of Charleston, and the introduction written by Frost ally Herbert Ravenel Sass explained that any man who loves Charleston thinks of the city as woman: 'he does not think of Charleston as "it",' but as a 'she,' and loves her for her 'wisdom' and 'virtue,' and for staying true to the 'old gods' of architectural 'beauty' and 'dignity,' rather than the 'false gods' of 'passing fancies and affectations.'[82] Many of Smith's engravings focused on prestigious landmarks, but others featured street views of everyday fabric. One of these was specially adapted by the Society for the Preservation of Old Dwellings for a newspaper article and a mailer card supporting a 1934 membership drive (Figure 3.6). It replicated the same row of houses three times, each revealing more demolitions until only one house was left.[83] What was once urbanism, was now merely architecture – what had once been a place, was now a lonely object. It was the city as a whole and not individual houses, no matter how important they may be, that defined successful preservation. This kind of rhetoric made an impact. By the end of the decade, the roster of the Society had soared to over seven hundred members. As they saved more old structures and defeated more incongruous projects in the historic district, the newspaper reported, 'Momentum Gains for Preservation.'[84] Looking back on the Society's efforts in 1939, the new president, William Means, gave credit to Frost and her first team:

> About twenty years ago a small group … of the so-called weaker sex got together and formed this society in Charleston … the spirit and determination of this group has not waned one iota, and it is still the backbone of the society.[85]

As the influence of the Society increased, however, a number of problems rose to the surface. One of them was a sense among some working-class Charlestonians that preservation was an elite practice that served to exclude them from the historic heart of the city. Aloysius Flynn, the president of the Central Labor Union, cried foul, declaring, 'we consider that the laboring man has as much right to live below Broad street

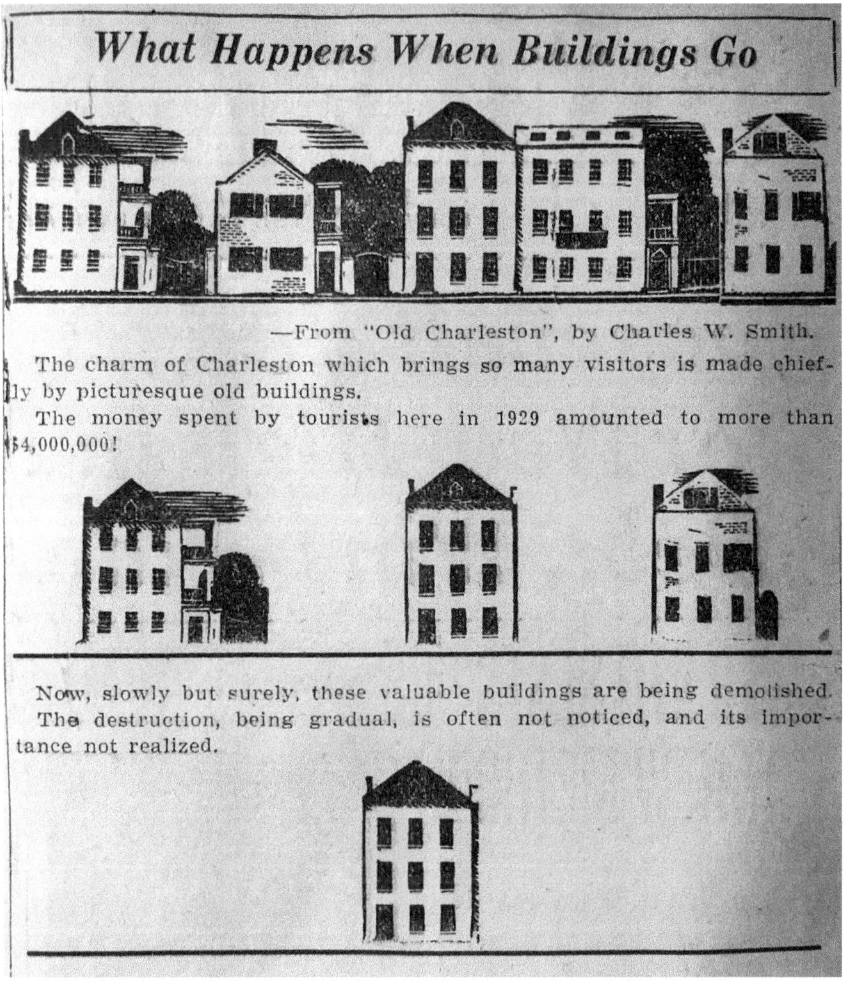
What Happens When Buildings Go

—From "Old Charleston", by Charles W. Smith.

The charm of Charleston which brings so many visitors is made chiefly by picturesque old buildings.

The money spent by tourists here in 1929 amounted to more than $4,000,000!

Now, slowly but surely, these valuable buildings are being demolished. The destruction, being gradual, is often not noticed, and its importance not realized.

FIGURE 3.6 Newspaper advertisement for the Society for the Preservation of Old Dwellings, 1934

Source: Courtesy of the Preservation Society of Charleston

as has the capitalist.'[86] Frost answered by insisting that no exclusion was intended, but incidentally revealed that race was also a bone of contention among some critics: 'I have even heard intelligent people express the opinion that [the zoning ordinance] has to do with the segregation of the races. It has nothing to do with segregation.'[87] The old institution of slavery and its ongoing legacies meant, however, that class and race were inextricably linked in Charleston, and many African-American families were driven out of Charleston's historic district by rising rents, increased property taxes, and sometimes blatant evictions. One of her allies defended his decision to redevelop old buildings for white tenants by declaring,

> My Charleston friends appeared to take more pride in the preservation of historic architecture, reflecting in the glory and dignity of the early days rather than in the habitation of fine old buildings by negroes, and they expressed approval of what I had done.[88]

Frost herself had a fairly good record of humane treatment towards black workers and neighbors, and even had a reputation for offering sustenance and shelter in her downtown home to the unfortunate and the marginalized.[89] There were limits, however, even to her progressive vision of community, and gentrification emerged as a pressing issue under her watch.

By the time Susan Pringle Frost died in 1960, the Preservation Society of Charleston, as it is known today, had become permanent fixture in the city. The artist and writer Elizabeth O'Neill Verner eulogized the Society's founder, declaring, 'That we still live in the old neighborhoods and have preserved for posterity our beloved city is due to one woman and one woman only: Susan Pringle Frost.'[90] This statement subtly reveals the scope of Frost's conception of architectural placemaking, because unlike the efforts of previous preservation advocates in Charleston and beyond, Frost's legacy could not be defined by a single building such as the Penn House, the Old South Meeting House, Mount Vernon, or the Old Exchange. She saved 'old neighborhoods' and her 'beloved city,' which is to say, she focused on huge portions of urban fabric that could not be turned into discreet museum pieces, but rather dense, dynamic, complex arrays of public and private space where people could live, work, and enjoy the company of others. Verner's eulogy is also a bit misleading, however, for it asserts that Frost's power was a singular, isolated force. Whether she was conscious of it or not, however, her interconnected love of historic buildings and faith in the goodness of public city life had important precedents in the writings of Mary Griffith, Louisa Tuthill, and Lucia True Ames Mead. They, together with Alice Wellington Rollins, saw urbanism as crucial to the wellbeing of women, and through them, to the wellbeing of society at large.

Frost's own track record of engagement with her city, including the several phases of her professional life and her political organizing in the suffragist struggle, suggests that she would have appreciated her feminist predecessors' thoughts on the importance of living, breathing social fabric, with common memories and purposes supported by shared spaces. She certainly relished the company and cooperation of the workers, residents, and leaders of downtown Charleston, whom she mobilized with such force, teaching them to see their city with enlightened and compassionate eyes, and to love and protect 'her.' With Frost's forbears and collaborators in mind, it seems wrong to say that Charleston was redeemed by 'one woman only,' but it is doubtlessly correct to assert that 'one woman' led the way. Many women had imaginatively and forcefully declared that meaningful improvements to American cities might be achieved if female minds, hearts, arms, and voices attained greater freedom to exercise their power in the preserving and shaping of communities. Frost proved to Charleston, and to the world, that they were right.

Notes

1 John H. Stubbs, *Time Honored: A Global View of Architectural Conservation* (Hoboken, NJ: John Wiley & Sons, Inc., 2009).
2 Melanie Hall, ed., *Towards World Heritage: International Origins of the Preservation Movement, 1870–1930* (Farnham: Ashgate, 2011).
3 For studies of Frost and her world, see, for example, Stephanie E. Yuhl, *A Golden Haze of Memory: The Making of Historic Charleston* (Chapel Hill, NC: The University of North Carolina Press, 2005); Stephanie E. Yuhl, 'Rich and Tender Remembering: Elite White Women and an Aesthetic Sense of Place in Charleston, 1920s and 1930s,' in W. Fitzhugh Brundage, ed., *Where These Memories Grow: History, Memory, and Southern Identity* (Chapel Hill, NC: The University of North Carolina Press, 2000), pp. 227–248; Sydney Bland, *Preserving Charleston's Past, Shaping Its Future: The Life and Times of Susan Pringle Frost* (Columbia, SC: University of South Carolina Press, 1999); Martha Severens, *The Charleston Renaissance* (Spartanburg, SC: Saraland Press, 1998).
4 Vernon Louis Parrington, Jr., *American Dreams: A Study of American Utopias* (Providence, RI: Brown University Press, 1947), p. 22.
5 Duangrudi Suksang, 'Mary Griffith's Pioneering Vision: Three Hundred Years Hence,' *Utopian Studies*, vol. 11, no. 1 (2000), pp. 24–25.
6 Mary Griffith, *Camperdown; or, News from Our Neighborhood: Being Sketches* (Philadelphia, PA: Carey, Lea and Blanchard, 1836).
7 See Joel Nydahl, 'From Millennium to Utopia Americana,' in Kenneth M. Roemer, ed., *America as Utopia* (New York: Burt Franklin and Company, 1981), pp. 237–251, and James L. Machor, *Pastoral Cities: Urban Ideals and the Symbolic Landscape of America* (Madison, WI: University of Wisconsin Press, 1987).
8 Griffith, *Camperdown*, p. 5.
9 Mary Griffith, 'Three Hundred Years Hence,' in Griffith, ed., *Camperdown*, p. 11.
10 *Ibid.*, p. 15.
11 *Ibid.*, p. 17.
12 *Ibid.*, pp. 52–53; the house Griffith was most likely describing is now known as the Letitia Street House, which was relocated to Fairmount Park in the 1880s to prevent its demolition. Later, however, it was discovered that the house was too young to have served as Penn's residence, and has been subsequently neglected.
13 Miles Glendinning, *The Conservation Movement: A History of Architectural Preservation* (Abingdon: Routledge, 2013), p. 110.
14 Louis-Sébastien Mercier, *Memoirs of the Year Two Thousand Five Hundred*, trans. W. Hooper (Philadelphia, PA: Thomas Dobson, 1795), p. 168.
15 Glendinning, *The Conservation Movement*, pp. 90–92.
16 Thomas J. Brown, *Civil War Canon: Sites of Confederate Memory in South Carolina* (Chapel Hill, NC: The University of North Carolina Press, 2015), pp. 52–53.
17 Patricia West, *Domesticating History: The Political Origins of America's House Museums* (Washington, DC: Smithsonian Institution Press, 1999), pp.
18 Griffith, 'Three Hundred Years Hence,' p. 83.
19 *Ibid.*, pp. 87–88.
20 Dolores Hayden, *Building Suburbia: Green Fields and Urban Grown, 1820–2000* (New York: Pantheon Books, 2003), pp. 21–44.
21 *Ibid.*, p. 43.
22 Burnhap, *The Sphere and Duties of Woman, A Course of Lectures* (Baltimore, MD: John Murphy, 1848), pp. 37–38.
23 *Ibid.*, pp. 39–40.
24 See, for example, Anne M. Ousterhout, *Most Learned Woman in America: A Life of Elizabeth Graeme Fergusson* (University Park, PA: The Pennsylvania State University Press, 2004), p. 8.
25 Burnhap, *The Sphere and Duties of Woman*, p. 36.

26 Louisa C. Tuthill, *History of Architecture, from the Earliest Times* (Philadelphia, PA: Linsday and Blakiston, 1848), p. v.
27 *Ibid.*, p. viii.
28 *Ibid.*, pp. 225–226.
29 *Ibid.*, p. 222.
30 *Ibid.*, pp. 317–318.
31 *Ibid.*, p. 325.
32 Sarah Lynn Farmer, 'Communicating Justice: The National American Woman Suffrage Asociation's Use of Public Relations to Win the Right to Vote,' in Dulcie Murdock Straughan, ed., *Women's Use of Public Relations for Progressive-Era Reform* (Lewiston, NY: The Edwin Mellen Press), p. 36.
33 Kathryn Kish Sklar, *Women's Rights Emerges within the Antislavery Movement, 1830–1870* (Boston, MA: Bedford/St. Martin's, 2000), p. ix.
34 Anne Firor Scott, *Natural Allies: Women's Associations in American History* (Urbana, IL: University of Illinois Press, 1991), p. 79.
35 *Ibid.*, p. 141.
36 Elizabeth Baigent and Ben Cowell, *'Nobler Imaginings and Mightier Struggles': Octavia Hill, Social Activism and the Remaking of British Society* (London: University of London, 2016).
37 Mary Adelaide, *Baroness Burdett-Coutts: A Sketch of Her Public Life and Work* (Chicago, IL: A.C. McClurg and Company, 1893), pp. 105–107.
38 Scott, *Natural Allies*, p. 3.
39 Alice Wellington Rollins, *Uncle Tom's Tenement* (Boston, MA: The William E. Smythe Company, 1888), p. 153.
40 *Ibid.*, p. 273.
41 Lucia True Ames [Mead], *Memoirs of a Millionaire* (Boston, MA: Houghton, Mifflin and Company, 1889), pp. 19–20.
42 Lucia Ames Mead, 'Historic Boston,' *The Perry Magazine*, vol. iii, no. 4 (December 1900), p. 148.
43 Mead, 'Historic Boston,' p. 145.
44 Michael Holleran, 'Roots in Boston, Branches in Planning and Parks,' in Max Page and Randall Mason, eds., *Giving Preservation a History: Histories of Preservation in the United States* (New York: Routledge, 2004), p. 86.
45 Mead, 'Historic Boston,' p. 148.
46 *Ibid.*, p. 148.
47 Ames [Mead], *Memoirs of a Millionaire*, pp. 301–302.
48 *Ibid.*, p. 148.
49 *Ibid.*, p. 151.
50 *Ibid.*, p. 154.
51 *Ibid.*, p. 159.
52 *Ibid.*, p. 240.
53 'Mrs. Lucia Ames Mead Is Taken by Death,' *The Gazette and Daily*, Tuesday, November 3, 1936, p. 6.
54 Randall Mason, 'Historic Preservation, Public Memory, and the Making of New York City,' in Max Page and Randall Mason, eds., *Giving Preservation a History*.
55 *Ibid.*, p. 138.
56 A Southern Matron, 'To the Ladies of the South,' *Charleston Mercury*, Friday, December 2, 1853.
57 Brown, *Civil War Canon*, pp. 36–90.
58 Eleanor Pringle Hart, 'A Beginning in Preservation-As I Remember,' *Preservation Progress*, vol. vii, no. 2 (March 1963), p. 11.
59 'Warm Meeting of City Council,' *Evening Post*, Wednesday, January 24, 1900, 5; 'Bought by Colonial Dames,' *Evening Post*, Saturday, June 8, 1901, p. 2.
60 'Celebrated by D.A.R.,' *Evening Post*, Monday, June 30, 1913, p. 10.

61 Anne Firor Scott, 'The "New Woman" in the New South,' in *idem, Making the Invisible Woman Visible* (Urbana: The University of Illinois Press, 1984), pp. 213–214.
62 Susan Pringle Frost, *Highlights of the Miles Brewton House* (Charleston, SC: self-published, 1944), p. 4.
63 Sydney Bland, *Preserving Charleston's Past, Shaping Its Future: The Life and Times of Susan Pringle Frost* (Columbia, SC: The University of South Carolina Press, 1999), pp. 13–14.
64 *Ibid.*, p. 15.
65 'Kindergarten Occasions and News,' *Kindergarten Magazine*, vol. xiv, no. 7 (March 1902), p. 440; 'The Woman's Department,' *The Exposition*, vol. 1, no. 9 (August 1901), pp. 320–322; Bland, *Preserving Charleston's Past, Shaping Its Future*, p. 15.
66 Bland, *Preserving Charleston's Past, Shaping Its Future*, pp. 16–19.
67 *Ibid.*, pp. 19–24.
68 Alston Deas, 'They Shall See Your Good Works,' *Preservation Progress*, vol. vii, no. 3 (May 1962), p. 1.
69 'Miss Frost Tells History of Her Restoration Work,' *The News and Courier*, Monday, February 24, 1941, p. 4.
70 'In Interest of Mass Meeting for Preservation of Old Dwelling Houses of Charleston,' PSC Constitution and Meeting Notes 1920–32, archive of the Preservation Society of Charleston.
71 'History of Society to Preserve Old Dwellings Recited,' *The News and Courier*, Sunday, January 14, 1945, p. 10.
72 For public attacks on preservation culture, see, for example: 'Charleston Assets,' *The News and Courier*, Friday, December 8, 1933, p. 14; 'Why Antiquity?' *The News and Courier*, Monday, July 29, 1946, p. 4; 'Why Old Buildings,' *The News and Courier*, Tuesday, July 30, 1946, p. 4.
73 'Teaching the Younger Generation to Appreciate the Artistic Value of Old Buildings in Charleston,' *Evening Post*, Saturday, January 30, 1926, p. 15.
74 See, for example, James M. Hutchisson and Harlan Greene, eds, *Renaissance in Charleston: Art and Life in the Carolina Low Country, 1900–1940* (Athens, GA: The University of Georgia Press, 2003), and Severens, *The Charleston Renaissance*.
75 Bland, *Preserving Charleston's Past, Shaping Its Future*, pp. 85–86.
76 Robert R. Weyeneth, *Historic Preservation in a Living City: Historic Charleston Foundation 1947–1997* (Columbia, SC: The University of South Carolina Press, 2000), p. 19.
77 See, for example, Paul Hamilton Hayne, 'Charleston,' and John Dickson Bruns, 'The Foe at the Gates,' in Burton Egbert Stevenson, ed., *Poems of American History* (Boston, MA: Houghton Mifflin Company, 1922), pp. 515–517.
78 'History of Society to Preserve Old Dwellings Recited,' *The News and Courier*, Sunday, January 14, 1941, p. 10.
79 Eleanor Pringle Hart, 'Editorial: Charleston,' *Preservation Progress*, vol. vii, no. 1 (January 1962), non-paginated.
80 'Glowing Charleston Tribute Is Broadcast by Edwin C. Hill,' *The News and Courier*, Monday, September 2, 1940, p. 10.
81 'Charleston's Charm,' *The News and Courier,* Thursday, December 21, 1933, p. 4.
82 Charles W. Smith, *Old Charleston: Twenty-Four Woodcuts* (Richmond, VA: The Dale Press, 1933), non-paginated.
83 Society for the Preservation of Old Dwellings, Newspaper Clippings 11/3/1932–2/11/1945, archive of the Preservation Society of Charleston.
84 'Momentum Gains for Preservation,' *The News and Courier*, Thursday, December 7, 1939, p. 13.
85 Ibid., p. 13.
86 'Against Zoning Attitude,' *The News and Courier*, Monday, March 4, 1935, p. 4.
87 'The Zoning Ordinance,' *The News and Courier*, Friday, March 8, 1935, p. 5.

88 'Cabbage Row,' *The News and Courier*, Wednesday, December 27, 1933, p. 4.
89 Bland, *Preserving Charleston's Past, Shaping Its Future*, pp. 52–53; for Frost's 'humanitarian' reputation, see 'Miss Mary Frost Compiling a History of Family and Ancestral Home,' *The News and Courier*, Sunday, August 6, 1939, p. 2.
90 Elizabeth O'Neill Verner, 'Susan Pringle Frost,' *Preservation Progress*, vol. v, no. 4 (November 1960), non-paginated.

PART II

Pathfinding in the professions

4

THE 'MINISTER OF MUNICIPALITIES'

Shared space and social fabric in the work of Caroline Bartlett Crane

Ann Marie Borys

Caroline Bartlett Crane (1858–1935), born and raised in the Midwestern region of the United States, earned an education degree from Carthage College in Kenosha, Wisconsin.[1] She began a career of public service first as a teacher, then as a principal, and after that, she became a pistol-packing journalist. It was while working as a reporter in Minneapolis in the 1880s that she met a prominent Unitarian minister, William Channing Gannett, who encouraged her long-held private dream to enter into ministry. He 'guided her independent study' in Unitarian theology even after she moved to South Dakota to care for her widowed father.[2] By 1886, she was accepted as a candidate for ministry by the Iowa Unitarian Conference, an alliance with a concentration of women ministers that came to be known as the Iowa Sisterhood. Crane first served a fledgling congregation in Sioux Falls, South Dakota, and within a year she had increased its membership substantially and overseen the construction of their first church building. She would do the same when called by a struggling congregation in Kalamazoo, Michigan, establishing a pattern of community building that was empowered by increasingly intense engagements with architecture and urbanism. Ultimately, her capacity for building communities through the creation of physical spaces and the fostering of social bonds within them would lead to the final phase of her career as a sanitary and housing reformer. In that role, she would achieve a public voice comparable to that of Jacob Riis or Upton Sinclair, although she has never been recognized with the fanfare of those figures. Steadily, Crane seized the opportunities for urban engagement that had been slowly opening up for women in this pivotal age of social reform, carrying them tenaciously forward until she had claimed a legacy of design and placemaking in addition to her history as a teacher, journalist, and minister. The self-conceptions and physical fabric of the communities she touched were profoundly changed, and while her lack of formal design training has caused her to be neglected in the official histories of architecture and urbanism, her story is of significance to those fields, and helps us to see them in a new light and understand them at a greater depth.

Crane (Figure 4.1) appears to have been 'forgotten' for the last fifty years outside of Kalamazoo, Michigan, though she was widely known in her own time. Linda J. Rynbrandt's 1999 study of her life and work provides a portrait of a complex and compelling woman determined to make a difference in the world.[3] She is most importantly recognized as a pioneer of urban sanitation and food safety. She developed a reputation as 'America's Housekeeper,' becoming a leader in the international 'municipal housekeeping' movement that saw women extending their traditional roles as custodians of domestic health and

FIGURE 4.1 Portrait of Caroline Bartlett Crane

Source: Kalamazoo Public Library

wellbeing into the 'shared home' of the public realm, where they became leaders of social outreach, civic improvement, and environmental reform.[4] As Dolores Hayden has explained, 'Most feminists wished to increase women's rights in the home and simultaneously bring homelike nurturing into public life.'[5] Crane was just such a feminist, believing that women possessed unique strengths that made them indispensable to the future wellbeing of the nation. In all of her pursuits, Crane consistently advocated for the contributions of women to society to be recognized as equal to the farm- or wage-labor of men. Not surprisingly, she was an advocate for women's suffrage, and became friends with the famous suffragist Susan B. Anthony while participating in a national meeting for the movement in 1891.[6] Rynbrandt's book and her subsequent articles focus on establishing Crane's place among feminist sociologists, and her published projects, papers, and speeches provide clear testimony of her alliance with them. However, Crane's mix of interests and accomplishments permit other frameworks as well, including those of architecture and urban planning. Crane pursued her vision by questioning the social and physical boundaries of 'church,' 'city,' and 'home' in order to address a fuller spectrum of human needs. She believed that social justice and wellbeing could be enhanced through better designs for towns, homes, and institutions.

Crane is difficult to define by modern disciplinary categories and standards, but one can perhaps refer to her as an early urbanist as well as a sociologist. She lived and worked in a time when the negative physical and social characteristics of the industrial city were growing in their intensity and demanding attention, just as key forces in urban life were shifting and providing opportunities to address those problems. Crane was a part of the change in urban management from civic-minded volunteerism to professionals in public health and social work empowered by municipal regulation. She was an energetic and willful progressive from the start, choosing a life of hard work and service. She was also able to adapt to many of the changes that shaped the public spheres in which she worked from the 1880s to the 1920s. With the hindsight afforded by the century that has passed since she lived and worked, it is not hard to find some inconsistencies in her generally progressive social attitudes. To measure her by today's standards would, however, be to discount a remarkable record of altruism, including contributions that engaged all scales of built environments to improve conditions for individuals and communities. Like others of her era, she was involved with multiple and sometimes overlapping causes: women's equality, women's suffrage, poverty, public health, education, and environmental degradation. This chapter focuses on her accomplishments in building a new infrastructure for collective betterment where these different realms overlapped, using the built environment as a catalyst for positive social change.

The 'church-home' hybrid

As one among many municipal housekeepers, Crane was not completely exceptional in her overall aspirations and methods, but her particular priorities and areas of impact made her unique. She worked within various networks of women to achieve her complex and multifaceted goals. This began with the Iowa Sisterhood's model of socially engaged Unitarian ministry.[7] Women such as Mary Safford, Eleanor Gordon, and Eliza Wilkes were serving congregations of prairie farm families. Taking positions that their male colleagues shunned, they adapted their ministries to the needs that they found. They teamed up to solve problems, facilitated new congregational posts, and between 1880 and 1910 they built at least twenty new churches in Iowa's small towns. They were extremely practical women, suited to the hard life of farm communities, and so were able to offer members meaningful support and to grow their congregations.

From that base, Crane moved on to establish her longest ministry in Kalamazoo, Michigan, where she would spend nine years creating her own expansive version of supportive social ministry. Her time in this city saw her voraciously consuming ideas about religion, architecture, and reform from all available sources. She spent a summer in London investigating the work of the Salvation Army, and her proximity to Chicago allowed her to visit that city frequently. She studied social work there briefly and befriended women of the settlement house movement, including Jane Addams and Florence Kelley.[8] Her early mentor Gannett and his close colleague, Jenkin Lloyd Jones, were also accessible in Chicago. Along with socially oriented ministry, they were allied in promoting two related architectural themes: the transformation of Unitarian church architecture and the reformation of the American home.[9] They believed that Unitarian churches should distinguish themselves from other denominations and wished to reject the intimidation and fear associated with church monumentality. They objected to Gothic Revival churches on the grounds that they were too expensive, too ornate, and associated more with Catholicism than Protestantism. Their scale and aesthetics, Jones argued, made them more fit for human prostration to God than for fellowship.[10] Ultimately, they wanted churches that would not, in fact, look or feel like churches, and would be useful to their communities on many levels, and seven days per week. They were also critical of typical domestic architecture of the time, envisioning a simpler home as the wholesome and proper place for a meaningful family life in contrast to the ornate, status-oriented house emerging from Industrial Age consumerism. They desired to replace the typical Victorian middle-class residence with one that fostered spiritual harmony. Uniting the critiques of contemporary church and home environments, they proposed that the model for an ideal church should be grafted onto their vision of the ideal home.[11]

Gannett fully explicated the social meaning of the domestic allusions they sought in Unitarian churches in his 1896 sermon entitled 'The House Beautiful.' The full text was published in book form with graphic ornament by Frank Lloyd Wright, a nephew of Jones.[12] Gannett described an ideal house with beautiful spaces and convenient furnishings suited to a healthy and happy household as a place of warmth and welcome, a place of 'simplicity and repose.'[13] Rather than fancy furnishings and consumer goods, he recommended decorating a home with fresh flowers and books, which offered the universal beauty of nature and the means to understand the world through science and literature. Such a home would be, in his words, an 'immanence of miracle,' and a 'domestication of the infinite.'[14] The Western Unitarians echoed these domestic prescriptions in their vision for a reformed church architecture, calling for the elimination of overwrought elements intended to communicate worthiness through expenditure. A simpler approach to environment would valorize the spiritual over the material, elevating the exemplary beauties of 'Nature' and vital human relationships into central values of family and community.

Their vision of a 'church-as-home' was more of a social proposal than a literal physical one. Church buildings would still have special characteristics that set them apart from daily domestic life, but would be welcoming and supportive like a home; they would be places where each individual would feel noticed and valued. Jones took the lead in realizing this concept, commissioning two new churches in 1885–1886. One was a small private chapel on his family's farmland in southern Wisconsin, and the other was for his congregation in South Chicago.[15] He hired an architect, Joseph Silsbee, for both, but the ideas and vision were his own. Unity Chapel, the smaller of the two, demonstrated the idea most clearly. Its stone foundation and shingled wall conveyed a domestic character on the exterior. More importantly, the worship space was not expressed as a discreet, detached volume of singular purpose, because the fellowship hall, or parlor, was combined with it in the main building block. An additional wing for the entry and kitchen were placed at 90 degrees to the main block rather than axial to it. Entry into the square space for worship was on the diagonal, with a view out of the windows opposite rather than focused on the pulpit. The exterior massing of the larger Chicago church, All Souls, was decidedly residential in character with projecting porches and recesses. The worship space, or auditorium, was not visible in the massing. In his inaugural sermon, Jones described that space as

> a home where its members will gather for the studying of God's laws, for spiritual culture, for mutual comfort, to lay their plans to do better the work of the world, and to worship. It will be a social hall, a workshop, and an oratory for the soul in one.[16]

Crane became familiar with All Souls and the ideology it represented through her initial ministry among the Iowa Sisterhood and more directly while visiting Chicago. Moreover, she remained friends with Jones through 1890s when he was planning to rebuild All Souls as a larger institutional civic center serving the south side of the city. This expanded vision, the Abraham Lincoln Center, was only built later, however, in 1904. By then, Crane had already carried the 'church-home' concept forward in her own unique ways.

At Crane's ministry in Kalamazoo, which began in 1889, she quickly revived a dying congregation.[17] Her views and preaching style were attractive in and of themselves, but she also transformed her institution into a magnetic social hub. From the start, her building was open to the community seven days a week to fulfill her belief that, as untaxed properties, churches had an obligation to see that their buildings enhanced their neighborhoods to the fullest extent possible. There was a lack of public support agencies in the growing city and she was prepared to fill in the gaps. Providing social support systems and engaging in what would today be called social case work, the church served the needs of many individuals, ultimately influencing the moral integrity of the community at large.[18] Within five years she had transformed a small and struggling congregation into a vibrant part of the community.

By 1894, the congregation outgrew their small Gothic Revival structure. Crane was poised to build her own version of a church that would offer social support to members and non-members alike, making all visitors feel welcome and easily at home. Here she was able to combine Jones' ideal of a domestically tuned church building with emerging ideas about good design for home efficiencies, all while providing additional space for extra social programs (Figure 4.2). The financial means to build a larger church came from a donation from a grateful member of the congregation who had been inspired to reform his own life.[19] Crane had to engage a professional architect for such a substantial structure, just as Jones had done, but she led the design effort herself, organizing a community process that welcomed input from many quarters. She asked the building committee to imagine themselves in every role imaginable, from

FIGURE 4.2 Interior of the People's Church

Source: Western Michigan University Archives and Regional History Collections

the minister and ushers to the cook and teachers, and to take into account every age group being served. As Crane later wrote,

> We asked the minutest questions concerning conveniences – from where will the kindergartener keep her supplies, to where will the janitor keep his brooms. We had drawn everything exactly as we wanted it, for the sake of use, before we took our plan to an architect, to tell him that it was fixed as fate, and he was to put the best looking outside to it that he could.[20]

Crane's committee not only set the direction for the architect, but also studied and critiqued the plans as they were developed. By fostering community investment in the imagining and creation of this church home, Crane literally built collective aspiration and endeavor into the structure.

The plans that resulted centered upon a large auditorium space with adjoining parlors, both on level and in galleries above. These parlors were intended to provide meeting spaces for social and civic groups, but they could also be opened to the auditorium, thereby enlarging it to create enough seating for seven hundred persons. Additional spaces that served the broader needs of the community, particularly women, included the first free kindergarten in the city, a kitchen and dining room that hosted free lessons in modern home economics and served hot lunches for a low cost to working girls, and the city's first gymnasium for women. The basement contained shops where boys could learn metalwork, carpentry, and mechanical drawing instead of spending idle time in the streets. Other groups that used the meeting rooms included a literary club for African Americans, a local branch of the national grassroots conservation Audubon Society, a choral union, and an orchestra. Crane did not duplicate any of the institutions or services already available in Kalamazoo, such as a library, but specifically aimed to fill unmet needs.[21] Moreover, she saw this as a place for social service programs to get started and take hold so that the city itself would eventually be compelled to provide them. This illustrates not only her tendency to think in terms of systems and efficiencies, but also shows how she created a position of great influence in the city from outside of the economic and political structures, where men clung tenaciously to power. The institution was renamed the People's Church in accordance with Crane's ambitions and the donor's wishes. It was fittingly inaugurated with a communal meal or 'housewarming banquet' to which everyone who had worked on it, from the architect to the laborers, were invited along with their families. Within two years, the church was hosting over one hundred meetings per month.[22] The masonry structure that had been designed to contain all of this activity was larger than a house, but the pattern and scale of its windows and its generous porch-like entry portal were more residential than ecclesiastical in character (Figure 4.3).

Although the church had several identities as a place of worship, school, and workshop, its identity as a public home remained foremost for Crane. She kept the interiors 'plain and simple' so that those seeking support services would feel

FIGURE 4.3 The People's Church
Source: Western Michigan University Archives and Regional History Collections

at ease. All decisions followed the principles of Gannett's ideal home – a practical, simple workability, a democratic provision of comfort, encouragement, and self-sufficiency, all provided with warmth and generosity. In these ways, Crane extended the ideas she had encountered in the Iowa Sisterhood and in Chicago. She also carried forth Gannett's and Jones's principles of the ideal home and the ideal church, taking lessons from them but finding her own way of gathering and sheltering individuals and families in a unique, flexible, multifaceted community structure, and nurturing them through the provision of greater health and wellbeing.

Crane was both a highly involved client and a key designer of the People's Church. Her personal vision led and shaped community input to guide the architect regarding overall character, relationship to public space, number and position of interior spaces, materials, degree of architectural embellishment and ornament, and specific amenities. No doubt the architect brought the capacity for ordering the many parts into a unified whole, but both the institution and the architectural body of the People's Church are attributable to Crane's vision, design ideas, and energetic oversight. It represents an early and powerful example of the kind of lifestyle-oriented architectural reforms that Alice T. Friedman attributed to the 'New Women' claiming public lives and creative roles in twentieth-century design.[23] The Peoples' Church was to remain a vital part of downtown Kalamazoo for seventy-five years.

The city is a larger home

Although Crane's life and work through the 1890s were primarily dedicated to the People's Church, her congregation, and the greater community of Kalamazoo, three important events concerning Crane's future took place. One was the chance to spend additional time in Chicago, this time studying more closely the social theories and programs of the University of Chicago. The second was her 1896 marriage to Augustus Crane, a physician and pioneer in radiology. Last but not least, she suffered a persistent illness that prompted her to resign her ministry at the People's Church in 1898, although she would remain an active member for the rest of her life.[24]

When she returned to work, her professional career took a new shape. Her previous efforts helping individuals gave her powerful insight into a wide variety of social ills, and she could perceive systemic urban problems. This led to her major calling: public health, or sanitation, in urban America, work for which she would come to be known as a 'professional sanitarian' or 'minister of municipalities.'[25] She was comfortable with the idea that women were particularly suited to carry their skills in domestic management to the public sphere in order to clean up messes that the men in power were ignoring. As had been the case for the unique spaces and functions of the People's Church, Crane found gaps and worked to fill them. In 1903, she tried to find someone to speak to a Household Economics group on the subject of meat inspection. When she was unable to find anyone, she personally led a committee on visits to the unregulated slaughter houses and butcher shops that served Kalamazoo to find the information herself. Not surprisingly, they encountered many appalling conditions that constituted a threat to public health. However, when she presented their findings to the City Council, she discovered that they did not have jurisdiction over the slaughterhouses because they were outside the city limits. Not content to let the matter lie, she looked into the situation in other cities, hoping to find a solution. When she discovered that the problem was state-wide, she conferred with the state Board of Health and researched the regulation of meat inspection in other states and countries. She then personally wrote a bill for the Michigan legislature to give cities the right to regulate and inspect their meat supply, and subsequently wrote the corresponding ordinance adopted by the city of Kalamazoo.

Other cities began to seek her services, eventually at a rate that necessitated charging professional service fees. As the years went past and her experience accumulated, Crane developed an approach to comprehensive health inspection that included water supply, waste management, dairy inspections, slaughterhouse inspections, food service shops, and fire safety in tenements and public buildings, including schools. Her reports to the city would often prompt the formation of civic leagues to take on her recommended reforms. The processes she informed and guided were often viewed as a positive experience of communal effort, a sentiment evident in the fact that many cities asked her to return years later.

Crane's 1911 sanitary survey for the mid-sized industrial city of Rochester, New York (Figure 4.4), illustrates the scope and tenor of this work.[26] She was engaged by the Women's Educational and Industrial Union (WEIU), an organization founded in Boston by a physician to address social conditions detrimental to women's health. Rochester had formed its own chapter in the early 1890s. Eleven other city government and social agencies joined the WEIU in supporting Crane's study. By then, she had developed a standard protocol of investigation: requesting certain kinds of information in advance of inspection, conducting on-site inspections lasting five to ten days, and then posing follow-up questions to various officials. In Rochester, she was accompanied on her inspection tours by members of the WEIU. She delivered a preliminary report at a public meeting upon completion of the inspections, and then followed with her full printed report about six months later.

Her survey includes descriptions and assessments of conditions of waste and water systems, urban hygiene, food supply, housing conditions, and almshouses and jails. The report is composed of technical information, investigative reporting, and humanitarian reflections. It begins with the topics that are most universal: drainage and sewer systems, city water supply, street cleaning, waste management,

FIGURE 4.4 View of Rochester, New York, ca. 1910

Source: The Collection of the Rochester Public Library Local History Division, rpf00288

and air quality. Of these topics, her report on street cleaning is particularly revealing. As with sewer and water systems, she began with a thorough description of existing conditions, including plenty of hard data. The various paving materials used throughout the city were fully quantified and evaluated, and unpaved conditions are also described. She discussed the conditions of the various paved surfaces, their lifecycles, and their maintenance issues. She addressed the practices for the cleaning of all of the different surfaces, pointing out many problems and, where possible, offering solutions. When she found that store owners in the downtown commercial areas resisted some of the city's sidewalk-cleaning, she offered city officials some leverage: 'So far as I have been able to learn, the City of Rochester collects nothing from merchants for use of the [subterranean] space under the sidewalk which belongs to the municipality, and is worth a very considerable sum annually.'[27] She also pointed out the city's shameful neglect of the poorer communities in trash removal.

After looking in detail at practices in milk and meat supply chains, she moved on to buildings – first tackling housing conditions, and then the status of municipal institutions. While Rochester did not have a reputation for housing problems, she found that there were pockets of poverty marked by overcrowded, dark, and dilapidated housing with inadequate air and plumbing. Most of Rochester's poor were still housed in two-story frame buildings, but they were also found in upper floors of commercial buildings and a small number of larger four-story masonry blocks. The conditions that she enumerated were sufficient to establish the existence of a housing problem, but even worse was the fact that, as Crane explained to the people of Rochester, a new building code had just been enacted that would enable poor conditions to multiply. A more stringent code, such as the one recently adopted in New York City, was urgently needed. In this instance, she cited a national authority on housing to drive the point home: 'No housing evils are necessary; none need be tolerated. Where they exist they are always a reflection upon the intelligence, right-mindedness and moral tone of the community.'[28] She understood that this problem had hitherto been invisible to those not directly affected, so she injected a more rhetorical tone. It was, ultimately, an extremely meticulous report, engaging with tangible architectural and urban problems, comparing those problems to conditions in other communities, recommending best practices going forward, and even initiating the political debate that remediation would entail.

One of Crane's most dominant themes was fire safety, and this was a focus in nearly every structure she analyzed. Here, Crane departed from her usual reportorial professional demeanor and summoned the full power of human emotions. Having found several examples of fire risk in the downtown commercial area of Rochester, she reminded readers of the horrific and very recent Triangle Shirtwaist Factory fire, which had claimed the lives of one hundred and twenty-three women and twenty-three men in Manhattan on March 25, 1911. When the Rochester fire marshal assured her that required fire escapes were on order for some apartment buildings, she exposed his falsehood by checking with the building's owner.[29] Finally, her anger at inept, corrupt, or lazy public officials prompted her to publicly chasten them, noting that the 'Chamber of Commerce has published altogether the best pamphlets upon "Prevention of Fire" that I have seen. I recommend their careful study to all the people of Rochester, including the Fire Marshal.'[30] Further on in her inspection, she encountered some combustible construction in close proximity to a school's furnace and exhaust ducts that had passed a recent inspection. Dispensing with diplomacy, she cited the relevant code verbatim and suggested that whichever fire inspector failed to see the danger should retire. She also admonished the School Board for attempting to relinquish its own responsibility for building safety by assigning fire officials the inspection duty and blindly accepting their report.

In addition to technical, political, and legal issues, there is a great deal of humanity in her observations on housing and institutions, recalling her power, finely honed while designing the People's Church, to imagine herself in the shoes of many different people, including different age groups. She noted school furniture that was not properly sized for the littlest children, and imagined the discomfort of sitting all day with dangling feet. She was concerned about discomfort of a different kind when she saw that grade school toilet rooms had no privacy stalls. She worried about the residents of the almshouse having no porches, parlors, or private sleeping arrangements, and found their underwear, stamped with the institution's name, humiliating. She strove to understand and advocate for all of the people in all of the places she visited, asking how architecture served them, or failed to serve them, and considering how it might be improved to serve them better.

Crane was realistic about certain limitations; hers was not an airy utopian vision of the city. She accepted the basic capitalist proposition; she simply wanted those with political and economic power to take more responsibility for those without. In short, she wanted fairness to reign over exploitation. An editorial in the Rochester newspaper praised her astute diagnosis of the city's conditions and her comprehension of the politics involved in urban policy and management. She was held up as conscientious and fair.[31] She justified her work in public health and civic improvement on the basis that it was her female duty: 'The cleanliness, health and beauty of the city are the natural concerns of women, because the city is the larger home for us all.'[32] While this statement suggests she was, perhaps, bold rather than radical, Crane serves to illustrate the tremendous breadth and depth of 'municipal housekeeping,' leveraging the metaphor of the city as a 'larger home' to the extent that it afforded her the right and the obligation to assess the full spectrum of urban life. She was, indeed, not only a housekeeper for the larger home, but also, as she claimed, a 'professional sanitarian' and a 'minister of municipalities.'

The 'factory-home': women's workplace

In 1924, Crane's many years of inspecting housing for cities and contemplating and prescribing reforms for housing culminated in her design of a private, single-family house meant to demonstrate the feasibility of homeownership for lower-income families. Her design was a contribution to a major national movement, Better Homes in America, which flourished in the years following the Great War as a response to a widely perceived national housing crisis.[33] A sense of urgency was the result of a combination of factors: low production and supply after the war, increased demand from returning soldiers and immigrants, and the low percentage of homeownership that was revealed by the 1920 census.[34] There was a sense that market-driven solutions would be insufficient in quantity and shoddy in design and construction. To increase homeownership, more houses were needed that were both well-designed and affordable. Cost constraints suggested minimizing building footprints, but at the same time, modern plumbing, heating, electricity, and appliances for cooking and laundry were expected.

Trends in the first two decades of the twentieth century had already brought a reduction in the floor area of the average American middle-class house. The increased expense of modern plumbing and heating systems was partly responsible; other factors included the downward trend in the size of the average family and the declining need for in-home production of consumer products.[35] The rise of home economics as an academic discipline indicates that American society agreed on the need for better domestic life, and this growing discourse became a source of solutions. Efficiencies and scientific management were expected to make smaller houses workable.[36] Architect and Columbia University professor Greta Gray's 1923 textbook *House and Home* exemplifies this scientific approach: it was an encyclopedia of 'best practices' and technical knowledge aimed at improving the homebuilding industry.[37] In addition to discussing planning, materials, and construction, there are chapters on plumbing, heating, lighting, and 'built-in conveniences and labor savers.'[38]

Another indication of just how critical the housing shortage had become was the formation of the Architects' Small House Service Bureau in 1919 and its endorsement by the American Institute of Architects (AIA).[39] Pattern books for houses had been available since before the Civil War, and had evolved into mail-order businesses by the turn of the twentieth century. These were widely despised by professional architects who were invested in the characterization of architecture as a fine art and each of their productions as an 'original' artwork. However, when the housing problem became so acute following the First World War, some architects argued for professional involvement in order to uphold the quality of homes, neighborhoods, and cities. The Bureau began in Minneapolis but quickly expanded to a national scale after AIA approval. Its pre-designed plans were limited to addressing what the AIA called the 'small house problem:' a variety of efficient plans with a maximum of six rooms and 3,000 square feet.[40]

Better Homes in America was very visible in its efforts to address the housing problem. Like the more famous Case Studies Houses after the Second World War, the program was initiated by a magazine editor.[41] Launched in 1922 by Marie Meloney in the popular women's magazine *The Delineator*, it quickly garnered political and governmental endorsement at the state and federal levels. Each year from 1922 to 1935, civic groups sponsored the construction of a demonstration home in their towns or cities; these would all be open to the public during a single week in the fall, publicized by the magazine. There were five hundred homes built in the inaugural year, and over seven thousand in 1930. The movement naturally declined as the Depression took hold.

The Better Homes Movement was conservative in nature, promoting the single-family home, in contrast to progressive ideas in housing reform of the late-nineteenth century that had explored cooperative schemes and apartment houses. Those visions had focused on easing domestic labor by sharing cooking and laundry, and by using industrial machinery to serve an appropriate number of households. However, by the end of the Frist World War, the greater dispersion of families in suburbs and the manufacture of machinery scaled for individual use reduced the logical basis for cooperative living. The Better Homes Movement focused instead on the single-family home and minimizing its space requirements to make it more affordable for the working class.

While the architects' concerns were aesthetic and commercial, and Gray's textbook and similar manuals were pragmatic and technical, the Better Homes Movement was deeply ideological and political.[42] Their intention was to promote the vision of the ideal home as a crucible of traditional American family values and the hygienic and efficient machine-oriented work spaces for kitchen and laundry as conducive to national wellbeing. Productive citizenship and healthy family life were thus equated with home ownership. Herbert Hoover, then secretary of commerce, explained that the program served a 'universal yearning for better homes, and the larger security, independence and freedom that they imply.'[43] The Movement was launched with the construction of an ideal home in a prominent location in Washington, DC. This 2,000 square-foot home represented the myth of American tradition through its Colonial Revival style, but was also completely up to date in domestic technologies. This program's influential promotion of homeownership and the single-family home as the national ideal reinforced Victorian expectations of the sort promoted by Catherine Beecher and helped these proliferate in the twentieth century to the point that they are now commonly known as the 'American dream.'

Patriotism and nationalism were inherent in the Better Homes Movement: strengthening the family around the central figure of the mother meant stabilizing the fundamental social component of an American culture perceived to be increasingly inundated with immigrants. Advocates would encourage cohesiveness in the home by 'training the housewife to her role' and making her housework more efficient.[44] The 'training' was especially aimed at immigrant families in a blatant attempt to assimilate them more quickly to American norms, but increased efficiency was of great importance to all women, especially in the classes that could not afford domestic help. In addition to increasing homeownership, the Better Homes Movement aimed at curing what was seen as 'neglect of the home' by the modern woman, who was enjoying new freedoms brought by the automobile and compulsory school laws, among other things. Women were encouraged to lead the design efforts to assure that the results responded to American women's desires.

Despite its many conservative ideological foundations, some of the rhetoric of Better Homes echoed a decades-old feminist argument for the socio-economic importance of domestic labor and childrearing.[45] Even the president of Better Homes in America, Herbert Hoover (who would soon be president of the United States) implied as much when he observed that the American 'ingenuity and resourcefulness' evident in factory design was needed for 'the laundry and the kitchen.'[46] Early 'domestic scientists' such as Ellen H. Richards had been advocating for improvements in the quality of housing and the conditions for housewives, while home decorator Mable Tuke Priestman advocated for the elimination of dust-catching carved wooden ornament and draperies, and architect Una Nixon Hopkins promoted smooth white walls instead of wallpapers and upholsteries.[47] Simplification as seen in the American Craftsman bungalow, which began to displace the typical Victorian house, became broadly popular and heralded as cost effective. After 1910, special purpose rooms such as libraries, pantries, and sewing rooms were unusual; living room, dining room, and kitchen were seen as sufficient for family activities and required less cleaning.[48]

Caroline Bartlett Crane submitted a design to the third annual Better Homes in America contest, and she solicited free materials and labor from the Kalamazoo business community for the construction of her demonstration house. Her entry won first place among the one thousand five hundred demonstration homes built across the country in 1924 (Figure 4.5). It was clearly inspired by the Colonial Revival precedents that had been celebrated by the Better Homes Movement, but her practical approach went much further in finding efficiencies and creating a supportive environment for the mother of the household. She then uniquely published her prize-winning design in a book, *Everyman's House*, explaining the basis of every design decision. Herbert Hoover's foreword praised her 'practical good sense in arranging the house and its equipment.'[49]

While Greta Gray, among others, focused on the reduction in the amount of time needed in the kitchen due to new consumer conveniences, Crane maintained that a 1920s housewife without domestic help still spent most of the day in the kitchen just to provide the family's three daily meals. While both acknowledged it as the primary workplace for the woman, and they placed equal emphasis on hygiene and modern equipment, Crane portrayed a woman's labor there as an intense and demanding full-time occupation. She devoted four chapters of her book to detailed accounts of the activities of meal preparation, serving, and cleanup. She planned her kitchen with Taylor-inspired motion studies and tested it herself (Figure 4.6). For her, a healthy kitchen went beyond good ventilation and sanitary surfaces; she considered daylighting, electric lighting, hazards, and multiple options for easing the most strenuous tasks. She has been praised by occupational therapists for being sixty years ahead on concepts

FIGURE 4.5 Everyman's House, demonstration design for the 1924 Better Homes of America program

Source: Western Michigan University Archives and Regional History Collections

of universal design.[50] They point to many efficiencies of arrangement, but also admire details like the stool and stepladder that she designed with lower front legs, which would minimize fatigue while sitting to do the dishes.[51]

Announcing, 'Here is a house built around a mother and her baby,' she described the mother and child as the 'first social group,' and recognized that the mother of an infant is 'on duty' twenty-four hours a day.[52] A possible influence may have been the ideas of Swedish feminist Ellen Key, whose views on women's maternal role in the home were central to her influential book *Century of the Child*, published in 1900 and translated into English by 1909.[53] Crane designed her house with what she called the 'mother's suite' as a central concept; it consisted of a bedroom, bathroom, and adjacent kitchen. This allowed the mother to keep a toddler in a gated bedroom, away from the hazards of the kitchen, while still supervising at all times. Reciprocally, she could tend to the child's needs while maintaining close awareness of any cooking underway on the stovetop or in the oven. In the same spirit, Crane invented a baby's crib, the length of which straddled the width of the parent's bed, suspending the baby slightly above (Figure 4.7). When the baby cried at night, the mother could avoid stepping out into the cold night air by rocking the baby back to sleep with her foot, or she could simply sit up and reach for the

FIGURE 4.6 Kitchen of the Everyman's House

Source: Western Michigan University Archives and Regional History Collections

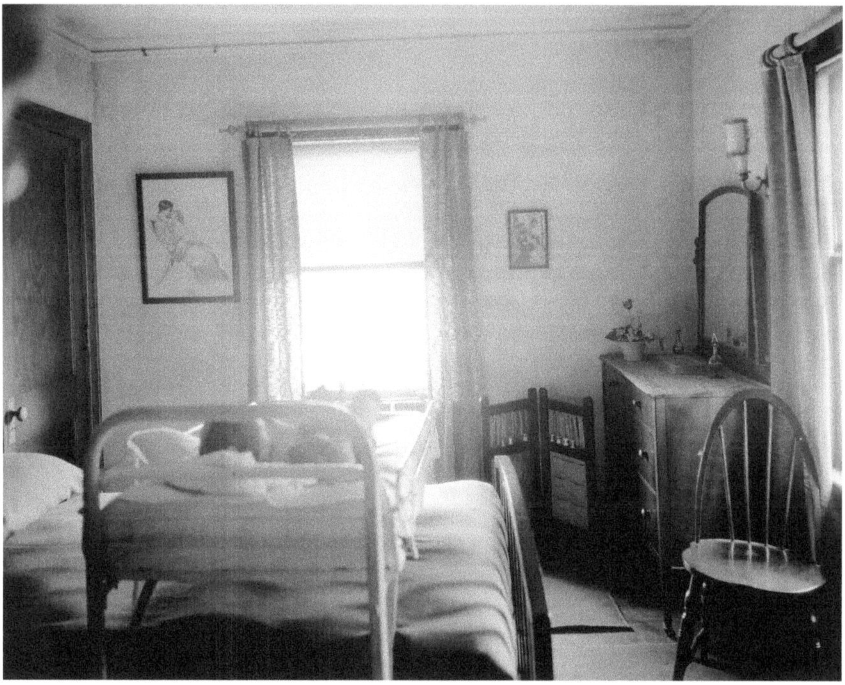

FIGURE 4.7 Everyman's House, view of Mother's suite

Source: Western Michigan University Archives and Regional History Collections

baby to rock or feed it. Crane thought through daily patterns of activity rather than merely providing various functional areas of a home.

The ideology of the 'mother's suite' was presented most fully in a chapter titled 'Occupation, None.' This was what the 1920 census workers recorded for housewives in their door-to-door surveys, a characterization that the entire chapter was devoted to refuting.[54] Crane told women that their needs in performing the sustaining work of wife and mother were as important as the needs of the husband and father in successfully pursuing his trade. Using parables and analogies, she made the case that although it was not recognized by society as such, homemaking was 'productive business.'[55] Crane had already agitated for this view during the First World War when she chaired the Women's Committee of the National Council of Defense in Michigan, by encouraging housewives to register their work as national wartime service. As she put it then: 'Their daily tasks and sacrifices in child care were actually a part of what was going to be the wealth and salvation of America in the next generation.'[56] In keeping with such views, she chose to see her demonstration house as a 'factory' for the production of good citizens.[57]

The floorplan of Crane's house was similar to that of other house plans produced at the time, the chief physical differences being the elimination of hallways so that rooms connected directly and the provision of space on the ground floor for the bathroom that avoided compromising the size of the other rooms (Figure 4.8).[58] However, her attitudes towards the use of rooms was quite distinctive. In the course of designing for a family of limited means, she blurred the boundaries of public and private living spaces, and with that, traditional gendered distinctions. She eliminated a dedicated dining room because it was unused 80 percent of the time; dining was merged with living. She used the space that she freed for the ground-floor 'mother's suite,' calling its master bedroom a 'mother's room.' While she was careful to describe how the layout of spaces would work for the needs of other family members as well, the mother and baby were consistently foremost. She also described how the arrangement would continue to serve family needs over time as the children grew and the parents aged, which was little considered by other small house designs. Crane's design appears rather conventional in some ways, but her erosion of separate and distinct rooms for every function indicates a modern sensibility that went further than the installation of time-saving equipment. She did not imagine a radically different spatial idea for a house, but she was able to envision a radically new organization of the household, and to renovate a traditional house plan just enough to support a new family order. Ever the urban thinker and community advocate, who strove to grasp complex systems from every angle, she argued for a recognition that the family home be seen not as an island, and still less as a 'man's castle,' but as the building block of the nation as a whole, in which the role of women was domestic, yes, but also social, political, and economic – even, increasingly, industrial. If the home was the foundry of the nation, and the elemental social unit was that of mother and child, then the house was the

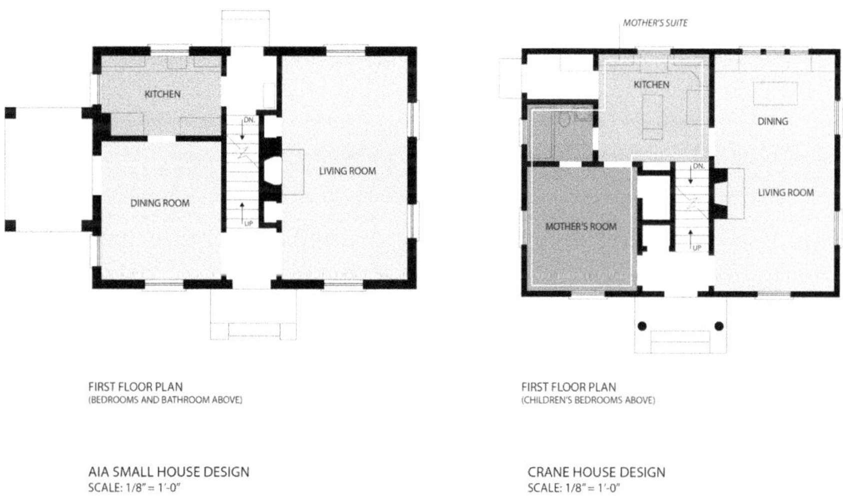

FIGURE 4.8 Comparison of floorplans from the Architects' Small House Service Bureau (left) and Caroline Bartlett Crane's Everyman's House (right)

Source: Drawing by Alissa Tucker

center of all life, and everything else, from farm to factory, needed to support it. That the architecture of that home could and should be designed by a woman was – considering Crane's proposition for viewing communities and nations as extensions of the domestic realm, where woman was both queen and conscience – almost common sense.

Conclusion: reform, not revolution

Crane's contributions to architecture were in the realm of processes and ideas at least as much as in striking formal proposals. Her goals and methods were part of the broad progressive social movements of her time, but she was special in her ability and commitment to applying them to real buildings. The Unitarian ministers of the Iowa Sisterhood and her Chicago-based mentors Gannett and Jones led the way in transforming their churches from echoes of remote monumentality to warmly inviting and socially supportive community centers. The People's Church of Kalamazoo was more architecturally expressive of the civic engagement they all practiced, partly because of the inclusive process as well as the flexible, dynamic results of the design; it was more enduring as well. Sarah Allaback's compilation of seventy-five biographies of the first American women architects does not include Crane, but she deserves to be known as a contributor to modern church architecture, and included in the storylines that celebrate, for example, Frank Lloyd Wright's later Unity Temple, but never so much as mention Crane.

She is also left out of the histories of modern house design, despite the fact that her work prefigured much of what would later emerge as key tenets of the modern movement. The house designed by Gerritt Reitveld to meet the progressive vision of a single mother, Truus Schröder, for example, has a spatial flow and functional flexibility similar to Crane's mother's suite. Interest in using modern technologies to improve the health and sanitation of the modern dwelling would also become increasingly widespread. Le Corbusier's well-known trope that a house could be re-thought as a 'machine for living in' was foreshadowed by feminists such as Helen Campbell, who envisioned a house as orderly and efficient as an office, a laboratory, or store, and whose work spaces were like 'the kitchen of a buffet car or steamship,' and Isabelle MacDougall, who described the ideal kitchen as a 'temple' with the 'scientific cleanliness of a surgery.'[59] Crane, being of a distinct Taylorist bent, embraced the factory model as her ideal at a remarkably early point.

In the design of People's Church and Everyman's House, Crane saw beyond the limitations of given architectural typologies, partly by seeing beyond the limitations of their traditional social biases. As a result of her painstaking efforts to make these buildings work better for each and every person that used them, and to create in them certain affordances, she developed designs that resisted conventions. The People's Church was designed without the coded symbolism of churches that are meaningful only to their members; the spaces were arranged and equipped to serve all citizens without distinguishing outsiders. The 'church-home' was collectively created as a public expression of warmth and welcome. Crane's urban reform work saw her taking the lessons she learned serving in the People's Church into the public realm, helping citizens see their cities fully, indeed as common homes, for the first time, and demanding that they take responsibility for them. Finally, Everyman's House embodied Crane's view of the actual social dynamic of the family, and of the communities of which every family was a part. Rather than accepting standard spatial patterns that passively downplayed the significance and the difficulty of women's duties, her 'house-factory' was built to fully serve its dual roles as family dwelling and women's workplace, and thus live up to its status as the wellspring of society. Through her architectural originality, Crane advanced the feminist goal of recognizing the equal value of work inside and outside of the home, all while serving the broader cause of social justice. She was truly a 'minister of municipalities.'

Notes

1 Biographical information on Crane is drawn from a number of sources: Linda J. Rynbrandt, *Caroline Bartlett Crane and Progressive Reform: Social Housekeeping as Sociology* (New York: Garland Publishers, 1999); Carrie Chapman Catt, "Caroline Bartlett Crane," in *American Women in Civic Work*, ed. by Helen Christine Bennett (New York: Dodd, Mead, and Co., 1915) accessed in the Library of Congress, Rare Books and Special Collections Division, rbnawsa n7485, http://hdl.loc.gov/loc.rbc/rbnawsa.n7485 accessed Feb. 16, 2016.; Charles R. Starring, "Caroline Julia Bartlett Crane," in *Notable American Women, 1607–1950: A Biographical Dictionary*, ed. by Edward T. James (Cambridge, MA: Harvard University Press, 1971), 401–402; and Renee Ruchotzke, "Caroline Bartlett Crane," *Dictionary of Unitarian and Universalist Biography* http://uudb.org/articles/carolinebartlettcrane.html, accessed Feb. 16, 2012.

2 Ruchotzke, "Caroline Bartlett Crane," np.

3 Rynbrandt, *Caroline Bartlett Crane and Progressive Reform*, xxi.

4 Agnes Hooper Gottlieb, *Women Journalists and the Municipal Housekeeping Movement, 1868–1914* (Lewiston, NY: The Edwin Mellen Press, 2001).

5 Delores Hayden, *The Grand Domestic Revolution* (Cambridge, MA: The MIT Press, 1981), 5.

6 Anthony attempted to discourage her from marrying in 1896.

7 Cynthia Grant Tucker, *Prophetic Sisterhood: Liberal Women Ministers of the Frontier, 1880–1930* (Boston, MA: Beacon Press, 1990).

8 For an analysis of the Chicago reform scene, see Chad Montrie, *Rethinking Municipal Housekeeping: Hull-House Women and Sanitation Reform in Chicago, 1889–1913* (Columbus, OH: Ohio State University, 1997); see also Lynda J. Rynbrandt and Mary Jo Deegan, "The Ecofeminist Pragmatism of Caroline Bartlett Crane," *The American Sociologist* 33, no. 3 (Sept. 2002): 58–68.

9 Joseph Siry, "Frank Lloyd Wright's Unity Temple and Architecture for Liberal Religion in Chicago, 1885–1909," *The Art Bulletin* 73, no. 2 (1991): 257–282, doi:10.2307/3045793.

10 Jenkin Lloyd Jones, "The New Problems in Church Architecture," MS (May 17, 1885).

11 This was not to suggest a reversion to the New England meetinghouse, which was a variation on the homes of the initial colonial settlement era; their reference was the midwestern homes of their own time.

12 William C. Gannett and Frank Lloyd Wright, *The House Beautiful* (Park Forest, IL: W.R. Hasbrouck, 1963).
13 *Ibid.*, n.p.
14 *Ibid.*, n.p.
15 Joseph Siry, *Unity Temple: Frank Lloyd Wright and Architecture for Liberal Religion* (Cambridge, UK: Cambridge University Press, 1996), 13–22.
16 Jenkin Lloyd Jones, "The Ideal Church," MS (1882).
17 Starring, "Caroline Julia Bartlett Crane," 401.
18 Tucker, *Prophetic Sisterhood,* 112–113.
19 "People's Church History," People's Church website, http://peopleschurch.net/who-we-are/about-peoples/peoples-church-history/, accessed Feb. 21, 2016,
20 Caroline Bartlett Crane, "The Story of an Institutional Church in a Small City," *Charities* XIV, no. 4 (May 1905): 4.
21 Catt, "Caroline Bartlett Crane," 6.
22 *Ibid.*
23 Alice T. Friedman, *Women and the Making of the Modern House* (New Haven, CT: Yale University Press, 2007).
24 Starring, "Caroline Julia Bartlett Crane," 401; Tucker is alone in stating that the year was 1899 and the reason was to rest and improve her chances for pregnancy, *Prophetic Sisterhood*, 236.
25 Catt, "Caroline Bartlett Crane," 4, 45; also Rynbrandt, *Caroline Bartlett Crane and Progressive Reform*, 95.
26 Caroline Bartlett Crane, *A Sanitary Survey of Rochester, NY* (Rochester, NY: Women's Educational and Industrial Union, 1911).
27 *Ibid.*, 19.
28 *Ibid.*, 64; Crane is quoting Lawrence Veiller, *Housing Reform: A Handbook for Practical Reform in American Cities* (New York: Charities Publication Committee, 1910), 8–10.
29 *Ibid.*, 84.
30 *Ibid.*, 85.
31 "A Civic Expert's Survey," *Rochester Democrat-Chronicle*, May 14, 1911.
32 Lynda J. Rynbrandt and Mary Jo Deegan, "The Ecofeminist Pragmatism of Caroline Bartlett Crane," *The American Sociologist* 33, no. 3 (Sept. 2002): 58.
33 Janet Hutchison, "The Cure for Domestic Neglect: Better Homes in America, 1922–1935," *Perspectives in Vernacular Architecture* 2 (1986): 168–78, doi:10.2307/3514328.
34 *Ibid.*, 168.
35 Gwendolyn Wright, *Building the Dream: A Social History of Housing in America* (Cambridge, MA: The MIT Press, 1983), 159–172.
36 *Ibid.*, 159.
37 Greta Gray, *House and Home: A Manual and Textbook of Practical House Planning*, (Chicago, IL: J.B. Lippincott, 1923).
38 *Ibid.*, p. 131.
39 Lisa Marie Tucker, "The Small House Problem in the United States 1918–1945," *Journal of Design History* 23, no. 1 (2010): 43–59.
40 *Ibid.*
41 Karen E. Altman, "Consuming Ideology: The Better Homes in America Campaign," *Critical Studies in Mass Communication* 7, no. 3 (1990): 286–307, doi:10.1080/15295039009360180.
42 *Ibid.*
43 *Ibid.*, 289.
44 Hutchison, "The Cure for Domestic Neglect," 168 and 178.
45 Wright, *Building the Dream*, 159.
46 Altman, "Consuming Ideology," 289.
47 Wright, *Building the Dream*, 160–162.

48 *Ibid.*, 172.
49 Herbert Hoover, "Forward," in *Everyman's House*, ed. by Caroline Bartlett Crane (Garden City, NY: Doubleday, 1925), ii.
50 Carla Chase and Suzane Roche, "Caroline Bartlett Crane's Everyman's House: Historical Home Design and Home Modification Today," *OT Practice* 16, no. 17 (2011): 14–17.
51 *Ibid.*, 16.
52 Caroline Bartlett Crane, *Everyman's House* (Garden City, NY: Doubleday, 1925), 133.
53 It is speculation that Crane read Key's work, but not unlikely. Key was first published in the United States in the *Atlantic Monthly*, a progressive journal founded by Unitarians.
54 *Ibid.*, 123.
55 *Ibid.*, 125.
56 *Ibid.*, 129.
57 This observation was attributed by Crane to the architect who drew her plans.
58 The house was 29′ x 22′, with approximately 1,000 square foot of living space on one and half stories and 600 square foot of basement storage.
59 Helen Campbell, "Household Furnishings," *Architectural Record* 6 (Oct/Dec 1896): 101; and Isabel McDougall, "An Ideal Kitchen," *The House Beautiful* 13 (Dec 1902): 27.

5

THIS STRANGE INTERLOPER

Building products and the emergence of the architect-shopper in 1930s Britain

Katie Lloyd Thomas

> We thought Bond Street, the world's most exclusive shopping centre, was a place to buy Rolls' cars and diamond pendants; not to exhibit bricks and slates and patent floors. As we entered [The Building Centre], we noted an aristocratic lady looking at the cartoons of building activities in the window and then with a look of determination, she entered evidently intent on finding out what this strange interloper was doing in Bond Street. We do not think she was disappointed. There are more ideas in this free exhibition than in any shop in this famous thoroughfare.[1]

On 6 September 1932, a 'strange interloper' opened amidst the boutiques, auction houses and jewelers on New Bond Street at the heart of London's fashionable West End shopping district.[2] On display across the four floors of this elegant emporium were not the 'Rolls' cars and diamond pendants' of its neighboring stores, but the latest building products – from 'bricks and slates and patent floors' to boilers, plumbing and electrical equipment. The Building Centre's arrival caused a great stir in the national press, in trade journals and in women's magazine. Its reviewers were particularly surprised on two fronts. First, as *The Builder* reported, many commentators were puzzled that such prosaic, technical products should be on display next to luxury stores such as Asprey, Louis Vuitton and Tiffany and Company. While building products bureaus could already be found in other major cities such as Berlin, New York and Oslo, and indeed the Architect's Technical Bureau, in nearby Bloomsbury, had added building materials and materials, to its comprehensive collection of manufacturers' catalogues,[3] The Building Centre was the first to introduce an elaborate display designed to appeal to and welcome members of the lay public. Second, there was considerable astonishment that so many of the Centre's enthusiastic visitors were women (Figure 5.1). As the *Edinburgh Evening News* reported:

FIGURE 5.1 Woman entering The Building Centre on London's New Bond Street, date and photographer unknown, but probably 1939 or 1940

Source: Image courtesy of the Architectural Association Archive

> In less than a month, I hear, nearly 20,000 people have visited [The Building Centre], most of them being architects and builders, of course, but a surprising proportion being people with no professional interest in the exhibition. Very curiously, too, women have predominated amongst these 'outsiders'.[4]

Of course, Bond Street already attracted large numbers of female shoppers to its fashionable stores, and women too made up much of the audience at exhibitions such as the *Daily Mail* Ideal Home Show, with its hugely popular displays of domestic fixtures, fittings and furniture.[5] One way to understand The Building Centre's perplexing appeal to women would be to put it into the context of the other contemporary marketing drives that targeted female consumers and sought to sell them domestic goods. There is, however, no evidence to suggest that the Centre's founder Frank Yerbury, better known today as secretary of the Architectural Association (AA), then London's leading school of architecture, had intended his new Centre to appeal to women in particular. The prospectus he produced to entice investors in the project set out its purposes as: 'For the mutual benefit of architects and manufacturers of materials and equipment, and all those engaged in the building industry, and to stimulate public interest in building.'[6] As the numerous press reviews of its opening suggest, The Building Centre's notable achievement was to take products that had hitherto been only of interest to those involved in the building industry and make them attractive and enticing to a public that included women. The technical products on display there – gutters, paints, roofing products – were altogether another order of goods to the refrigerators, curtains and washing machines that were so energetically promoted to women in the inter-war period.

The peculiar hybrid nature of The Building Centre – a blend of proprietary product information library and department store – and its popularity with women, represents more than simply an extension of the existing domestic appliances and furnishings market. As this chapter shows, the emergence of the Centre should be understood as part of an enormous growth in the range of proprietary building products being manufactured and sold in the UK in the early twentieth century. Moreover, this was a process that saw architects recruited as brokers of these commodities. The architect took on a new role selecting one branded building product over another, a practice that was finally formalized in the writing of contractually binding building specifications in the 1930s. Thus, the architect became a conduit for guaranteed sales between the manufacturer and client/consumer, and The Building Centre acted as one of the mechanisms that facilitated this reconfigured set of relationships.

At the same time as it would provide information to experts in the industry, Yerbury intended The Building Centre as a place to which architects could bring their lay-clients to find out about the range of products on offer. Goods were not directly for sale but nevertheless the Centre needed to develop display techniques that could re-present them to appeal to a non-expert audience. As in the electrical industry, which recruited vast numbers of women, not only to make goods in its factories, but also to promote and demonstrate the benefits of electrification and its labor-saving appliances to the female consumer, my research has found some evidence that women were also involved with this work of repositioning building products for a domestic market, albeit on a much smaller scale. This chapter traces some of these women and explores the nature of their work, explaining to some extent their presence at The Building Centre. It thereby expands the existing literature on women's work in design and architecture in the inter-war period, and makes more sense of the surprising fact that in 1936 the Centre hosted the first ever exhibition in the UK of work by women architects. Indeed the widespread involvement of women in hitherto 'technical' arenas such as the electrical, gas and building products industries may be another of the factors that made it acceptable for women to enter the architectural profession in the inter-war period.

Recovering the proprietary turn: architects as consumers and designers

The significance of the inter-war 'proprietary turn,' as I term it, was, in fact, well recognized and hotly debated by architects at the time. It is architectural history that has overlooked the 'turn' and its effects, and 'forgotten' that there was ever a time when the architect did not select proprietary products on behalf of their client. This chapter therefore speculates on two aspects of this 'turn' that may well have consigned it to the historiographical scrapyard. First, to recognize architects' role as commodity-brokers for the manufacturing industry is also to place the work they do firmly in the service of capitalism. Tellingly, there has been more research in this area in the North American context, where architects at the time were much more comfortable with being seen as businessmen than in the U.K.[7] Too often, changes in architectural design are attributed to the ideas of professional designers, with the result that major transformations at other levels are neglected.[8] The approach taken here asks instead how industrial production impacts the practises and definitions of the architecture profession, and consequently requires an expansion of traditional architectural history methodologies. Useful here is the work of the Marxist theorist and historian Sérgio Ferro, for whom the privileging of design over production (the 'building site' in his formulation[9]) has been a fundamental problem in architectural discourse since the Renaissance.[10] Production is not so much forgotten as willfully obscured so that design can be foregrounded and valorized. Ferro's concern is that in this formulation, the exploitation of labor in building becomes invisible. Even if our position is to accept the architect's inevitable co-option into capitalist industry, being made more aware of the ways that the forces of production have shaped their practise could sharpen architects' capacity to have some critical agency in these developments. Hence this chapter places architects' role in the circulation of building products in the center, and new knowledge is thereby gained about architects, clients and the larger social and economic structures of which they were a part during a crucial period in the history of a leading industrial nation, and particularly in its capital city.

Second, this is a story in which men (and some women!) become 'shoppers' – albeit on behalf of their clients and as part of their professional activity. As Rachel Bowlby explains, we can expect to find in histories of consumption that, 'women have overwhelmingly been the principal shoppers both in reality and in the multifarious representations of them.'[11] Whereas architects had previously consulted dry, technical catalogues, or visited dusty offices and trade libraries to view and select product samples, they now set off to 'the West End's most iconic street'[12] to browse The Building Centre's opulent displays.

The gendered binary of female consumer and male producer or designer has a strong hold. It is already a quarter of a century since feminist design historians Suzette Worden and Jill Seddon called for a shift in history and criticism away from understanding women primarily as consumers, arguing that, 'What additionally needs redressing is the tendency, even in feminist work, towards historical and critical analysis that sees women primarily as consumers of design rather than makers or designers.'[13] They noted the 'gendered coupling of women and consumption' in binary terms, which place 'women as the passive "other" to the active, male creator and producer.'[14] In her introduction to *Women's Places: Architecture and Design 1860–1960*, Penny Sparke has more recently made use of this binary to frame her summary of feminist design history suggesting, for example, that Alice Friedman's positing of clients as key protagonists in the innovative design of some of the twentieth century's most canonical and influential houses marks a shift, 'from an interest in the agency of the producer to that of the consumer.'[15]

This chapter is cautious about this characterization, since it reproduces a separation of the producer from the consumer that is already false. As Miriam Glucksmann has pointed out in her study of female factory workers in the new industries of the 1930s, 'women *both* produced *and* consumed the new goods.' The changes in their status at the time should not be understood as distinct, but, she writes, 'were linked as two complementary chains in a circuit.'[16] The importance of understanding this 'both *and* condition,' of accepting its reality and both the limitations and opportunities that it presented for women is emphasized here. Becoming a producer or designer did not lift women out of being consumers, nor out of being seen in these terms. Nevertheless the proprietary turn engendered new conditions in which women did develop new forms of agency, expertise and knowledge. And if women were now entering the (masculine) space of building products, we should also take note that architects were being interpolated into (feminine) spaces of consumption.

East wall: the new practise of proprietary specification

3.10.36

Dear Betty,

I understand from our phone conversation that it is not your intention to remove the false ceiling in the hall and entirely lag the domestic hot water pipes at East Wall.

I feel I must write you that clause H27 was inserted in the specification after taking the advice of several persons who had special knowledge of ELECTRIC water heating and in view of our rather excessive sum for this type of heating …

Yours Sincerely,
A. Colaço Osario

P.S. Have you been in touch with Crabtree. My catalogue shows the switch covers we want.[17]

This letter from Arnold Colaço Osorio (1906–1985) to his architect Elisabeth 'Betty' Benjamin (1908–1999), concerning the modernist house she was designing for him, is one of a number documents in the building's remarkably complete job file. The references in the letter to Crabtree switch covers, and the specification for electric water heating, are typical of many other documents in the file; Benjamin's collection of trade brochures and catalogues and her correspondence with manufacturers; their letters demanding she returns samples she has been hoarding for many months; letters from Colaço Osorio, which, like the one cited above, insist she consider yet another self-feeding boiler or electric clock that he has come across in his perusal of trade literature and advertisements. The file demonstrates the degree to which the specification of proprietary products had started to play a key role in architectural practise in the inter-war period in the U.K.

East Wall was built in Gerrards Cross (a suburb to the north of London) in 1936 (Figure 5.2). Its designer, Elisabeth Benjamin, was a recent graduate of the Architectural Association.[18] Her client, Arnold Colaço Osorio, was the director of the U.K. arm of the paint company made so famous by Le Corbusier's 'Law of Ripolin,' in which he exhorted every citizen to do away with damasks and wall hangings, to make everything clean and 'think against a background of white.'[19] According to Colaço Osorio's sons, their father had dreamed of becoming an architect himself and took on the family business with reluctance. He devoted much time and money to the project of building his own house, designing the landscaping and, with his wife Frances, had visited Les Terrasses at Garches, the modernist house of his cousin Gabrielle de Monzie (née Colaço Osorio) which she and Sarah and Michael Stein had commissioned Le Corbusier to design.[20] At the time of the commission, Benjamin had designed just one other house, in Wimbledon (completed 1935), in collaboration with the architect Eugen Kaufmann. Although she was later dismissive of the design, the

FIGURE 5.2 East Wall, Gerrards Cross (1936)

Source: Architect: Elizabeth Benjamin with Godfrey Samuel. Family photograph courtesy of David Colaço Osorio

Wimbledon house was included at the *Modern Architecture in England* exhibition at the Museum of Modern Art in New York in 1937, however, as Benjamin complained to the exhibition curators, only Kaufmann was named as its architect.[21]

East Wall was considered of enough significance by the architect and writer F.R.S Yorke to be included in his influential survey of modernist architecture, *The Modern House in England*, published in 1937, this time correctly attributed.[22] Benjamin and Colaço Osorio preferred to call it 'The St George and the Dragon House.' Through its center runs an exposed serpentine wall made of blue 'Southwater' engineering bricks that are more commonly used in sewers. The dragon's head encloses the dining area at ground level with a balcony to the master bedroom above, and its tail encircles the stair. St George, as Benjamin put it, was the, 'rigid white concrete structure bestriding it.'[23] There are many readings we might make of this house. We might see in it the triumph of the new 'rational' modernist vocabulary over the organic vital and vernacular use of 'underground' sewer brick. Or we might note that the spine separated the women's world of cooking, cleaning, nursery, children and maids from the spaces of master bedroom and public appearance. This elegant orthogonal box was also a very early use of reinforced concrete in British domestic architecture, probably worked on by the young Ove Arup, although the design took little advantage of the material's structural possibilities.[24]

Benjamin described the design of East Wall as a collaboration. On this occasion she worked with the Tecton architect Godfrey Samuel with whom she was close, but the evidence in the job file shows that his main involvement was in completing the project, after Benjamin had married and moved away from London. She was also generous about her client, recalling that Colaço Osorio gave her 'absolute carte blanche' with the design of the house.[25] His correspondence in the job file suggests this was true in terms of the architectural form, but when it came to specifying the products, fixtures and fittings for East Wall, Colaço Osorio was very much involved. Below, for example, is the clause he wrote out in full in a letter to Benjamin so that she could insert the terminology into her specification for the contractor.[26] Naturally he specified his own company's paint:

PAINTER.

M 1. GENERAL.

All materials to be bought direct the manufacturers Ripolin Ltd. at 3 Drury Lane, WC2

M 1.A DISTEMPER.

Distemper where used to be Duresco and to be applied strictly in accordance with the manufacturers instructions and obtained direct from Messers. John Lines.

M 1.B USE.

All undercoatings and finishings to be obtained ready for use both in respect of body and color. No tinting, thinning, or intermixing except on the specific instructions of the architect.

M 1.C APPLY.

At least one day is to be allowed between application of each coat.[27]

The specification as a whole is full of examples of named building products, from the concrete shuttering – 'The whole of the plywood is to be obtained from Messrs. Venesta Plywood. Co.' – to the fire grate – 'from Bell Fireplace Co and build in same.' The bricks of the central 'dragon' wall were to be 'Southwater Engineering (sewer finals) from Sussex Brick Co.,' while Eldorado cork slabs were to be used for insulation – entirely ineffectively as it turned out – by laying them directly into the shuttering. The electrical specification is particularly dense with proprietary clauses:

COOKER. Cables to be Callenders 7/044.V.I.600meg.Non-Association.
Cooker Unit to be of M.E.M. [in pencil: G.E.C?] manufacture, vitreous enamelled finish with pilot lamp holder and 3-pin plug for electric kettle.
Cooker fuses to be M.E.M.30amp.Double pole in Iron Case. [in pencil: and fix cooker supplied][28]

The sheer volume of letters and trade literature in the East Wall job file was clear evidence of the importance of product selection between client and architect. In addition, my previous research into the changing forms of clause in specifications since the eighteenth century made it apparent that the naming of brands in the document was a relatively new practise, at least in the U.K.[29] Prior to the inter-war period it is rare to find building materials given by manufacturer's name in British specifications. There are exceptions: as early as 1769 the carpenter's specification for the Sessions-House at the Old Bailey prescribed that windows were to be 'glazed with Ratcliff Crown Glass.'[30] Some proprietary clauses can be found in nineteenth-century specifications such as David Mocatta's for the London Fever Hospital (London, 1833–1843), which refers to Parker's Roman Cement, a material that was commonly named in the documents of the period.[31] Following the First World War, architects were recommending at least the domestic 'fittings and decoration' on behalf of their clients and already some were feeling they had too much influence. Deborah Sugg Ryan cites Wareham Smith, the advertising manager of the *Daily Mail* and head of its Special Publicity Department, on the need to 'undermine the influence of the architect, without delay' and to 'remove his stranglehold from the whole industry.'[32] Smith wanted to give clients and householders the power to select products, and envisaged the *Daily Mail* Ideal Home Show as one way to make this possible. But it was not until 1935, when F.R.S. Yorke took over the editorship of *Specification*, the authoritative guide to best practise in architectural specification that had been produced annually in Britain since 1898, that we find the first clear evidence of the formalization of proprietary specification as a central part of the architect's role.

For his first volume of *Specification*, Yorke made changes that he considered the 'most sweeping and comprehensive in the history of the publication.'[33] He completely revised or rewrote some sections, and added new ones. The embossed portrait of Inigo Jones on the front cover was replaced with a fashionable pale grey woven binding and a crisp black sans serif font. Most significantly, for this chapter, he argued that architects must now take proprietary products on board as part of their practise:

> Proprietary materials are playing a more and more important part in building construction. The early editions of *Specification* ignored them, as architects were inclined to ignore them … Today it is impossible to ignore proprietary building products and to continue to practise as an architect.[34]

What this meant for the newly organized 1935 edition of the guide was that notes on the plethora of branded products then available to the building industry – from new wood products, fiberboards, plasters, concrete surface treatments and paints to cables, switch covers and electric clocks – would no longer be gathered together in a single section entitled 'proprietary products' appended to the master specification. Instead they were moved into the main body of the specification within the appropriate traditional trade 'divisions' of the guide – such as 'carpenter,' 'painter,' 'concretor' and 'electrician.' These 'divisions' offered notes and standard clauses that architects could select to build their own specifications, following the structure and order of the guide. It is this shift that is evident in the East Wall specification, written just a year later.

On the face of it, this was a modest change, but Yorke's inclusion of proprietary clauses within the conventional trade divisions (and by extension within the specifications that architects would write) was a decisive and even contentious acknowledgment that these products were now part of the architect's remit and practise. While The Building Centre put products on display to facilitate their promotion, the proprietary specification was a means by which professionals in the construction industry secured their sale. The East Wall job file shows us that the rapid increase in the use of proprietary clauses also put the architect in a new role with respect to their clients. In preparing the East Wall specification, Benjamin, like any other architect at the time, was not only prescribing the materials, standards and processes of building. She was also selecting one product over another, and 'shopping' from a range of goods on offer on behalf of her client.

The Building Centre: the 'artistic' promotion of building products

> Would-be home-makers, whether they are contemplating the building of a house or merely the interior decoration of one already built, would do well to pay a visit to the Centre. All the latest ideas in building construction, heating, lighting, sanitation and structural decoration are exhibited in a way which requires no technical knowledge to appreciate their conveniences and artistic merits.[35]

The Building Centre may have been unusual in its West End environment and for pioneering new ways of showcasing building products, nevertheless there already existed a great appetite for exhibitions of domestic goods, fixtures and fittings. Such general excitement for these new products both within the industry and among the lay public is clear, for example, from the extensive press coverage of the twentieth Building Trades Exhibition held at the Olympia exhibition hall in west London in 1936. Represented on the 350 stands were the recently established Building Research Station, various trade associations, schools offering courses in the building trades and of course, manufacturers. The exhibition was visited by thousands of people during the two weeks it was on; including King Edward VIII on the day after it opened. Most of the stalls were architect-designed and the press ran photographs, drawings and reviews of the best designs, as well as detailed surveys of the new products on offer. Many of the products specified by Benjamin at East Wall were on display. Venesta was there with a stand designed by R.D. Russell, and so was Sussex Brick and the 'well-known'

Cork Insulation Co. Ltd., which provided East Wall's cork flooring used in the rooms behind the 'dragon.' The design of its stand, however, was not considered interesting enough to be illustrated.[36]

As one anonymous exhibition reviewer explained in *The Architect and Building News*, the inter-war period saw radical change in the British building industry from 'a predominantly traditional industry' in which both builders and architects underwent long apprenticeships to one with a focus on the invention of new materials and systems.[37] The first phase of Registration for architects was introduced in 1931,[38] while the post-war context of material and labor shortages, coupled with the need for an unprecedented level of house building after work had effectively stalled during the war, led to changes in the building industry.[39] New building methods and systems were developed that could rely on factory-based production and use less-skilled labor on the construction site. New materials such as fiberboards, plasterboards, ply and other wood products were developed that could utilize limited resources efficiently.[40] The number and range of paints and plasters available expanded. Other shifts were related more subtly to the effects of war. Adrian Forty has described how the enormous investment in enlarging the capacity for the production of electricity during the war left suppliers needing to find new ways to encourage domestic consumption of electricity. All manner of electrical appliances – particularly for use at breakfast when usage by industry was at its lowest – were invented and foisted on to the householder, from toasters to the electric cookers and clocks that Benjamin included in her specification for East Wall.[41]

Generally, and particularly in the south east, the U.K. saw a shift from the heavy industries that had relied on exports to markets within the Empire, to new lighter industries producing goods for the domestic market.[42] The proliferation of building products seems to have been as much a means for manufacturers to diversify and take advantage of the house-building boom as a response to needs in the construction industry. As a trade journalist explained, it also meant that architects and builders were faced with an enormous range of new and unfamiliar materials:

> The change is, of course, comparable to that which took place in most of the other major industries during the latter part of the nineteenth century. It is, however, enormously complicated by the fact that we deal with not just a few materials but with a whole host, differing more widely in their characteristics than the traditional chalk and cheese.[43]

While it might seem surprising to us today that arch modernists such as Yerbury and Yorke were as interested in these proprietary materials as they were in promoting and disseminating new design, it is clear from the journals, exhibitions and publications of the time, and from their involvement in organizations such as the Design and Industries Association (DIA), that architects engaged enthusiastically with the opportunities presented by these new materials.[44] They were keen to design stands for manufacturers at Olympia, and they frequently describe the changed world they were in and the challenges and potentials the increase in these products raised for them. Struck by these new developments after his visit to the 1936 Building Trade Exhibition, one journalist noted that the 'modern-minded' architect was now an 'essential collaborator in the fellowship of art, science, and industry in whose hands the technique of building rests.' The architect, they continued, was to be 'the synthesist on whom falls the responsibility for co-ordinating industrial activities, many of which have in our time become highly specialised departments of applied science.'[45]

In this context, the new practise of selecting proprietary building products in the specification was, therefore, of more significance than it might initially seem. Manufacturers sought to persuade architects to specify their products and sometimes worked closely with them, and architects needed to navigate their way – just as Elisabeth Benjamin had done – around what could be an overwhelming array of options supported by a range of means from trade catalogues and fairs to office visits from salesmen. On the one hand then, The Building Centre was a service for architects and a development of the Materials Bureau that Yerbury had set up in the 1920s and run inside the AA, where students and members could peruse samples of the latest building products (Figure 5.3). The Centre was intended to showcase products and provide information about them – but a clear principle was that no money should change hands. Although manufacturers had to apply to have their products approved for display and pay an exhibit fee, nothing was on sale. Visitors who were interested in a product could request the in-house information sheets at the enquiries desk on the ground floor and 'retain these as a complete catalogue of all the materials or firms to be used on one particular job,' but no money was to change hands.[46] Minutes from the committee setting up The Building Centre reveal the anxieties around architects appearing to endorse one product over another that could transgress their professional code of conduct, and the fine line between promotion and information.[47]

On the other hand, the East Wall job file also demonstrates (particularly vividly, since Colaço Osorio was so interested in the latest products and technologies) the extent to which the client was now involved with the business of product selection. The lay public also needed to be informed about paints, concrete finishes, sealants, roofing asphalts, bricks, glass bricks, plumbing, electrical appliances and fittings and so on. Yerbury intended the Centre to appeal to clients as much as to architects and building industry professionals. It was also hoped that the Centre would stimulate public interest in building and design. As a journalist reported, its purpose at another level was to '"sell" *building*,' and 'awaken public consciousness in matters of building and architecture by quickening its interest in the fittings, material and furnishing which go to the erection of a structure.'[48]

To achieve this, Yerbury and his team established an innovative approach to the display of building products that contrasted with the cluttered collection at the AA. It was this, according to the press, that made the Centre stand out

FIGURE 5.3 Products displayed for architects at the AA Building Materials Bureau

Source: Image from Building Materials Bureau Pamphlet (n.d. probably late 1920s), AA Archives, Box F2 03(A). Copy courtesy of the Architectural Association Archive

from other materials bureaus in cities around the world. There were changing displays in the shop window on to New Bond Street, just as in its neighboring shops and galleries. A statue of a reclining nude greeted visitors in the opulent art deco foyer, with temporary exhibition spaces to either side (Figure 5.4). A grand panelled corridor, illuminated with the latest neon fittings, led visitors to the library-style enquiries desk on the left, past smaller semi-enclosed display areas for each of the categories of products on display, and on, to the stairs to

FIGURE 5.4 Entrance lobby at The Building Centre (1932). Reprinted from *Hardware Trade Journal* (7 September 1932)

Source: Image courtesy of the Architectural Association Archive

further floors of exhibits. Journalists noted the 'artistic' nature of the displays and that products were placed as if in situ, enabling visitors to imagine easily how and where products would be used in their own homes. Brick panels were mounted on the walls as they would appear in a finished building; tiles were laid on to small sections of roof and bathroom and lighting fittings were arranged on the walls in graphically arresting compositions (Figure 5.5). The Centre's design elevated an otherwise dreary library of building products to department store or art gallery. Furthermore, as a reporter noted, the new Centre opened with a private view, 'like painters do for their pictures.'[49]

FIGURE 5.5 Products displayed for experts and the public at The Building Centre (1932), paints and marbles in the Octagon Room. Reprinted from *The Architect's Journal* (2 September 1932), p. 279

Source: Image courtesy of the Architectural Association Archive

Indeed, much of the enthusiastic and extensive press coverage of the Centre's opening in trade and national press noted the 'artistic' mode of its display, pointing out that it made the selection of building products accessible to those with no technical expertise, and in particular to women. As the *Nottingham Evening Post* article (cited at the start of this section) explained, the

Centre would not just be of use to architects and builders but 'of equal use and value to housewives.' So while industry catalogues and advertisements used the languages of expertise and technical know-how to appeal to 'insiders,' the Centre's development of an 'artistic' language of display would appeal to 'outsiders.' In this sense we might say that within its walls the world of building products was, to some extent, feminized.

Between manufacturers and their market: new roles for women

The more observant reader might already have noticed that to the side of the 'aristocratic lady' in her fur coat who is about to enter The Building Centre, there is another woman (Figure 5.1). Standing up a ladder, putting the finishing touches to 'the cartoons of building activities'[50] and wearing a work coat and skirt and some sparkly earrings, is the painter Marjorie Morrison. She had been the slide librarian at the AA since 1935 and worked at The Building Centre when the AA decanted to the London suburbs during the Second World War, when this photograph might have been taken.[51] Morrison was not the only woman to be employed at the Centre. AA graduates Mary Crowley (later Medd), Justin Blanco White and Rose Gascogine were also appointed as research assistants for *Housing: A European Survey*, published by The Building Centre Committee in 1936.[52] Jill Seddon records that DIA member Cycill Tormley, selected the display of goods at a Building Centre exhibit on the 'prosperous working man's home' (1937).[53] Alma Dicker, another AA-trained architect, worked at the Centre from its inception, at first just managing one floor of the building. She also took part in organizing the temporary exhibitions held at the Centre, in which capacity she oversaw the *Work of Women Architects* exhibition in 1936, and, as the *Morning Post* reported, was also responsible for the design for the Centre's extension in the same year:

> Mr. Yerbury and Miss Alma Dicker are responsible for the redecoration of the roofs and walls and this has been effected in delightful fashion wholly by means of colour values of artistic nuances. The blackening of the dome of the octagon room was a daring idea, justified by the forceful concentration of the lift from the glazed panels.[54]

Like Benjamin, Dicker's architectural training led her into the almost entirely male sphere of the building industry in the 1930s. Edward Bottoms notes that she was later involved in designing stands for the *Daily Mail* Ideal Home Exhibition of 1939, before becoming general manager at the Centre and then emigrating to Australia in 1949 to work with the Melbourne Building Research Liaison.[55] While journalists might have assumed the women they saw at the Centre were 'outsiders,' visiting only as clients, it appears that in fact a number of women worked there and must have visited in their own right as architects.

That women's presence at the Building Centre owed not a little to Yerbury is suggested by the fact that already in the early 1920s he had made 'Women in the

Profession' the subject of the second chapter in his *Architectural Students' Handbook*. In this he argued against the received wisdom that 'the woman student taking up architecture is necessarily bound to make a greater success of domestic work than a man' since students of neither sex will have had any experience of household tasks before prior to their studies! In spite of some sexist assumptions typical of the period, he ended with the rousing claim that 'the whole field of architecture is open to her … as for men.'[56] But women's involvement at the Centre needs to be considered beyond its enlightened director. First, as has been well documented by historians such as Penny Sparke, Jill Seddon and Suzette Worden, the design professions as a whole were increasingly open to women in the inter-war period and quite conducive to their participation. Jill Seddon suggests that freelance design work offered women employment they could pursue even after marriage.[57] Elizabeth Darling argues that the formalization of architectural education and qualifications in the 1930s made the profession more accessible to women.[58] Second, a wide range of new intermediate roles had opened up as part of the drive to stoke women's interest in consumption. Who better to recruit women as the domestic market for the household goods being produced by the 'new' industries than other women who understood their needs and aspirations?

Influential women, such as the well-known illustrator and kitchen designer Dorothy Braddell,[59] promoted design and domestic planning as a career for women, while others demonstrated new products and appliances to other women at shows such as the *Daily Mail* Ideal Home Exhibitions. In 1930, the exhibition organizers had even invited housewives to design their own ideal home; Phyllis Lee's winning entry under the title 'The House That Jill Built' was actually constructed.[60] The electrical industry also employed female demonstrators to persuade women of the benefits of electrification. NESCo, the North East Electricity Supply Company, sent out demonstrators to the furthest corners of its distribution network in its 'Travelling Electric Kitchen' to lecture potential customers on how to use the new appliances – cookers, irons, washing machines and toasters – and assuage their fears about this new form of energy. Demonstrators could be trained and certified at the sleek, modernist 'Electrical Housecraft' kitchen, which was designed by another AA graduate Edna Mosley, and set up by the middle-class campaigning organization, the Electrical Association for Women (EAW). Its guide to electricity, *The Electrical Handbook for Women* (1934), had already sold a remarkable 33,000 copies by 1935.[61] Mosely also designed the refurbishment of EAW's headquarters which opened at 28 Regent Street in 1933. As well as the Electrical Housecraft kitchen (Figure 5.6), there was a members' lounge furnished with abstract rugs and modern furniture, where a portrait of its founder Dame Caroline Haslett hung over the cubist sideboard. Another project was a full scale all-electric Bachelor Girl's Flat that featured in the Bachelor Girls Exhibition at the New Horticultural Hall, Westminster, in November 1930.[62] In this light, Dicker's role at the Centre can be understood to have had a similar function, making use of design skills and

FIGURE 5.6 The 'Electrical Housecraft' kitchen as designed by Edna Mosely at the opening of the EAW headquarters

Source: Reprinted from *The Electrical Age*, vol. II, no. 11 (Jan. 1933). Image courtesy of the Institution of Engineering and Technology Archives

knowledge, and her experience as a woman, to translate and render familiar and desirable the technical realm of building products to a new lay public that included women.

The EAW saw itself first and foremost as a women's organization.[63] Its activities supported the expansion of the electrical industry, but its members advocated the new domestic products – from light fittings to irons to toasters and washing machines – primarily because of their potential to improve the lives of women. Indeed one of its most well-known members and its vice-president, as well as the first president of its Manchester branch, was the Labour member of parliament and suffragist Ellen Wilkinson,[64] who was reported to have 'believed that the twin keys to women's earthly paradise were the Vote and Electricity.'[65] Whereas many of the EAW's members saw the advantages of electrification in freeing middle-class women from the drudgery of housework now that servants were less readily available, Wilkinson's passion lay 'in pressing for schemes which will enable the poorer working families to have the benefits of electric help in their homes,' towards reducing the toil of domestic labour and the ailments and dangers of smoke in the home.[66] This kind of rhetoric was as endemic in the promotion of household goods and products as it was in campaigns for women's emancipation. In a public lecture at The Building Centre in 1932, the General Electrical Company executive Sir Hugo Hirst made the surprising claim that by encouraging women to become consumers of the products on display, the Centre could play a part in freeing women from their domestic drudgery for more rewarding pursuits:

> The British housewife must not undertake the drudgery that she did generations ago ... Our girls are better educated. They have been promised a higher standard of life and when they come home from their day's work in the factory, office or shop, things must be made easier for them. Only the work of the architects' centre will bring that task nearer to completion.[67]

Hirst was an active supporter and benefactor of the EAW and his words are very similar to an earlier speech of Haslett's,[68] although in contrast to his vision of an 'easier' life, she saw in the relief from housework, 'time for reflection; for self-respect' and the 'leisure to acquaint herself more profoundly with the topics of the day.'[69] There is a complex web of associations at work here. 'New' feminism was adopting the language of suffrage. The electrical industry was promoting its products and services through the rhetoric of women's emancipation (and certainly electrification did bring benefits for many women, even if much more slowly for working-class women). Building products were seen, by extension, to offer some of the same advantages. Nevertheless, it remains the case that these developments altered and feminized the design and aesthetics around the new products, and also ushered in many new opportunities for women to engage in technical and design fields that had hitherto largely been open only to men.

Given this, The Building Centre appears as a more natural site for an exhibition of the *Work of Women Architects* than it might at first have seemed. No exhibition catalogue has yet been found, and only two original photographs remain to give us any sense of what the exhibition was like.[70] In each image we see the face of a woman peering at a model (Figure 5.7). She is not a visitor or an 'outsider,' but one of the exhibitors, the architect and sometime employee of the Centre, Mary Crowley (1907–2005).[71] From the extensive press coverage of the exhibition, we can piece together a list of most of the thirty or so exhibitors, who had been selected from a call for contributions set up by Dicker.[72] Although many of the projects on display were houses, neither of Elisabeth Benjamin's two house designs featured.[73] Other non-domestic schemes ranged from Elisabeth Scott's design for a Coffee Stall on Hampstead Green, described by one reviewer as 'surely one of the purely most masculine buildings it is possible to imagine,'[74] to a private zoo and a printing works by Aiton & Scott, Hilda Mason's design for a combined church and mission hall using reinforced concrete, in Felixstowe, a roof garden and nursery on top of a block of flats by Janet Pott and Alison Shepherd, as well as a number of projects by Jane Drew.

FIGURE 5.7 The architect Mary Medd looking at a model of R.E. Sassoon House (1933) as designed by Elizabeth Denby and Maxwell Fry and exhibited at the Work of Women Architects exhibition, The Building Centre (February 1936)

Source: Photograph courtesy of The Building Centre

Larger schemes on display included Elizabeth Denby's design with Maxwell Fry for modernist flats in Peckham, a group of almshouses by J.E. Townsend and Swarland, an austere resettlement village of seventy-seven houses, store, wood workshop and village hall built in Northumberland for the Fountains Abbey Settlers Trust and designed by Molly Procter-Reavall to house unemployed workers from Newcastle upon Tyne. As well as Mosely's Electrical Housecraft kitchen, the exhibition featured an all-electric house designed by Claire Nauheim. One journalist mentioned Dicker's setting out of 'the building materials and fittings displayed,' as a 'novel type of work' alongside the more conventional forms of architectural work exhibited.[75]

Once again the national press, trade journals such as *The Builder* and women's magazines gave the exhibition much enthusiastic coverage. Reporting in the architectural press was, however, scant and limited to tiny paragraphs in the journals' news and events sections, in which comments were often disparaging.[76] The only comment recorded from inside the profession – a professor at a leading school of architecture – claimed that women were not likely to be as first rate or as creative as men.[77] The impression is that this celebration of women's new entry and contribution to the profession was little supported by most architectural educators and practitioners. Instead, in creating a space in which women were welcomed as consumers of building products and of electrical appliances, it was The Building Centre that established conditions that supported their work in the building and design industries.

Conclusion: architects becoming shoppers

The case studies explored in this chapter have troubled normative expectations around gender. In the case of East Wall, the architect – who should be the 'expert' – is a woman; a brilliant designer but relatively inexperienced and evidently overwhelmed by the vast range of building products on offer. The client – who should have been the 'layperson' being escorted by their architect to The Building Centre – is a man, and a technocrat obsessed with all the latest products and technologies. Of course male architects also selected products on behalf of their clients and needed guidance through what was available – the mass of technical literature, trade advertisements, exhibitions and institutions such as The Building Centre are evidence enough of the support system this change required. What the East Wall job file does is make these developments visible. The intense (and gendered) exchanges between Benjamin and Colaço Osorio enable us to see this new nexus of industry, 'art' and expertise and to understand some of the tensions that were involved in the architect's emerging role as product-broker.

In the case of The Building Centre, a library of building products – previously a male preserve that continued to be presented in terms of technical expertise in trade literature and exhibits aimed solely at the industry – is repositioned in terms of its location at the heart of luxury consumption in London and in terms of a design language that offered an 'artistic' – even feminine – means of display. The 'outsiders' or shoppers were assumed to be women, and the 'insiders' – those employed at the Centre and the architects and construction industry professionals who visited for information – were expected to be men. But we have seen that the reality was more nuanced; there were male clients and there were female 'insiders.'

We need then to acknowledge that, on the one hand, the widespread recruitment of women as consumers in the inter-war period also opened up new roles for women that gave them expertise in technical areas and allowed them to enter and influence debates about the built environment and contribute towards the development of new design languages. And on the other hand that the 1930s saw the recruitment of a new kind of 'shopper' – the architect. Architects have since the Renaissance – as Sérgio Ferro has argued – been the 'courtiers of capital' – in so far as their professional techniques have made possible the transfer of autonomy and know-how from artisans and guilds to contractors,[78] but proprietary specification recruited them in an additional form of service to capitalism, as product brokers for the manufacturing industry. That 'shopping' is so very much culturally identified with women, and with femininity, may explain the degree to which architectural history has seemingly overlooked this significant development, preferring to hold on to a conception of the designer that can be neatly and conveniently differentiated from the consumer.

Notes

1 *The Builder*, (n.d., ca. 15 October 1932), TBC Press Cuttings (book 1, no title), Box 2013:98. This and other press articles about The Building Centre (TBC) cited in this chapter are collected in four press cuttings books held at the Architectural Association (AA) Archives. Not all articles are dated but they are organized in chronological order, so the date can be assumed.
2 See Bronwen Edwards, 'Making the West End Modern: Space, Architecture and Shopping in 1930s London' (unpublished PhD: University of the Arts London, 2004) accessed online July 2, 2018: http://ualresearchonline.arts.ac.uk/2299/
3 W.J. Boyle, 'The History of the Standard Catalogue Company', n.d., cited by Steve Parnell, 'The Battle to Define Architecture', chapter 2 in his monograph on *Architectural Design* in preparation. I am grateful to him for sharing his research with me.
4 Review of the opening of The Building Centre, *Edinburgh Evening News* (15 October 1932), TBC Press Cuttings (book 1, no title), Box 2013:98, AA Archives.
5 See Deborah Sugg Ryan, *The Ideal Home Through the 20th Century* (London: Hazar Publishing, 1997) and *Ideal Homes, 1918–39: Domestic Design and Suburban Modernism* (Manchester: Manchester University Press, 2018).
6 Prospectus for The Building Centre Ltd., n.d., front cover, Box F2 03(A), AA Archives.
7 See, for example, Gabrielle Esperdy, 'The Odd-Job Alleyway of Building: Modernization, Marketing, and Architectural Practice in the 1930s', *Journal of Architectural Education*, 58; 4 (2005), pp. 25–40; James P. O'Brien, 'Consuming Sweets: The Work of Architecture in the Age of Selection among Manufacturers' Manufactured Differences', *Journal of Architectural Education*, 53:1 (1999), pp. 25–34; Andrew Shanken, *194X Architecture, Planning, and Consumer Culture on the American Home Front* (Minneapolis: University of Minnesota Press, 2009).
8 For an extended development of this position see Tilo Amhoff, Nick Beech and Katie Lloyd Thomas, 'Industries of Architecture', in Katie Lloyd Thomas, Tilo Amhoff and Nick Beech, eds, *Industries of Architecture* (London: Routledge, 2016), pp. 1–10.
9 For a useful outline of the significance of 'dessin/chantier' or 'design over the building site' in Sérgio Ferro's analysis, see Felipe Contier, 'An Introduction to Sérgio Ferro', in Lloyd Thomas, et al., eds, *Industries of Architecture*, p. 93, fn.5.
10 For the only English translations to date of Sérgio Ferro's work from Portuguese, see Sérgio Ferro, 'Dessin/Chantier: An Introduction', in Ricardo Agarez and Silke Kapp,

trans., Lloyd Thomas, et al., eds, *Industries of Architecture*, pp. 94–105; Sérgio Ferro, 'Concrete as Weapon', Alice Fiuza and Silke Kapp, trans., *Harvard Design Magazine*, no. 46 (Fall/Winter 2018), insert, pp. 8–33.

11 Rachel Bowlby, *Carried Away: The Invention of Modern Shopping* (London: Faber and Faber, 2000), p. 7.

12 Edwards, *Making the West End Modern*, p. 73.

13 Suzette Worden and Jill Seddon, 'Women Designers in Britain in the 1920s and 30s: Defining the Professional and Redefining Design' (Graz, Austria: 2nd European Feminist Research Conference Proceedings, 1994), p. 363.

14 *Ibid.*

15 Penny Sparke, 'Introduction', in Brenda Martin and Penny Sparke, eds, *Women's Places: Architecture and Design 1860–1960* (London: Routledge, 2003), p. xii. Alice Friedman, *Women and the Making of the Modern House* (New Haven: Yale University Press, 1998). Friedman's position has been invaluable in my own thinking to opening up the possibilities of the multiple agencies that can shape architectural design and discourse.

16 Miriam Glucksmann, *Women Assemble: Women Workers and the New Industries in Inter-War Britian* (London: Routledge, 1990), p. 228, author's italics.

17 Client/architect correspondence from job file for East Wall, Gerrards Cross, Bucks (1936), RIBA British Architectural Library Drawings and Archives Collections, Samuel Godfrey papers, SaG/9/4.

18 On Benjamin's work see, Lynne Walker, 'Interview with Elisabeth Benjamin', *Twentieth Century Architecture*, 2 (1996), pp. 74–84. East Wall is also included in Alan Powers, *Modern: The Modern Movement in Britain* (London: Merrell Publishers, 2005), pp. 50–51. It is rephotographed in Nick Dawe and Kenneth Powell, *The Modern House Today* (London: Black Dog, 2001), p. 96 and discussed and illustrated with the original blueprint in Lynne Walker's chapter 'An Irresistible Movement', in Elizabeth Darling and Lynne Walker, eds, *AA Women in Architecture 1917–2017* (London: Architectural Association, 2017) pp. 22, 24–25.

19 Le Corbusier, *The Decorative Art of Today*, trans. James Dunnett (London: The Architectural Press, 1987), p. 192.

20 For the story of Les Terrasses, see Chapter 3, 'Being Modern Together: Le Corbusier's Villa Stein-de Monzie', Friedman, *Women and the Making of the Modern House*, pp. 92–125. James Ward has shown that it was in fact de Monzie who paid for Les Terrasses, which suggests a more direct connection between the Ripolin family money which de Monzie had inherited and Le Corbusier. See James Ward, 'Le Corbusier's Villa 'Les Terrasses' and the International Style' (unpublished PhD thesis, New York University, 1984). Colaço Osorio family history supplied by Arnold's sons, David and Nicholas Colaço Osorio in interviews with the author, July 2012.

21 Thanks to Mary McLeod for this information and sharing her research with me. Letter from Betty Nagelschmidt (née Benjamin) to Miss Fantl, 03.10.1937, Museum of Modern Art Archives, NY, Ref. CE II.1.75.4. It appears that MOMA did produce an errata slip for the catalogue but no record has been kept of it.

22 F.R.S. Yorke, *The Modern House in England* (London: The Architectural Press, 1937), pp. 131–132. Happily, after some decades of neglect, East Wall has now been painstakingly restored by its current (female) owner and the architect Keyvan Lankarani. It was Grade II listed in 1985.

23 Lynne Walker, 'Interview with Elisabeth Benjamin', p. 80.

24 *Light, Air and Simplicity: House at Gerrards Cross [1936]*, produced and directed by Angela Daniell (London: Momentum, 1997). In this film, Benjamin claims that the concrete work was designed by Alvar Aalto, who was then, she says, just starting out. Lynne Walker, who also interviewed Benjamin, is almost certain that this would in fact have been Ove Arup who had acted as concrete consultant for many of the Tecton group.

25 *Ibid.*

26 It is quite common to find manufacturers supplying exemplar clauses for their products in trade catalogues of the period. Presumably they hoped that architects would be keen to save time and copy these clauses, therefore specifying their own products rather than those of another manufacturer. See for example the Mander Bros.' 'Specification of painters' work for architects and quantity surveyors' (London: London, Architects' Dept, n.d. but probably early 1930s), Canadian Centre for Architecture Archives, Montreal. See https://archive.org/details/SpecificationOfPaintersWorkForArchitectsAndQuantitySurveyors/page/n1 (accessed 29 November 2018), advertising masquerading as technical information!

27 Specification for house at Hedgerley Lane, Gerrards Cross, Bucks (1936), RIBA Archives, RIBA British Architectural Library Drawings and Archives Collections, Samuel Godfrey Papers, SaG/9/4.

28 *Ibid.*

29 See for example, Katie Lloyd Thomas, '"Of Their Several Kinds": Forms of Clause in the Architectural Specification', *ARQ*, 16:3 (September 2012), pp. 229–237. My research has focused on the development of specifications in the U.K, but initial study browsing specifications at the CCA Archive suggests that in the North American context this practise starts at any scale as early as the 1880s.

30 Specification for Newgate Gaol and the Sessions House at the Old Bailey (1769), RIBA British Architectural Library, Early Works (EW) No. 790.

31 Specification of work for the London Fever Hospital (1833–1844), *A Volume of Transcripts of Several Specifications of Works and Estimates by David Mocatta and Others, Made Between ca.1833–1843*, RIBA British Architectural Library Drawings and Archives Collections, David Mocatta Papers, MoD/1/1.

32 Sugg Ryan, *The Ideal Home Through the 20th Century*, p. 11.

33 F.R.S. Yorke, 'Preface', in *Specification 1935* (London: Architectural Press, 1935), p. iii.

34 *Ibid.*

35 *Nottingham Evening Post* (9 September 1932), TBC Press Cuttings, (book 1, no title), Box 2013:98, AA Archives.

36 'Building Trades Exhibition, Olympia, 1936-II', *The Architect and Building News* (25 September 1936), p. 411.

37 'A First Review of the Building Trades Exhibition, Olympia, 1936', *The Architect and Building News* (18 September 1936), p. 350.

38 See David Dean, *The Thirties: The English Architectural Scene* (London: Trefoil Books, 1983).

39 Mark Swenarton, *Homes Fit for Heroes: The Politics and Architecture of Early State Housing in Britain* (London: Heinemann Educational Books, 1981) and *Building the New Jerusalem: Architecture, Housing and Politics 1900–1930* (Bracknell: IHS BRE Press, 2008); Marion Bowley, *Housing and the State,1919–1944* (London: George Allen & Unwin, 1945).

40 See Christopher Powell, *The British Building Industry Since 1800: An Economic History* (Abingdon: Spon Press, 1980); Marion Bowley, *The British Building Industry: Four Studies in Response to Resistance and Change* (Cambridge, UK: Cambridge University Press, 1966).

41 Adrian Forty, *Objects of Desire* (London: Thames & Hudson, 1986), pp. 183–197.

42 Glucksmann, *Women Assemble: Women Workers*, pp. 72–81.

43 'A First Review of the Building Trades Exhibition, Olympia, 1936'.

44 See particularly Elizabeth Darling, *Re-forming Britain: Narratives of Modernity before Reconstruction* (London: Routledge, 2007) and *Wells Coates* (London: RIBA Enterprises, 2012).

45 'Olympia, 1936', *The Builder* (4 September 1936), p. 296.

46 Prospectus for The Building Centre Ltd., n.d., Box F2 03(A), AA Archives.

47 Agenda papers for the Building Materials Sub Committee, 14 No 1929-20 Nov 1930, Box C301, AA Archives.
48 *The Builder* (15 October 1932), TBC Press Cuttings (book 1, no title), Box 2013:98, AA Archives. My italics.
49 *Sheffield Daily Telegraph* (3 September 1932), TBC Press Cuttings (book 1, no title), Box 2013:98, AA Archives.
50 *Edinburgh Evening News* (15 October 1932), TBC Press Cuttings (book 1, no title), Box 2013:98, AA Archives.
51 I am grateful to Vanessa Norwood of The Building Centre for identifying the woman in the photograph, and to Andrew Higgott, who worked alongside Morrison at the slide library, for sharing photographs and details of her biography. Morrison was a central figure at the AA and worked there until 1985, her services to architecture were recognized with an MBE in 1983.
52 Catherine Burke notes that Mary Medd (née Crowley) was working full time at The Building Centre in September 1935, *A Life in Education and Architecture: Mary Beaumont Medd* (London: Ashgate, 2013), p. 57. The best evidence I have been able to find for this is Medd's CV which lists her employment there for the full year of 1936, Institute of Education Archives ME/A/10/1 CV. The fact she was photographed at the Work of Women Architects exhibition with the model of Elizabeth Denby and Max Fry's Sassoon House scheme could suggest she was working on site and was available to pose for the picture, or it could be because she had been involved with Denby's Kensal House as Elizabeth Darling recounts in her discussion of Mary Medd in 'Becoming Truly Alive', in Darling and Walker, eds, *AA Women in Architecture 1917–2017*, pp. 26–43.
53 This was the Working Class House exhibition in 1937. Jill Seddon, 'Mentioned but Denied Significance: Women designers and the "Professionalisation" of Design in Britain', *Gender and History*, 12: 2 (July 2000), pp. 426–447, 434.
54 'Building Centre's New Home', *Morning Post* (9 January 1936), TBC Press Cuttings (*No.* 7), Box 2013:98, AA Archives.
55 Edward Bottoms, 'Beyond the Drawing Board', in Darling and Walker, eds, *AA Women in Architecture 1917–2017*, pp. 66–83, p. 75.
56 F.R. Yerbury, *Architectural Students' Handbook* (Westminster: Technical Journals Ltd., n.d. – but appears to be 1922), pp. 7–9.
57 Seddon, 'Mentioned but Denied Significance', p. 437.
58 Elizabeth Darling, 'Women with Attitude: AAXX', *Architectural Review*, 13 March 2018, www.architectural-review.com/essays/women-with-attitude-aaxx/10028287.article (accessed 27 March 2010).
59 See for example, Jonathan M. Woodham, 'Women, Design and the State in the Interwar Years: A Case Study of Elizabeth Denby and the Council for Art and Industry', in Jill Seddon and Suzette Worden, eds, *Women Designing: Redefining Design in Britain between the Wars* (Brighton: University of Brighton, 1994), pp. 41–45.
60 Sugg Ryan, *The Ideal Home Through the 20th Century*, pp. 64–65.
61 Suzette Worden, '"Not the Arty Type but the Practical Female Person": Women's Role in the Design of Domestic Appliances', in Worden and Seddon, eds, *Women Designing*, pp. 34–39 and p. 38.
62 Carroll Pursell, 'Domesticating Modernity: The Electrical Association for Women, 1924–1986', *The British Journal for the History of Science*, 32:1 (March 1999), pp. 47–67.
63 Ibid., p. 47.
64 Peggy Scott, *An Electrical Adventure* (London: Hodder and Stoughton, 1934), p. 100.
65 Introduction to Ellen Wilkinson's annual EAW address in 1934, reported in *Electrical Age for Women*, No.2 (1934), p. 653.
66 *Ibid.*

67 Report of Sir Hugo Hirst's lecture at The Building Centre in the *Birmingham Post* (28 October 1932), TBC Press Cuttings, TBC Press Cuttings (book 1, no title), Box 2013:98, AA archives.
68 Hirst's contributions to the EAW's activities are in a history of its first ten years; Scott, *An Electrical Adventure*, pp. 102, 61–62. For his financial support of the Association see https://sites.google.com/a/staff.westminster.ac.uk/electricity-for-women/home/electrical-promotion-between-the-wars (accessed 24 April 2017).
69 Reprinted in Scott, *An Electrical Adventure*, p. 108.
70 These photographs are in the stores of The Building Centre, as it exists today, much changed, in Store Street, London. I am grateful to Colin Tweedy, director of the Centre, for enabling me to see the collection.
71 I am grateful to Elizabeth Darling for identifying the woman's face in the picture.
72 Both *The Builder* and *Architect and Building News* (20 December 1935) carried advertisements looking for contributions to an 'Exhibition of Work Executed by Women Architects' that opened at The Building Centre in 1936. Potential contributors are asked to send preliminary prints to 'Miss Alma Dicker, FRIBA, Honorary Secretary', TBC Press Cuttings (*No.* 7), Box 2013:98, AA Archives.
73 For example: Frances Barker, semi-detached house in Mill Hill, London; Margaret Murray, house for a woman doctor in Boar Hill, Oxfordshire; Mary Crowley, three houses in Tewin, Hertfordshire; Gillian Harrison, houses in Kingsgate and Littlestone, Kent; Margaret Tomlinson, thatched house in Devon; Sadie Speight, conversion of a Victorian house into a modern home. Other exhibiting architects noted in reviews of the exhibition include J.B. Albery, Ruth Easton, Doris Robinson, M.F. Rigg, Eleanor Hughes, Ithell Colquhoun and Mrs Cosens. These references compiled from press reviews of the exhibition in TBC Press Cuttings (*No.* 7), Box 2013:98, AA Archives.
74 'Women Make Good as Architects', *Daily Mail* (11 February 1936), TBC Press Cuttings (*No.* 7), Box 2013:98, AA Archives.
75 'Women Build New Reputation in Reinforced Concrete', *News Chronicle* (11 February 1936), TBC Press Cuttings (*No.* 7), Box 2013:98, AA Archives.
76 For example, there are no mentions of the exhibition in *Journal of the RIBA* (8 & 22 February 1936) or *Architectural Review* (February 1936); and brief entries 'Building Centre Exhibition' under 'News and Notes' in *Architectural Design and Construction* (Vol VI.4, February 1936, p. 110) and 'Work of Women Architects' under 'General News' in *The Builder* (21 February 1936, p. 378), TBC Press Cuttings (*No.* 7), Box 2013:98, AA Archives.
77 'Women as Architects What they are Doing Today?', *Homes and Gardens* (April 1936), TBC Press Cuttings (*No.* 7), Box 2013:98, AA Archives.
78 Ferro, 'Dessin/Chantier: An introduction', in Lloyd Thomas et al., *Industries of Architecture*, p. 101.

6

ADAPTING AND ANTICIPATING

The home planning consultancy work of Hilde Reiss and Jane Drew, 1943–45

Erin McKellar

Although private architectural work became scarce during the Second World War, many architects in the U.K. and the U.S. engaged creatively with the war effort to create unorthodox projects for themselves. These years saw architects tackling an array of ventures ranging from defense-related work designing munitions factories and developing urban camouflage to more domestic home-front pursuits such as designing emergency housing and planning postwar cities. By examining the wartime endeavors of the German-born American architect and designer Hilde Reiss (1909–2002) and the British architect Jane Drew (1911–96), this chapter reveals that while male architects were more likely to be recruited for projects related to defense and weaponry, female professionals often resourcefully developed or even invented alternative positions. Reiss obtained a wartime job as a consultant for the Housing Authority of the City of Vallejo in the San Francisco Bay Area of California, and in this role she focused on advising the inhabitants of Vallejo's war housing projects on how to transform their temporary dwellings into homes. Meanwhile, Drew obtained consultancy work from the British Commercial Gas Association, for which she researched and publicized new ideas related to kitchen planning. Working within similar contexts and using similar strategies, Reiss's and Drew's impacts extended beyond what would normally have been possible for women, as both professionals transformed the ostensibly auxiliary role of consultant into a powerful agent for shaping community design discourses.

It should be noted that these women did not merely fill vacancies left by the mobilization of male architects. Rather, women architects claimed leading roles in adapting wartime domestic spaces and anticipating the postwar domestic landscape globally and publicly throughout unoccupied nations. In perhaps the best-known example of this phenomenon, the American corporation Revere Copper and Brass Incorporated hired architects and designers to market their anticipated postwar goods to American households, producing a series of booklets on 'better living' that illustrated how Revere products would bring forth a better world.[1] Revere's project relied solely on well-known male professionals such as Buckminster Fuller, William Lescaze, George Nelson and Antonin Raymond.[2] The similar consultancy projects with which Reiss and Drew were engaged therefore showcase how women resourcefully made space for themselves in a crowded field, claiming roles in the formulation and dissemination of modernist architectural ideas that aspired to, and in many cases would, help shape the world to come. Because Reiss's and Drew's projects involved significant public outreach in the form of publishing and exhibiting, this chapter contends that domestic design consultancy, while initially limited in scope, provided such women with a platform from which to guide the architectural expectations of non-professional audiences and engage in community-building. Since their audiences were comprised primarily of women, examining these figures at this moment reveals key intersections among women as architectural makers, mediators and users. As makers, Reiss and Drew created spaces for the use of specific clients and more general mass consumers or users. Because Reiss and Drew were women, both architects largely received small-scale, domestic projects – a fact that reflected the tenacious historical association between femininity and domesticity. As mediators, Reiss and Drew engaged their substantial knowledge of modern architecture and design by distilling complex, cutting-edge ideas, and at times simplifying them, so they would reach lay audiences. In their consultancy projects, both designers wrote material and devised exhibitions so that their audiences could read about modern architectural concepts and see how principles could be applied in the home. Finally, because Reiss and Drew consulted on domestic projects – and because they were doing so during wartime – women comprised their audiences, and they were asked to play roles individually and collectively as users of these new proposals. Reiss worked to empower women as homemakers and war workers during a time of international crisis, while Drew cast eyes toward the future by addressing women as potential consumers of household goods, showing them how to modernize their households and reduce their workloads. In both cases, Reiss and Drew tailored their content to reach women by discussing and depicting female figures throughout their work. Through their work and their methods, the two architects encouraged women to participate in an architectural transformation that would modernize and thus, in some measure, liberate their lives.

Women architects in wartime: consultancy and expertise

Consultants supply expert advice in all professions. During the Second World War, architectural professionals applied their expertise across a range of areas. In Britain, for example, architects and engineers such as Ove Arup spearheaded discussions on Air Raid Precautions by designing shelters and analyzing buildings to understand how they might react to being bombed.[3] Other architects and designers, such as Antonin Raymond, Erich Mendelsohn and Hans Knoll, helped the American Army to develop more devastating weapons by providing expert advice on Japanese and German construction methods and materials.[4] While women architects were often not invited to take part in similar defense- and weapons-related projects, architectural historians such as Gillian Darley have demonstrated that the war did open some doors to women. Schools such as the Architectural Association in London availed more places to women, and architects such as Judith Ledeboer contributed their expertise during wartime by researching and compiling a major report on prefabrication for the Ministry of Works.[5] In both Britain and America, many women architects were called upon to design small-scale objects, plan evacuation camps, advise on the interiors of emergency housing and curate exhibitions – roles that were often seen as less important to national defense and thus more appropriate for women. Therefore, women architects frequently occupied less visible positions than their male counterparts. The projects with which Reiss and Drew engaged, particularly during the latter part of the war, exemplified this type of activity. They were hired by the Housing Authority of the City of Vallejo, California and the British Commercial Gas Association, respectively, to employ their knowledge by providing expert advice on how to plan modern dwellings. By the 1940s, housing fell well within the parameters of the architectural work that was acceptable for women. On both sides of the Atlantic, women had actively pursued housing reform as 'municipal housekeepers' in late-nineteenth and early-twentieth century cities. For example, women had helped lead the Better Homes of America movement in the 1920s, and prominent reformers such as Edith Elmer Wood and Catherine Bauer had helped to shape U.S. housing policy throughout the 1930s, while figures such as Ledeboer and Elizabeth Denby had committed themselves to researching and developing low-cost housing solutions in Britain during the same decade.[6]

From the time Reiss arrived in the United States from Germany in 1933, she cultivated an architectural career for herself as a teacher, writer, editor, consultant and curator. Prior to moving to the United States, Reiss had trained at the State Academy of Building in Weimar and the Bauhaus in Dessau, where she studied under Ludwig Mies van der Rohe and Ludwig Hilbersheimer.[7] By the time Reiss began her studies at the Bauhaus in 1930, the school had adopted a much more architectural focus under the directorship of Mies van der Rohe. Likely grounded in these studies, Reiss seems to have emphasized creating a unified aesthetic in her projects by employing built-in and other functional furniture and textile elements, which she believed were easily modifiable elements of a space. Based in New York throughout the 1930s, she worked in the offices of high-profile industrial designers such as Norman Bel Geddes and Gilbert Rohde, as well as interior designer Eleanor LeMaire, and she taught at the New School for Social Research and the Design Laboratory. While engaged in these activities, she also took on private commissions to redesign existing apartments throughout the city of New York. In these projects Reiss built a reputation as an expert on interiors, which would later feed into her work with the Housing Authority of the City of Vallejo.[8]

When private-sector design work became scarce as the nation focused on preparing for war, Reiss began taking on consultancy projects. The first example of such a project, undertaken from 1942–43, was a voluntary role that she obtained through her husband, architect William Friedman, after he was offered a position at the Heart Mountain Relocation Center in Wyoming.[9] Located between the towns of Cody and Powell in northwest Wyoming, the Heart Mountain Relocation Center comprised one of ten camps that the U.S. Federal Government set up to intern people of Japanese ancestry, most of whom were U.S. citizens. Issued on February 19, 1942, Executive Order 9066 authorized officials to deport and imprison all people of Japanese ancestry from the West Coast, including all of California and parts of Arizona, Oregon and Washington, under the guise of national security. Reiss did not receive the offer of paid employment that Friedman did, and indeed she was also excluded from the types of projects with which other Bauhaus *émigrés* were occupied, for example Aluminum City Terrace, which had been designed by Walter Gropius and Marcel Breuer for the employees of the ALCOA factories in New Kensington, Pennsylvania.[10] However, once in Wyoming, Reiss carved professional space for herself by creating her own unpaid position. She volunteered to help transform the internment camp's existing rudimentary Army barracks into facilities for the internees, including schools, nurseries, community centers and shops.[11] No records appear to illustrate the modifications that Reiss made, but the knowledge that trained experts helped to make the camps 'livable' outlines the planning and the design expertise involved in the internment process. It is worth asking to what extent Reiss's work at Heart Mountain can be viewed as a humanitarian intervention in an unjust system and to what extent she merely engaged in professional opportunism. However, this is a question that has not yet been resolved.

While Reiss's work at the Heart Mountain Relocation Center comprised unofficial voluntary consultancy, she later monetized her expertise when she became technical consultant for the Housing Authority of the City of Vallejo in California's San Francisco Bay Area. Reiss obtained this position through her existing professional network, as some of her friends in San Francisco knew the director of the Housing Authority.[12] Vallejo was strategically important during the Second World War because it hosted the Mare Island Naval Shipyard, which became a major center for wartime shipbuilding and the main submarine port on the United States' West Coast. The city expanded rapidly as the naval yard grew in strategic significance. A town of about thirty thousand in 1940, Vallejo ballooned in size, nearly quadrupling by 1943, by which time the Mare Island Naval Shipyard alone employed forty thousand people.[13] As part of a much larger government-sponsored program to house workers of defense industries, architects and contractors swiftly stepped in to alleviate the stress on the town's overcrowded housing stock, constructing twelve thousand new housing units in Vallejo.[14]

As technical consultant, Reiss's initial role mirrored her voluntary position at the Heart Mountain Relocation Center. She was initially responsible for furnishing Vallejo's community centers and other public facilities, such as schools and nurseries. However, Reiss increased the significance of her role when she began advising inhabitants of Vallejo's Housing Authority on how to furnish and finish their wartime dwellings.[15] Reiss could easily justify this service by pointing to Vallejo's material realities. First, because the U.S. government needed to maintain high morale among workers in order to ensure defense preparedness, it was essential to instill positive feelings about the authority housing in the inhabitants. Second, because much of the authority housing had been constructed quickly and inexpensively, it had been built to standards to which some Americans would have been unaccustomed. Material rationing regulations restricted the numbers of both permanent and temporary units and kept room sizes small – especially in temporary housing, where speed, economy and conserving critical materials meant that architects and builders kept room sizes smaller and maintained higher densities than in permanent projects.[16] Within the altered material conditions of war, Reiss clearly saw an opportunity to exert influence over her audience of homemakers and war workers by teaching them those principles of modern design that had long been formulated for efficiency.

Architect Jane Drew also found opportunity in the war, enabling her to set up her own architectural practice and to monetize her expertise as a female architect. As an architectural practitioner Drew followed a more conventional career trajectory than Reiss had done. However, like Reiss, one of Drew's key wartime projects comprised consultancy work that allowed her to promote the principles of modern design to non-professional audiences. Trained at the Architectural Association (AA) from 1929–34, Drew had set up a small architectural practice that focused on residential design with her first husband and fellow AA classmate, architect James Alliston. After separating from Alliston, Drew partnered with architect Maxwell Fry. Perhaps best known for her postwar work and collaborations with Fry in Ghana and Nigeria, as well as their projects in Chandigarh, India with Le Corbusier and Pierre Jeanneret, Drew ran her own architectural office in wartime London while Fry was engaged in projects with the Royal Engineers in Derby and West Africa.[17] It was through this office that Drew obtained her consultancy work for the British Commercial Gas Association (BCGA).

The BCGA regarded Drew as the ideal expert to advise on matters of kitchen planning. Not only did she understand current architectural trends, but she had also engaged in at least some household coordination as a wife and mother. In 1944, the BCGA explicitly connected female expertise and domestic goods in an advertisement that pictured gas-fueled consumer appliances as the future of household comfort (Figure 6.1). During the conflict, manufacturers had been producing in the service of the war; however, the BCGA anticipated helping manufacturers transition to peacetime production by making modern gas appliances widely available to consumers during the postwar

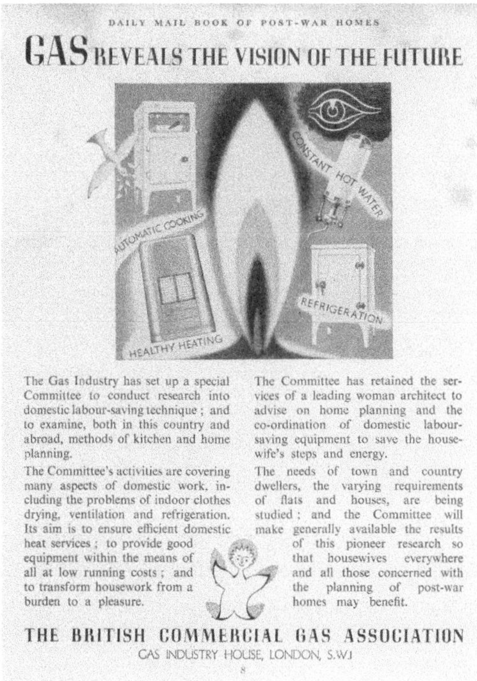

FIGURE 6.1 Advertisement for the British Commercial Gas Association, 1944

Source: *Daily Mail Book of Post-war Homes*

years. The advertisement, which appeared in the *Daily Mail Book of Post-War Homes*, a publication aimed at women, explained that the gas industry had retained the services of a 'leading woman architect to advise on home planning and the coordination of domestic labour-saving equipment to save the housewife's steps and energy.'[18] By referencing Drew only as a 'leading woman architect,' the British Commercial Gas Association acknowledged that their audience of housewives cared more about the general expertise of women professionals than they did about name recognition.

Drew considered her consultancy project an opportunity to elevate the lives of ordinary women through careful study and analysis. British architects and housing advocates had perceived that the majority of kitchens in new houses remained 'only barely equipped' by the early 1940s.[19] These kitchens provided a shelf or two and a cupboard, but only rarely included the standardized kitchen cabinetry that was popular in the U.S. and that would become increasingly commonplace in British households after the war. Drew and other architects thus believed that the postwar years would provide impetus to hasten improvement in this area. While Drew assumed her role as architectural consultant within this context, she also understood that the war had transformed the lives of women by expanding their worldviews through their work in factories and on farms, where they had gained experience living communally and had developed skills with modern machinery.[20] Realizing that young postwar women would not be satisfied dedicating all of their time and energy to toil in the home, Drew explained that she was conducting extensive research on kitchens because 'every women agrees that house drudgery must be banished after the war.'[21] She thus saw her role as part of a larger social project that would help to improve women's lives by reducing their domestic labor.

In order to alleviate toil, Drew focused on modernizing kitchen technologies and rationalizing kitchen floor plans. Aware of the social impact of new materials, she carefully researched synthetics such as Formica, in wide use as substitutional materials during wartime, to discover potential postwar uses for them. She also spent time in the U.S. learning about gas air conditioning and heating, as well as enamels, which she believed could be used to produce durable and heat resistant appliances.[22] Her research revealed that manufacturers could employ such materials to produce kitchen components inexpensively and in quantity, and, moreover, to promote easy cleaning to eliminate drudgery. While Drew investigated the potential for mass production, she also sought to apply these concepts meaningfully in a process of 'kitchen planning,' intending for each element of the postwar kitchen, from its materials to its floor plan, to improve housekeeping. Planning the kitchen meant discovering a family's pattern of life and tailoring the kitchen to suit those requirements rather than creating a one-size-fits-all solution. By focusing on variations in economic and social rhythms of different communities, Drew ensured that the scope of her work, and her expectations for its impact, moved beyond the domestic realm and into those communities at large. Like Reiss, Drew found that re-imagining domestic life within the context of war, when major changes were broadly felt across society and expected in the future, required that she consider the interior as a unit within a broader economic and social fabric, where even small changes might resonate with women both individually and collectively. Drew thus worked within Britain's existing social structure to disseminate modern architectural ideas that would improve women's lives.

Disseminating advice through publishing

Because both Reiss and Drew viewed their consultancy projects as platforms for the wider promotion of modernist principles of architectural design, both professionals performed significant public outreach in the form of publishing and exhibiting. Reiss's aim was to bolster the war effort by convincing Vallejo inhabitants to transform their small temporary wartime dwellings into homes and, more broadly, to sow the seeds of change in the minds of homemakers. She thus provided advice, free of cost, showing women how to adapt their constrained wartime homes, moving beyond the limited mandate of her technical consultancy to the City of Vallejo. Although she had no staff or budget available to create an individual consultancy service, Reiss ensured that she could reach the thirty-five thousand residents of Vallejo's authority housing through other methods: she published a magazine titled *Your Home*, in which she suggested how to furnish the various types of dwellings found throughout Vallejo, and she set up model apartments to demonstrate furnishing, decorating and planning ideas. Meanwhile, Drew's goal as a consultant for the British Commercial Gas Association was to prepare consumers for goods that were not yet available, which required her to help her audience imagine what such kitchens and their furnishings might look like. In order to illustrate her research, Drew prepared a publication and exhibition, both called *Kitchen Planning*, which visualized her conclusions by presenting a range of kitchen proposals to an audience of British wartime women in early 1945. For both professionals, publishing and exhibiting thus became allied presentation methods for their consultancy projects, allowing them to demonstrate modern design principles through multiple media.

Your Home and *Kitchen Planning* outlined the ideas that appeared in Reiss and Drew's exhibitions and also provided opportunities for their authors to offer in-depth advice to audiences of women who did not always have the time or means to access exhibitions. Moreover, because these publications were reproducible, relatively durable and inherently portable, Reiss and Drew ensured that the impact from their temporary displays would endure. The two professionals used publications to introduce their audiences to the idea that a home should be 'planned' – that is, designed to support a family's needs and activities. Both architects approached the domestic interior as a problem that could be solved by the application of rigorous methods, either by professionals or by users. Specifically, Reiss and Drew advocated that their readers should ascertain their needs and develop a plan from there, rather than simply acquiring objects or settling for inadequate spaces. By picturing and discussing women, either on their own or as members of families, Reiss and Drew made it clear throughout their publications that women formed at least half of their intended readership. In this way they sought to transform women into active, empowered agents who would fashion their homes according to their individualized family requirements.

In surviving issues of *Your Home*, published in 1943 and 1944, Reiss explained to her readers that her goal was to help them to make 'your home' as comfortable as possible.[23] *Your Home* was published bi-monthly, printed in numbers of ten thousand and made available to inhabitants of authority housing free of cost, reflecting the material circumstances of Reiss's audience.[24] Families that had been assigned to Vallejo's authority housing often had little money and few resources. In order to take up work in Vallejo, many of them had relocated over long distances and could not bring their own furniture with them. The third issue of *Your Home* reported that hundreds of families had moved to Vallejo from Texas, Louisiana, Missouri, Colorado, Oklahoma, Illinois, New York and Pennsylvania to work at the Mare Island Naval Shipyard.[25] For many families this relocation was temporary as it was intended to last for the duration of the war. Reiss, however, suggested that her readers' accommodation in Vallejo need not feel temporary and advised them to transform their apartments into homes by employing imaginative solutions.

Written and edited entirely by Reiss, *Your Home*'s advice was tied to Reiss's research into Vallejo's housing types and the families that occupied each kind of dwelling. She tailored her suggestions to suit actual floor plans that could be found in Vallejo housing developments such as Carquinez Heights and Chabot Terrace, both designed by architect William Wilson Wurster, as well as Solano Apartments and Amador Apartments, which had been built by the contractors Barrett and Hilp. Some of these apartments were rented unfurnished, while others included essential pieces of furniture such as beds, chairs, tables and dressers.[26] Reiss recognized that families often could not buy fine new furniture, either because they did not have the means or because scarcity rendered new objects more expensive during wartime. She illustrated that they could furnish their apartments by creatively employing the modest and limited furniture that was readily available and by engaging in easy do-it-yourself projects.

In the first issue of *Your Home*, for example, Reiss suggested that her readers avoid sets of traditionally designed furniture because they were often bulky. Instead, she insisted, 'small furniture with simple lines gives a feeling of spaciousness.'[27] Reiss aimed much of her guidance at combatting the small size of Vallejo apartments in this way, suggesting that selecting unembellished objects and unpatterned fabrics would help her readers' rooms seem larger. She helped them to master various facets of interior design by teaching them how to buy fabrics and how to distinguish between direct and indirect lighting. Throughout the magazine Reiss demonstrated how her readers could apply these principles to create functional and spacious rooms of their own. In the second issue of *Your Home*, Reiss offered an array of 'dos and don'ts' to show readers how to group furniture to generate comfortable conversation groups and unobstructed circulation paths (Figure 6.2).[28] Such pages also included photographs of women users to reinforce the connection between Reiss's audience and the people who would design and occupy these spaces.

FIGURE 6.2 Pages from *Your Home*, no. 2 (1944). City of Vallejo and Vallejo Housing Authority

By dispensing her advice, Reiss aimed to transform her readers into active adherents to modern design principles who could intelligently plan their homes – a goal that her mode of presentation also supported. Throughout the pages of *Your Home*, Reiss helped her readers to recognize the questions that they needed to ask themselves in order to plan their spaces, such as 'Have we made the best possible use of available space?', 'Who will use this room?' and 'What will take place in this room?'[29] As readers answered these questions, Reiss encouraged them to formulate inventive solutions so that they could customize their dwellings in ways that made sense for their lives. For example, the Housing Authority assigned many families with children to one- or two-bedroom apartments, each of which was typically small. Reiss thus coaxed her readers to jettison concepts such as bedrooms and living rooms while planning their spaces. In one article she suggested that 'Mr. and Mrs. A.,' a family of three living in a one-bedroom apartment, could instead envision both living room and bedroom as multipurpose spaces, transforming the living room into a combination living and sleeping room for the parents, while turning the single bedroom into a nursery with play space for their four-year-old daughter.[30] While this example provided only one instance of such a solution, it stood as representative of the ways in which readers might ask themselves how to best plan their spaces for use.

The anonymous, universal 'Mr. and Mrs. A.' was a trope drawn from popular advice literature, which at the time was read most frequently by women. By employing this device, Reiss demonstrated that she understood that she was addressing a predominantly female audience. Furthermore, Reiss repeatedly included photographs of women users throughout the ideal spaces shown in her magazines. She invited her readers to participate by reaching out to her audience and asking them to contribute to the community's design discourse by sending in suggestions and innovative do-it-yourself projects of their own. Alongside the men who submitted examples of furniture that they had built for their apartments, women such as Ellen J. Meagher, a graduate of the University of California who had studied under Catherine Bauer and worked for the City of Vallejo Housing Authority, provided images of apartments that demonstrated 'light and graceful' interiors employing contrasting materials and unified color palettes to create harmonized spaces.[31] By soliciting participation in this way, Reiss and her readers collectively became part of a larger endeavor of transforming Vallejo's wartime housing into communities filled with homes, rather than developments filled with temporary dwellings. Men were a part of this enterprise, but women were at its center.

While Reiss's expert advice hinged on understanding the practical limitations and personal aspirations of the community that she was serving, the kitchen proposals that Drew developed for the British Commercial Gas Association required that she extensively research new technologies, factory-line production and modern home economics. Returning to Britain after completing her American research, Drew and her partners further explored production methods in order to apply these ideas to British factory lines. From the beginning of the project, Drew had aimed to design kitchens and components that British aircraft factories could make as they transitioned from wartime to peacetime production. She suggested that designing the entire kitchen as a single unit would improve production.[32] In addition, she and her research team examined the uniforms and coveralls issued to British women for their wartime work in order to ascertain their average height, applying this data to design kitchens with comfortable heights for appliances and work surfaces that were suited to women's bodies.[33] Time-and-motion studies, which had been used for decades by other home economists, helped Drew to determine the layouts of new kitchens.

In order to position kitchen innovations as a social good, Drew and the gas industry attempted to articulate productive connections between the evolution of kitchen design and the future lives of modern women who had undertaken wartime work outside the home. Positioned opposite *Kitchen Planning*'s introduction, a photomontage by German artist John Heartfield depicted busy workers, many of them women, cheerfully engaged in wartime labor with a caption that read, 'these are the people for whom we are planning' (Figure 6.3).[34] While this image underscored the traditional, conservative idea that the kitchen was integral to female life, the photomontage's representation of those women as wartime farm laborers, factory workers and members of the armed forces revealed that the war had transformed the social roles and expectations of women, and that the kitchen must change with them. Drew's kitchen research was building a better world by rewarding these workers with modernized kitchens at the war's end. The image also suggested that Drew's research comprised part of the gas industry's contribution to the war effort by supporting and honoring those who served or sacrificed.

FIGURE 6.3 Photomontage from *Kitchen Planning*, 1945. Gas Industry of Britain

Focusing on the kitchen's social role, Drew continued to develop her strategy of modeling different kitchens to reflect the diversity of communities. She concluded that multiple kitchen types would be needed to support variations in technological capabilities, resources, family income, family size and so on. Contending that most kitchen-related needs fell into a few set categories, she conceived a range of six 'almost ideal' solutions.[35] These proposals included a package kitchen, a dining kitchen in a family flat, a kitchen-bathroom unit, a living-room-kitchen, a working kitchen for a suburban home and a kitchen in a large house. Like Reiss, Drew had conducted research into the practical realities of potential users of British kitchens, applying data to guide her proposals. For example, she suggested that her 'living-room-kitchen' would suit a lower-income family living in a semi-detached or rural house, while her 'kitchen in a large house' was intended for a well-off family with domestic help.[36] By creating different proposals in this way, Drew tacitly accepted traditional class distinctions and gender roles while simultaneously communicating a socially ambitious desire to provide women across classes with the benefits of modern design.

In addition to supporting a diverse range of kitchen users, Drew showed her readers that variation offered consumer choice by ensuring that they could tailor their homes to suit their individual tastes. Just as Reiss had focused on inexpensive ways to furnish dwellings, Drew positioned color as a cost-effective, and therefore easily applicable and changeable, ingredient in interior design. While researching in the United States, she had explored color extensively and advocated it as a simple way to brighten the kitchen. Like Reiss, who presented her readers with the all-encompassing principles of modern design, Drew suggested that color was one means by which to achieve visual unity 'right through the kitchen beyond the architecture into the cutlery, tea cloths, kitchen utensils, curtains' and so on.[37] Throughout *Kitchen Planning* she proposed sample color schemes to inspire her readers. She also revealed how certain hues could support functionality, for example demonstrating that dark shades minimized visible footprints on floors.

Because Drew's gas industry research was both abstract and technical in nature, explaining her ideas to non-professional audiences required her to develop a way for her readers to imagine themselves using modern kitchens. Drew visualized these concepts in *Kitchen Planning* by using figures to illustrate how her proposals functioned (Figure 6.4). For example, the image accompanying the description of the living-room-kitchen depicted a bright space with a dark brown floor (again, to hide footprints), cheerful yellow and burgundy seating, and striped curtains in gray and burgundy that served to link the colors of the kitchen and living spaces. Moreover, this illustration showcased a nuclear family using the space: a woman stood in the kitchen area preparing food, while a man read at the dining table and two children played on the floor. A half wall both divided the kitchen and living areas and linked the space, ensuring the family remained in contact. This group, read as a mother, father and two

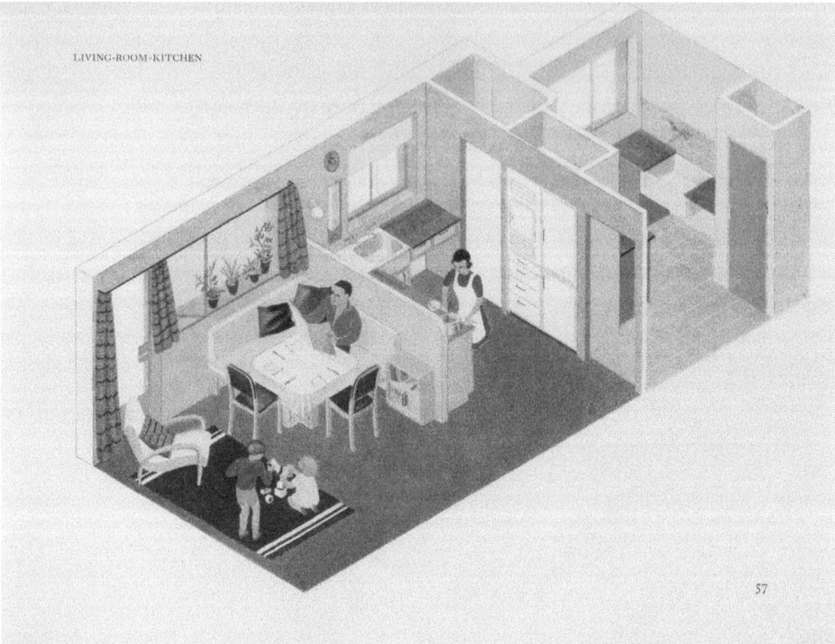

FIGURE 6.4 The living-room-kitchen from *Kitchen Planning*, 1945. Gas Industry of Britain

children, corresponded to the lower-income family living in a semi-detached or rural house that Drew suggested would occupy such a kitchen, and the illustration served to allow readers to envision themselves inhabiting new spaces that would reshape their lives. This was quite similar to the strategy that Reiss had pursued in *Your Home* by imagining 'Mr. and Mrs. A.' and their child, as well as including other photographs of women. *Your Home* and *Kitchen Planning* thus seem calculated to transform passive female readers into active collaborators who would understand and call upon modern planning principles to shape their dwellings and thus to modernize and improve their lives in the long term.

Displaying advice in exhibitions

Reiss and Drew considered publications and displays to be allied presentation methods. While the magazine *Your Home* and the book *Kitchen Planning* illustrated their ideas, print media could not show completed interiors or actual objects in three dimensions, nor could print convey their material qualities. Exhibitions provided a medium for Reiss and Drew to concretize their expert advice further for their non-professional audiences. Reiss curated model apartments within various Vallejo housing developments to help her readers visualize how they could apply the interior design and home planning principles that she presented throughout *Your Home* in actual residences. Meanwhile, Drew assembled both the book and exhibition of *Kitchen Planning* (along with a smaller sixteen-page exhibition brochure) concurrently, with the three-dimensional display allowing her to bring vividly to life the ways that modern kitchens would perform a social good in the postwar era.[38]

Reiss set up several model apartments throughout Vallejo's authority housing and ran them with the assistance of a committee of local women.[39] The first of these demonstration apartments opened on December 15, 1943 at the Solano Apartments (Figure 6.5). Completed earlier in 1943, Solano Apartments contained about six hundred and fifty dwellings in two sizes, with courtyard space for gardens, play areas and drying laundry.[40] The smaller apartments comprised a living room, kitchen and bathroom and were mainly occupied by couples, while the larger dwellings also included a bedroom and were better suited to small families. The Solano Apartments were also among those that the Housing Authority of the City of Vallejo furnished. The modest furnishings included two couches, two armchairs, one dining table, two side chairs, one chest of drawers, a kerosene range and an icebox.[41] Reiss planned and designed the display apartment using one of the smaller apartment types. She combined the available authority furniture with do-it-yourself objects and modest store-bought accessories. Both the exhibition and the magazine underscored that all furnishing had been accomplished inexpensively by employing the resources that were available to inhabitants.[42]

Throughout the model apartment, Reiss visually manifested the advice that she had been dispensing in *Your Home* by focusing on principles of modern interior design. As stated, with an eye toward enhancing the spaciousness of these small dwellings, Reiss suggested that readers of *Your Home* employ small-scale furniture with clean lines, unembellished objects, plain fabrics and so on.

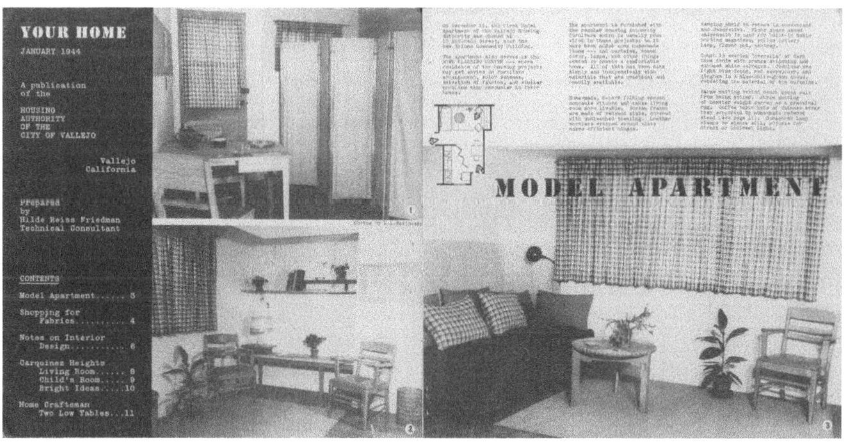

FIGURE 6.5 Pages from *Your Home*, no. 2 (1944). City of Vallejo and Vallejo Housing Authority

In the case of small dwellings, such as the model apartment, where rooms had to fulfill multiple purposes, Reiss encouraged her readers to eschew tradition and embrace flexible multiplicity in spatial uses. Reiss outfitted the dual-purpose living-and-sleeping room as a true living room by positioning the furniture to form conversation groups. Two armchairs and a built-in table formed the first group, above which she positioned a hanging shelf to save floor space. A couch positioned across from the table and chairs formed a second conversation area that users could quickly convert into a sleeping area whenever required. Finally, Reiss transformed the kitchen into a third sitting area by setting up a dining table and two chairs, using a handmade screen to conceal the counters, sink, range and icebox when they were not in use. Furthermore, she created a sense of spaciousness and unity in the small dwelling by using a restrained combination of plain and printed fabrics: hardwearing blue denim covered the couch, while blue, white and green gingham carried accents from kitchen to living room as curtains and cushion covers.

Paired with *Your Home*, which encouraged readers to ask themselves questions and send in tips for other readers, the display apartment served to enhance the participatory nature of Reiss's project. She set up the model apartment, which was located near the Solano Community Building, to serve as a 'home planning center' where residents could seek advice on furniture arrangement, color schemes, fabric selection, do-it-yourself projects and other problems that they might face when setting up a new home.[43] The name 'home planning center' encouraged visitors to engage with available experts and the material on display. Run by the Victory-Solano Community Building Committee, a host of female volunteers staffed the model apartment on a daily basis, and the space also hosted a library, which ensured continued visits.[44] Reiss thus intended for the exhibition apartment to inspire readers of *Your Home* and guide them toward devising innovative solutions as they sought to apply these questions to their temporary wartime dwellings. Moreover, because a committee of local women ran the model apartment, it meant that women could guide everyday conversations about designing modern and comfortable interiors.

While Drew's *Kitchen Planning* exhibition was less participatory in nature than Reiss's model apartment, it was no less committed to presenting accessible ideas about interior design and spatial planning to non-professional audiences. The exhibition was held free of charge from February 5 through March 3, 1945, at Dorland Hall in London, a centrally located and popular exhibition space. *Kitchen Planning* showcased ten full-scale kitchens that demonstrated the modernizing ideas that Drew had been exploring throughout her research, such as uniform levels of working surfaces, equipment layouts that promoted an easy working sequence and standardized fitted cabinets that maximized storage space. Because Drew also aimed to, in her words, 'provide the right plans ready for our factories to start manufacturing when the great switch over to peace comes,' the exhibition also promoted prototypes and products by more than one hundred manufacturers.[45] In this way *Kitchen Planning* aimed to transform female exhibition visitors into savvy consumers of household technologies.

However, the exhibition did more than simply elicit desire for postwar consumption. By displaying complete model kitchens rather than plans or diagrams, or even appliances and other goods, the exhibition allowed Drew, in the role of consulting architect, to demonstrate to women that their homes could and should be planned according to modern principles developed in part by women designers. The model kitchens and other exhibition materials helped to illustrate the efficacy of the planned modern kitchen by encouraging exhibition-goers to imagine how they might integrate such technologies into their own homes. Just as the book *Kitchen Planning* visualized the social potential of modern kitchen planning through its introductory photomontage, the exhibition did so through a mural by graphic designer Frederick Henri Kay Henrion, who had also designed many of the exhibition's display elements. In this mural, which dubbed the kitchen the 'hub of the house,' a woman stood working at the center of a wheel that was positioned within the outline of a home. By depicting the housewife as the wheel's fulcrum, Henrion's mural implicitly demonstrated that her labor was essential to keep the household functioning. Moreover, the kitchen's centrality within the dwelling reinforced one of the key arguments that Drew had advanced in the book, which was that the kitchen must be designed relative to the rest of the house.[46]

The exhibition also employed actual women to embody the roles that the figure drawings had played in the book. Within the exhibition this device served a double purpose, first to demonstrate that different types of kitchens would suit different families, and second, and perhaps more importantly, to reveal the usability of such kitchens to the curious women visiting the display at Dorland Hall. For example, a publicity photograph for the living-room-kitchen showed two actors within the space: a woman stood cooking while a young girl set the table in the other part of the room (Figure 6.6). Paired with the half wall that divided the space, the actors demonstrated that a mother could supervise and instruct her child while she prepared a meal. Just as in the book, this device was intended to help women imagine themselves as active agents within the spaces on display.

For both Reiss and Drew, translating technical design concepts into vivid displays was essential in order to make their advice more accessible to society at large. Reiss used the medium of the model apartment to create a dynamic, participatory center for the advice she dispensed in *Your Home*. The display that she set up served to show rather than tell her audience how they could transform their temporary apartments into homes using their available resources, and the women that ran the center palpably demonstrated the female agency at the center of this discourse. Meanwhile, Drew's exhibition stripped away some of the more technical jargon that she had included in the *Kitchen Planning* book, instead purely visualizing its content. Visitors to Dorland Hall met model kitchens that clearly embodied the uses of color, new materials, appliances and

FIGURE 6.6 Installation view showing the living-room-kitchen from *Kitchen Planning*, Dorland Hall, London, 1945

Source: *The Architects' Journal*

architectural design strategies that Drew proposed throughout her book. Moreover, by including actual women in the displays, she worked to demonstrate that these were lively and dynamic spaces designed to serve the carefully studied lives of human beings, not merely assemblages of products.

Conclusion and legacy

The expertise that Reiss and Drew cultivated and disseminated throughout their wartime consultancy projects directly fed into their later careers. After completing her stint in Vallejo, Reiss moved to Minneapolis, Minnesota in 1945 to work for the Walker Art Center. Here, as curator of the newly established Everyday Art Gallery and editor of the *Everyday Art Quarterly*, Reiss reiterated many of *Your Home*'s ideas in the displays she curated and the articles she wrote, all of which highlighted modern design principles and showcased examples of modern architectural design to help Americans learn about design standards. Drew, meanwhile, went on to collaborate with Fry and Jeanneret on a number of large-scale projects in West Africa and India. Here she applied her knowledge of kitchen technologies, factory production and domestic planning to design housing and university residences. In both of their cases, consultancy positions allowed them to research and practice design throughout the war years and afforded them platforms that that enhanced their professional experience and visibility.

Reiss and Drew's consultancy projects shine light from multiple angles on the roles of women as architectural makers, mediators and users. The Housing Authority of the City of Vallejo and the British Commercial Gas Association called upon Reiss and Drew as makers to create model interiors that demonstrated modern design principles, each organization drawing upon their established expertise as design professionals. In these roles Reiss and Drew became mediators by employing both print and exhibition media to translate their ideas to reach non-professional audiences. Finally, both organizations hired Reiss and Drew at least in part because they were women and, as such, their expertise would matter more to audiences of women, who were asked to wield their minds and bodies as active agents in this discourse. The fact that the two professionals held such similar roles in two different countries – with Reiss promoting European values in an American community, and Drew drawing upon American developments in her attempts to reform British lives – speaks to the increasingly global nature of modern design cultures, as well as the ways in which political and cultural constructs of gender were co-evolving on both sides of the Atlantic.

Despite the fact that their resourcefulness enabled them to test the limitations of gender in the architecture profession – and stretch the role of consultant in the process, transforming interior architecture and design work into a platform for community-building – Reiss and Drew still accepted certain expectations that their societies had for women. Looking at their projects through today's eyes, it may be easy to conclude that the two architects merely participated in a system that aimed to re-domesticate women at the war's end. Nonetheless, we know that Reiss and Drew intended to improve women's lives through their work. Situating their advice and proposals within an established heteronormative framework may have been a pragmatic approach to ensure that audiences would accept their ideas about modernist architecture – principles that many readers or exhibition-goers may have been encountering for the first time. In *Your Home*, for example, Reiss promoted the notion of the *Existenzminimum* (minimum space standards carefully planned) dwelling but did so within the construct of a nuclear family, reassuring her readers that each family would be able to fashion their own personalized, if tiny, space. In *Kitchen Planning*, meanwhile, Drew disseminated new ideas about kitchen design and manufacture, aiming to transform and elevate the home through intelligent kitchen planning but doing so without challenging the idea that domestic work belonged to women, even if she did assert that women had been transformed on some level by their wartime experiences. This sense of give-and-take likely made the new ideas that the two women publicized more palatable, including the rather bold idea that ordinary women should consider themselves qualified to reform their environments using modern design principles made accessible to them by other women, who claimed public roles as design and cultural authorities due to their education and experience. Bolder still was the implicit message that reforming domestic life was a social process to be conducted collectively and that doing so would profoundly impact every level of society. The woman, situated at the center of her hub, would link with other women in other hubs, and together they would create a kind of industrial complex, complete with high technology, factory methods and, perhaps, the promise of ongoing, dynamic change.

Notes

1 On this topic see Andrew M. Shanken, *194X: Architecture, Planning, and Consumer Culture on the American Home Front* (Minneapolis: University of Minnesota Press, 2009).

2 Although each of these brochures was credited to a male professional, it is likely that some women did contribute to this research. Antonin Raymond, for example, frequently collaborated with his wife, Noémi Raymond, who often did not receive credit for her labor. On their careers see Kurt G. Helfrich and William Whitaker, *Crafting a Modern World: The Architecture and Design of Antonin and Noémi Raymond* (New York: Princeton Architectural Press, 2006).

3 On this topic see Jean-Louis Cohen, *Architecture in Uniform: Designing and Building for the Second World War* (New Haven: Yale University Press, 2011), pp. 161–172, and Tecton Architects, *Planned A.R.P.* (London: The Architectural Press, 1939).

4 See Cohen, *Architecture in Uniform*, pp. 231–239.

5 Gillian Darley, "A Collection of Scimitar Minds," in Elizabeth Darling and Lynne Walker, eds, *AA Women in Architecture: 1917–2017* (London: Architectural Association, 2017), pp. 45–65.

6 On 1930s' housing policy in the U.S. see Gail Radford, *Modern Housing for America: Policy Struggles in the New Deal Era* (Chicago: University of Chicago Press, 1996), especially Chapter Three. On concurrent housing debates in Britain, especially the New Homes for Old exhibitions, see Elizabeth Darling, *Re-forming Britain: Narratives of Modernity before Reconstruction* (New York: Routledge, 2001), especially Chapter Four, and Elizabeth Darling, "Becoming Truly Alive," in *AA Women in Architecture: 1917–2017*, pp. 27–42.

7 Interview with Hilde Reiss, conducted by Martha Ruddy, March 17, 2000, Walker Art Center Archives. Reiss studied at the State Academy of Building, Weimar, in 1929 and at the Bauhaus in Dessau from 1930–32. She received Bauhaus Diploma No. 89. Inge Schaefer Horton, *Early Women Architects of the San Francisco Bay Area: The Lives and Work of Fifty Professionals, 1890–1951* (Jefferson: McFarland & Co., 2010), p. 353.

8 On these projects, which Reiss undertook with fellow Design Laboratory instructor Lila Ulrich, see "Experiment in Change" *Arts and Decoration* (February 1935), pp. 4–11 and "A Century Intervenes," *Arts and Decoration* (March 1935), pp. 12–17.

9 Interview with Hilde Reiss, conducted by Martha Ruddy, March 17, 2000, Walker Art Center Archives. Friedman had practised architecture since 1926, having trained at New York University, Atelier Whitman Goodman and the University of Minnesota; "Importance of Everyday Objects," *Interiors* (March 1946), p. 60.

10 Peter S. Reed, "Enlisting Modernism," in *World War II and the American Dream*, ed. Donald Albrecht (Cambridge, MA: The MIT Press, 1995), pp. 13–16.

11 The architecture of Second World War internment camps in the United States has not yet been extensively studied. On internment in the U.S. see, for example, Michi Nishiura Weglyn, *Years of Infamy: The Untold Story of America's Concentration Camps* (Seattle: University of Washington Press, 1996) and Greg Robinson, *By Order of the President: FDR and the Internment of Japanese Americans* (Cambridge, MA: Harvard University Press, 2001).

12 Interview with Hilde Reiss, conducted by Martha Ruddy, March 17, 2000, Walker Art Center Archives. The director of the Housing Authority of the City of Vallejo when Reiss was hired was likely to have been Maurice J. Wilsie, who held the position while Reiss was publishing *Your Home*.

13 An article that appeared in *California Arts and Architecture* in June 1943 estimated that the 1940 population of Greater Vallejo was thirty thousand in 1940 and had grown to ninety to one hundred thousand by 1943. The authors of this article based their estimate on material compiled by civilian defense, the ration board and utility company sources; "People Make Production," *California Arts and Architecture* (June 1943), p. 35.

14 In June 1940 Congress authorized the U.S. Housing Authority to use public funds to construct dwellings to shelter the rapidly expanding populations of wartime production centers. From October 1940 the National Defense Housing Act (also known as the Lanham Act) made federal funds available to construct housing and services such as schools, nurseries and recreation to serve defense industries. For an overview of this program see Cohen, *Architecture in Uniform*, pp. 111–127. On Vallejo's program see William Wilson Wurster, "Carquinez Heights," *California Arts and Architecture* (November 1941); Fred Langhorst, "A New Approach to Large-scale Housing," *California Arts and Architecture* (April 1942); "Vallejo: War Housing Case History," *California Arts and Architecture* (December 1942); "People Make Production," *California Arts and Architecture* (June 1943); and Greg Hise, "Building Design as Social Art: The Public Architecture of William Wurster, 1935–1950" in Marc Treib, ed., *An Everyday Modernism: The Houses of William Wurster* (Berkeley: University of California Press, 1995), pp. 138–163.

15 Polly Weaver, "Design for a Modern Career," *Mademoiselle* (February 1946), p. 310.

16 "Dwelling Design" in Federal Public Housing Authority – National Housing Agency, *Standards for War Housing, Excluding Temporary Housing* (Washington: Federal Public Housing Authority, 1942), pp. 2, 4. Federal Public Housing Authority of the National Housing Agency, "Temporary Housing," War Housing Technical Bulletin No. D-2, unpaginated.

17 In 1941 Fry worked with the Royal Engineers in Derby, and in April 1942 he was posted to West Africa. During this time Drew ran her own office out of 3 King Street in London while studying for her forthcoming post as Assistant Town Planner in West Africa. After Drew's first office was destroyed in an air raid, she relocated to 12 Bedford Square. In 1945 both Fry and Drew were posted in West Africa. When Drew returned to London at the end of the year, she ran 'The Office of Maxwell Fry & Jane Drew' from 63 Gloucester Place. Iain Jackson and Jessica Holland, *The Architecture of Edwin Maxwell Fry and Jane Drew: Twentieth Century Architecture, Pioneer Modernism and the Tropics* (Burlington: Ashgate, 2014), pp. 113–118.

18 "Gas Reveals the Vision of the Future," *Daily Mail Book of Post-War Homes* (London: Daily Mail Ideal Home Exhibition Dept. of Associated Newspapers Ltd., 1944), p. 8.

19 Maxwell Fry, *Fine Building* (London: Faber and Faber Limited, 1944), p. 62. In the foreword, Fry acknowledged that Drew's guidance made the book possible, and much of the content on kitchens appears to have been drawn from her research.

20 Jane B. Drew, "Housing," *Architect's Year Book* (1945), p. 43.

21 Jane Drew interviewed by Peter Stewart, "The Kitchen of the Future," *Women's Illustrated* (February 5, 1944), p. 13.

22 Jane Drew, unpublished memoirs, p. 51, Jane Drew Papers, Dr J/1/1, RIBA Archives. Jackson and Holland have also discussed Drew's interest in synthetics, attributing her readiness to use them to her father's work with stainless steel surgical tools. Jackson and Holland, *The Architecture of Edwin Maxwell Fry and Jane Drew*, p. 117.

23 Letter from Charles F. Daley, chairman of the Housing Authority of the City of Vallejo, *Your Home*, vol. 1 (November 1943), unpaginated.

24 Hilde Reiss quoted in Weaver, "Design for a Modern Career," p. 310.

25 Hilde Reiss Friedman, *Your Home*, vol. 3 (March 1944), p. 11.

26 Hilde Reiss Friedman, "Housing Project as Progressive Community," *Arts and Architecture* (August 1944), p. 18.

27 Hilde Reiss Friedman, *Your Home*, vol. 1 (November 1943), unpaginated.

28 Hilde Reiss Friedman, *Your Home*, vol. 2 (January 1944), pp. 6–7.

29 Hilde Reiss Friedman, *Your Home*, vol. 1 (November 1943), unpaginated.

30 Hilde Reiss Friedman, *Your Home*, vol. 1 (November 1943), unpaginated.

31 Hilde Reiss Friedman, *Your Home*, vol. 3 (March 1944), pp. 6, 11.

32 Leonie Cohn, "Talking of Jane," in *Jane B. Drew: Architect* (Bristol: Bristol Centre for the Advancement of Architecture, 1986), p. 16.

33 Karen Parker, "Jane Drew, Architect and Practical Idealist," in Jill Seddon and Suzette Worden, eds, *Women Designing: Refining Design in Britain between the Wars* (Brighton: University of Brighton, 1994), pp. 139–140.
34 Jane B. Drew, *Kitchen Planning: Plans and Suggestions Based on Joint Research by the Gas Industry* (London: Gas Industry of Britain, 1945), p. 2.
35 Drew, *Kitchen Planning*, p. 3.
36 Drew also proposed that package kitchens could help to convert existing houses into flats – a necessary step toward housing people during the immediate postwar years.
37 Drew, *Kitchen Planning*, p. 34.
38 While no documentation clearly calls the book a catalogue of the exhibition, a letter from Eileen (no surname given) of the British Commercial Gas Association to Drew dated September 28, 1944, explained that the exhibition had been postponed until 1945 due to bomb damage in London. While the exhibition was postponed until February 1945, the book's publication was also withheld until 1945, even though Drew's research was ready for presentation by the second half of 1944; Maxwell Fry and Jane Drew Papers, F&D/5/2, RIBA Archives. The sixteen-page exhibition booklet was printed in color and illustrated all of the kitchens that were on display; "Kitchen Planning: Big Gas Exhibition next Month," *Gas Journal* (January 17, 1945), p. 81.
39 This committee comprised Mrs. Rosabell E. Mattison, Mrs. Helen Crisp and Mrs. Virginia Kuemerle. Mattison and Kuemerle were both pictured in *Your Home* 3. Hilde Reiss Friedman, *Your Home*, vol. 3 (March 1944), p. 11.
40 "People Make Production," p. 46.
41 Hilde Reiss Friedman, *Your Home*, vol. 1 (November 1943), unpaginated.
42 Images of the apartment appeared in the second issue of *Your Home* in January 1944; Hilde Reiss Friedman, *Your Home*, vol. 2 (January 1944), p. 3.
43 Hilde Reiss Friedman, *Your Home*, vol. 2 (January 1944), p. 3.
44 Hilde Reiss Friedman, *Your Home*, vol. 3 (March 1944), p. 11.
45 Drew, *Kitchen Planning*, p. 3. The existing products shown in the exhibition were from 1939 due to the fact that no new appliances had been available in Britain during the war.
46 Drew, *Kitchen Planning*, p. 6.

PART III

Staking claims to urban space

7

ALMOST AS GOOD AS A FRANK GEHRY

Doris Duke, Maya Lin, and the gendered politics of public space in Newport, Rhode Island

Catherine W. Zipf

On May 11, 2011, the Newport Restoration Foundation (NRF) put forth a plan to redesign Queen Anne Square, a small but prominently placed public space in Newport, Rhode Island, designed by Doris Duke in the 1970s. The NRF had received an anonymous donation to fund a renovation of the park and had commissioned Maya Lin to spearhead the project. After a year of planning, they unveiled the new design and prepared to break ground. To their surprise, the plan met with immediate and hard resistance. The controversy was extremely ugly, and accusations flew in every direction as prominent community members on all sides were vilified. And yet, miraculously, the design went forward. On May 31, 2013, almost exactly two years from the project's announcement, dignitaries gathered to mark the completion of Lin's design with a ceremonial ribbon cutting. Today, many consider the redesign a success.

Arguments on both sides coalesced around four themes: economic concerns, the interpretation and representation of history, the ownership and use of public space, and the ideal image of women architects. Throughout the debate, biases both for and against Duke and Lin emerged, coloring the discussion in unintentional but revealing ways. In overt statements, the Newport community expressed what specific purposes it wanted this little space to serve; behind the scenes lay preconceived and obliquely expressed notions of gender, which subversively influenced broader views of how public space should be designed and who should have the power to design it. Signaling the arrival of a new front in architecture's gender wars, the Queen Anne Square controversy has much to teach us about the role of gender in twenty-first century urban design.

Given to the people of Newport

Queen Anne Square is not a historic space, despite its name and despite its location in the heart of colonial Newport. The site is bounded by Thames Street, Spring Street, Mill Street, and Church Street. Its primary focus is Trinity Church, built in 1726 by carpenter-builder Richard Munday. The church's design follows tradition such that the altar is located on the east side of the building and the entry tower is on the west, where it interfaces with the square. Today this grand vista gives viewers the impression that the open square and the ancient church have always been part of a thoughtfully composed urban package, but until the 1970s, the square did not exist, and the church was surrounded by a host of buildings ranging in size and function (Figure 7.1). In order to enter the church, one had to walk along a pathway threading through these buildings.

Newport's economy, like any other, has seen ups and downs. During much of the twentieth century, it revolved around operations at the United States Naval base on the city's northern edge. In 1951, the Navy transferred operations at the Torpedo Station, originally founded in 1869, to private industry. A year later, the Naval Training Station was moved to Maryland, leaving only the Fleet Training Center and Naval School Command in Newport.[1] These developments caused a significant downturn in Newport's fortunes. A glimmer of hope appeared in 1955 and then again in 1958 with the construction of two piers that could accommodate cruiser-destroyer ships and with the expansion of Newport's Navy facilities to provide support for that fleet. These developments brought

FIGURE 7.1 The future site of Queen Anne Square, ca. 1970. The Newport Restoration Foundation

a short period of relative prosperity to the city. Newport bustled, albeit in a Navy fashion; its infrastructure was not in the best of shape and there were problems stemming from the activities of sailors on shore leave. Nonetheless, the economic relief was real.

Thus, when rumors began to fly in the mid-1960s that the Navy was 'pulling out,' there was considerable concern, if not downright fear, among local citizens.[2] Amid the concern, leaders in the community began actively seeking new avenues for economic growth. While projects involving historic preservation and tourism were discussed, city leaders leaned heavily toward using federal dollars to revitalize the city through urban demolition and redevelopment projects.[3] In the late 1960s, in keeping with dramatic urban highway interventions then occurring all over the country, including the downtowns of cities like Washington, DC, and Chicago, Illinois, the City of Newport pushed a four-lane street called America's Cup Avenue through its downtown, destroying a major section of the historic urban fabric (Figure 7.2). Old buildings were demolished, the street plan was refashioned, and pedestrian access to the waterfront was altered in ways that still impact the city today. The construction of America's Cup Avenue paved the way for the creation of Queen Anne Square by opening the city's urban fabric in that

FIGURE 7.2 America's Cup Avenue, 1969, with the Walsh Brothers Furniture store visible in the center right. Historic American Building Survey

area and establishing the waterfront as a focal point and vista. These developments were, however, an unintentional side effect of what was first and foremost an attempt to rehabilitate the economy through the introduction of the automobile.

Considering how important historic preservation is to the city today, its tangential development from America's Cup Avenue is ironic. The loss of a considerable number of historic homes galvanized a grassroots movement to resist the dominant culture of neglect and demolition, and save Newport's oldest and most vulnerable structures. One such effort was 'Operation Clapboard,' founded in 1963 by Esther Fisher Benson and her son, Tom. The Bensons brought the quality of Newport's historic architecture to the public's attention and managed to save approximately forty buildings over its very short lifespan.[4] However, its preservation model of buying, restoring, and selling houses only worked in instances when the cost of restoration did not overpower the sale price – or, in other words, for houses in relatively good condition. It did not work for the hundreds of other colonial-era buildings, many occupied by transient naval personnel and in considerably worse shape.

Doris Duke (1912–1993) offered a new business model for preservation in Newport. Duke was a long-time summer resident and heir to a considerable fortune. Interested in art, music, dance, and craft, she watched Operation Clapboard's efforts carefully, as well as those undertaken by the fledgling Preservation Society of Newport County, which had been founded in 1945 by her friend, Katherine Warren.[5] She did not, however, self-identify as a preservationist. That changed in 1968, when two developers approached her to fund the renovation of an entire block in the city's Point neighborhood. Duke chose not to pursue this offer, but it did place in her mind the idea that a major restoration project could have an impact on the city as a whole. The goal of creating citywide change would be key to Duke's evolving vision for Newport's architecture and urbanism and would inform her preservation and design efforts, including the creation of the first Queen Anne Square.

At the end of 1968, Duke established the Newport Restoration Foundation with the intention of purchasing structures, funding their restoration, and then renting them to members of the community. Renting, instead of selling, produced a reliable income over the long term that enabled the NRF to take on costlier projects than could Operation Clapboard. The NRF purchased forty homes in its first fifteen months and twenty-five more over the next six years; today, the NRF owns and rents seventy-eight buildings around the city. This critical mass of buildings had a large economic impact. One or two preserved structures located around town would have made little difference, but the restoration of whole swaths of neighborhood fabric in key parts of town spurred other individual landowners and developers to follow suit. To that end, the NRF's philosophy was urban in focus.[6] Duke's activity was about preserving urban fabric and building community more than it was about saving old landmarks. Consciously or not, she followed the lead of another famous female pioneer of preservation and urban revitalization, Charleston's Susan Pringle Frost, who is discussed in Chapter 3 of this book. Frost, however, focused on rehabilitating and selling structures, while Duke created a long-term revenue stream through rentals. Duke's innovative preservation model required significant initial funding, and her considerable fortune served as a wellspring.[7] Her investments in the future of Newport had the added bonus of nurturing the local building industry by sustaining the livelihoods of a cadre of designers, restorers, and craftsman, many of whom had previously worked for the Preservation Society or Operation Clapboard. The system was, and remains, nearly unique, as no one nationally or internationally has replicated this preservation model on the scale of Duke's NRF.

Her success as a preservationist aside, not all was perfect in the life of Doris Duke. Her public presence as a strong, willful woman of independent means attracted scrutiny and gossip in Newport and beyond, and she had her fair share of scandals. On October 7, 1966, just two years before forming the NRF, while leaving her house with interior designer and 'constant companion,' Eduardo Tirella, Duke accidentally hit the accelerator of her car and crushed Tirella against the iron gates of her Bellevue Avenue estate, killing him instantly.[8] The event was ruled an accident and Duke was not charged, but it did have a significant effect on her reputation. Newport gossiped, and the talk about Duke was not always good.

Five years after the NRF's founding, in 1973, the Walsh Brothers furniture company, which occupied 222 Thames Street, burned completely to the ground, leaving a significant gap in the city's urban fabric and its economy (Figure 7.2). Although the Walsh family had owned and operated their business at that location for one hundred years, they decided not to rebuild.[9] The question then became what to do with the space. According to an oft-told local tale, one day while walking down Thames Street, Duke mentioned how nice it would be to have a public park there. The story is almost certainly apocryphal, but it does suggest that the idea of turning the Trinity Square block into a park was circulating around town early on. Today, the story links the notion of the park to the genius of Duke, and it was often repeated throughout the controversy over Lin's redesign.

Several other ideas for the space were also percolating in the wake of the Walsh Brothers furniture fire. Out of concern that a similar fire would strike them, the congregation of Trinity Church was exploring the purchase of adjacent properties with the intent of creating a protective buffer space around their building. The Newport Redevelopment Agency was also considering using the Walsh Brothers lot for a parking garage, a use that would have been consistent with the automobile-centric ethos of the adjacent America's Cup Avenue.[10] Partly at the urging of Trinity Church and partly in her own right, Duke decided to take action. Over the next three years, Trinity Church, the Newport Redevelopment Agency, and Duke purchased twenty-one properties on the block, moved historic structures to other lots, demolished the remainder, and created a public park. Queen Anne Square was dedicated on July 10, 1976, by

Queen Elizabeth II and Prince Philip in a special appearance and ceremony.[11] The plaque officially noted that the square was 'given to the people of Newport by the Newport Restoration Foundation, Trinity Episcopal Church, and Robert Goelet.'

One key issue in the later debate over Lin's design was the extent to which the park was actually designed by Doris Duke. The answer is not entirely clear, but it is indisputable that she played an active leadership role in every dimension of its creation. Initially, Duke found working with the government bureaucracy of the Newport Redevelopment Agency incredibly frustrating and considered pulling out several times.[12] But, she persevered, and eventually convinced the city to give her total control over the project's planning, construction, and aesthetics by offering to provide all of the financing. Between 1974 and 1978, Duke funded and spearheaded the effort to move five eighteenth- and nineteenth-century buildings to adjoining lots and instructed her NRF designers to draw up plans for the park. Those plans were very straightforward. Frank Street became a pedestrian lane and served as the spine of the site. Alongside, brick pathways ran in various diagonals through an asymmetrical, vaguely picturesque landscape of trees and larger shrubs (Figure 7.3). Duke personally supervised the location of the trees, often asking those driving the bulldozers to reposition them several times.[13] The remainder of the space was given over to grass, in keeping with what most 1960s-era Newport residents imagined was colonial landscaping. Flowers were another key design element. Duke loved flowers and had them planted all around the space (Figure 7.4).

By 2011, however, the flowers were long gone. They had proved too difficult to maintain, especially during the city's leaner financial years. The large swaths of grass lay in varied conditions throughout the site. It was difficult to know if and where to sit, since there were no benches in the park. The poor lighting insured that the park served well as a haven for illicit late-night activities and as a home for the homeless. Queen Anne Square had declined into an ill-defined, empty open space without a consistent public presence (Figure 7.5). The appearance of the square stood in deep contrast with the generally reverent opinion

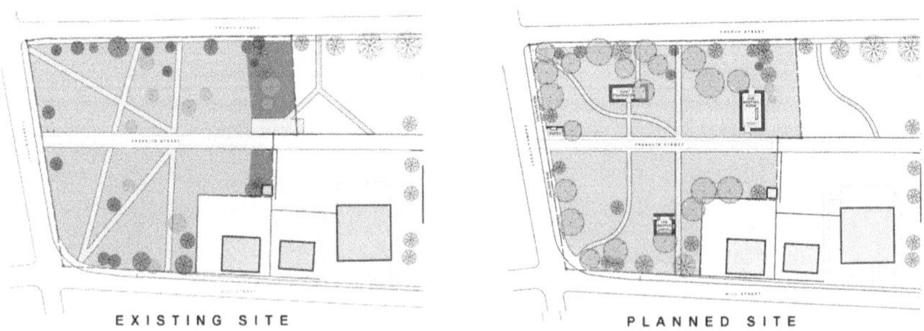

FIGURE 7.3 The Duke design and the Lin design in comparison

Source: *Newport This Week*, October 20, 2011

FIGURE 7.4 Postcard featuring Queen Anne Square, ca. 1977, showing the flowers Duke had planted in the park

Source: Collection of Nathaniel Robert Walker

FIGURE 7.5 Queen Anne Square, ca. 2010

Source: *Newport This Week*, October 20, 2011

the public had of Duke herself. By 2000, Duke was being venerated in heroic, if not mythic, terms. Often credited with having 'saved' Newport, she was a key figure in the town's story of how historic preservation had revived Newport's economy.[14] Such veneration contrasted with her 1960s-era reputation, which was, as recounted above, far more controversial. For Newporters, Duke is a hero whose reputation has been polished over time.

Not happy with the Dwarves

The NRF planned to address all of the problems with Queen Anne Square in its twenty-first century redesign. Framing the project as a 'reclamation,' the NRF outlined three goals and four potential benefits to the city. The project would revitalize a park to which their organization had a strong connection, pay homage to Duke and her legacy, and continue Duke's tradition of giving back to the community. The revitalized space would benefit the city by creating a more inviting space with better amenities, enhancing the profile of Trinity Church, creating a new destination in the city that would attract more tourists, and improving the city's public reputation. The NRF created the Doris Duke Monument Foundation to administer the site and secured private funding for the entire project and its maintenance. The city would only be responsible for mowing the grass, sidewalk and path maintenance, and trash removal, all tasks they already performed.[15]

Lin's design built on the colonial associations that Duke had attempted to establish thematically with her plantings and the park's name. The new scheme revolved around three recreated foundations, the stones for which came from the ruins of original colonial-era houses (Figure 7.6). The foundations followed the original footprints of the buildings Duke had moved elsewhere and, with the stone built high enough to function as seating, operated as outdoor rooms. The largest contained a water table with nine bubbling fountains, each representing one of the original families that settled Newport. A smaller one included a complete fireplace and was intended to represent the early years of Newport's Colonial era. Inscriptions evoking Newport's history, from religious tolerance to the founding of the NRF, were carved in key locations around the park by the local and much beloved stonemason, Nicholas Benson, who had worked with Lin in the past.[16]

Lin also collaborated with another longstanding design partner, landscape architect Edwina von Gal. Together, the two determined that nine mature trees needed to be removed. They also carefully considered what type of new trees to plant, assessing their historic significance, suitability to the climate, and, most importantly, the spread of the limbs, which were not to block the vista of the waterfront. For example, *sophora japonica*, or the Chinese scholar tree, was planted as a representative of the type of tree Newport merchants would have brought back from China. Sustainability was key; all the pavings were reclaimed from Newport's bluestone sidewalks while the retaining wall along Thames

FIGURE 7.6 Presentation image of Lin's design for Queen Anne Square. The Newport Restoration Foundation

Street was made from blocks recycled from a previously demolished bridge. Historic gas lamp fixtures were refitted with LED lights. The park has Wi-Fi.

The NRF unveiled Lin's plan in May of 2011. The plan circulated quietly until May 25, when the Newport City Council passed Resolution of the Council No. 2011–071, endorsing the plan in a vote of six to one. Public opinion against the proposal was immediate – and deafening.[17] Over the next two years, three hundred and forty newspaper articles were published on the plan, 60 percent between May 25 and December 14 of 2011, when the City Council voted to move forward with the design. The controversy was reported on by a wide range of media outlets, but most articles appeared in five local publications: the major dailies *The Providence Journal* and *The Newport Daily News*, the online *The Newport Patch*, and the weekly papers *The Newport Mercury* and *Newport This Week*.

The articles split about 40/60 percent pro-to-con, with each side consisting of a core of six to eight writers. The pro side had the initial advantage of early support from *The Newport Daily News* and from *The Providence Journal*'s local arts writer, Bill van Siclen. Other supporters included Tom Goddard, a member of the Doris Duke Monument Foundation and a board member of the Newport Restoration Foundation, Pieter Roos, executive director of the Newport

Restoration Foundation, Trudy Coxe, executive director of the Preservation Society of Newport County, and Ross Cann, a local architect and founder of a local group on Newport's architecture. All were well established figures.

The opposition side reflected a more grassroots effort. *The Providence Journal* was the first to question whether the project was a good idea at all, asking in an editorial dated May 24, 2011, the day before the City Council voted its initial approval, whether the $3.5 million costs of the park might be better spent elsewhere. The *Journal* viewpoint was quickly seconded by local residents Mary Shepard, Mary Weston, Anne DuBoise Joslin, Kyle Hence, and Timothy McGuinness. These five framed several arguments against the design in a series of printed articles. Shepard argued that the design was inappropriate to Newport and felt that the public had been cut out of the process. Weston objected to a non-profit telling the city what to do with its public space. Joslin wrote several articles on the site's land evidence history, asserting that the NRF did not have the right to remake public space. Hence felt that the NRF was ignoring significant environmental issues on the site. Personal attacks quickly entered the air, and as these increased in number and ferocity in the coming months, the problem of gender would emerge.

McGuiness was one of the first to take an aggressive tone, attacking NRF Director Pieter Roos, and architect Maya Lin:

> Can it be that our mayor and City Council members can't see that this unnecessary $3.6 million project is not a gift to our city but a trick by Pieter Roos to aggrandize himself, in cahoots with Maya Lin? Let Mr. Roos confine himself to the mission of the NRF. Let our mayor and City Council serve the resident taxpayers and voters of Newport by protecting all the trees and open space we still have left on our island. Let's all say no to Pieter's ruse.[18]

McGuiness' hostile pun calling the project 'Pieter's ruse' was a harbinger of what Roos would endure as the debate developed.

The opposition force was soon joined by a handful of credentialed voices, foremost among whom was Laurence Cutler, CEO of the National Museum of American Illustration, located on Bellevue Avenue in Newport. Cutler's first letter, written on October 13, 2011, to *Newport This Week*, represented a turning point in the opposition's fight.[19] Cutler felt strongly that the Lin design was not good artistically and should not be built. Eventually, Cutler would pen fifteen letters opposing the project. His authority as someone who worked in the visual arts insured that his viewpoint had an extremely powerful effect.

The opposition divided into several camps. Following Cutler's lead, several writers felt that the Lin design was inadequate or unworthy, an argument bolstered by comparison to another Lin design in Athens, Ohio, that the opposition deemed 'unsuccessful.' Another set liked the design but felt that what presently existed was a better memorial to Duke. A third group raised concerns over whether $3.5 million would really cover the cost of maintenance and whether Newport would still have to pay for the park. A fourth group was outraged over the lack of public inclusion and the questionable legality of the proceedings, wondering whether wealthy interests trumped democratic process, and whether the NRF had the right to redesign a public space. A fifth group did not like Lin's idea to rebuild houses within the park, arguing that a 'real' Doris Duke was preferable to a 'fake' Maya Lin. A sixth group felt the whole dispute could be resolved by replanting Duke's flowerbeds. Lastly, a core group of people simply liked the park as it was and categorically did not want change.

This opposition was met headlong by the proponents. Their arguments centered on those the NRF had initially framed: The project was being fully funded by donors at no cost to taxpayers, it would remake a space that needed rehabilitation in honor of an important leader in the preservation community, it would create a new tourist destination within the city, and it would invite a new generation of designers into the city's historic fabric. Fundamentally, this group liked the Lin design, wanted to see it move forward, and were flabbergasted by the opposition the design was encountering.

The absence of the Duke-era flowers is a useful frame of reference for each view's understanding of the problem (Figure 7.4). Each side perceived their loss in very different ways. The opposition, which included older Newport residents who remembered the flowers, felt that the lack of the flowers could be remedied by simply replanting them and that once the flowers were returned, the space would be fine. They did not acknowledge the reasons behind the disappearance of the flowers in the first place: the difficulty and cost of their maintenance. However, to proponents of the Lin design, including the leadership of the NRF, the absence of flowers meant that the space no longer reflected Duke's design and therefore significant change was possible. At heart, this disagreement stemmed from what each side defined as 'the Duke design.'

A key voice of support for the Lin design came from Ross Cann, who early in the debate wrote extensively on Lin's qualifications and the quality of her design. Of those in favor of the design, Cann was one of the most dedicated and committed. On August 13, 2011, he wrote:

> I have been shocked by letters opposing a general give of more than $3 million to the city from some of the same organizations that helped build the park … I have done work on buildings around the park and have seen homeless individuals living in the overgrown shrubbery. Is this what the few vocal opponents want to save? Others say, 'Preserve Miss Duke's historic vision!' Miss Duke was a practical woman who was not afraid to shuffle buildings to achieve pragmatic results and the park itself is an artificial creation that had no historical precedent in Newport. I believe that those who knew her best are the very ones pressing hardest to see her vision for the most beautiful park possible achieved in this new renovation.[20]

Cann was also one of the only voices to call for calm when the debate got ugly. In response to a cartoon entitled 'Doris Duke Would Not be Happy with the Dwarves,' printed in *Newport This Week*, Cann wrote 'I would propose a policy where letters and cartoons should be printed only if … they are not defamatory or unfounded in their attacks by name, gender or race …'[21] Regrettably, the opposition side found aggressive language to be a source of power. Roos recounts instances of personal vilification, including at the City Council meeting on December 14, 2011, when an opponent who felt Lin's fireplace and chimney recalled Auschwitz called Roos a Nazi.[22]

'It took me by surprise'

It did not take long for issues of gender to start boiling over amid such visceral heat. Very early in the discussion, *Newport This Week* published a photo and summary paragraph entitled 'Not as Old as She Looks.'[23] The goal of the article was to support the project and inform readers of the history of the site. But in referring to the park as 'she,' the article unintentionally gave Queen Anne Square a gender identity. To a certain extent, the space already had one; it was named Queen Anne Square by Queen Elizabeth II during the dedication.[24] But the article personified the space in a way that intensified the emerging gender dynamics of the situation. First, it established the metaphor of Queen Anne Square as a young damsel in pressing danger, and second, it began the process of conflating the two designs with the females who had created them.

Throughout the conversation, Doris Duke and Maya Lin were treated very differently. Duke was commonly referred to with the maiden prefix as 'Miss Duke,' which is how most had referred to her when she was alive. Newspaper articles likewise used the phrase 'Miss Duke's design' when referring to her park. The title 'Miss' conveyed virtue and respect to Duke, as well as to her design. Maya Lin, by contrast, was rarely referred to as anything other than 'Maya Lin.' No titles such as Ms, Mrs, or Miss were ever used for her. Furthermore, Lin was always referred to by both her first and last names, such that there was never any confusion over her gender. This approach was a departure from the general practice of calling great designers by their last names – a 'Michelangelo design,' for example. Queen Anne Square's redesign was always a 'Maya Lin design' or 'Maya Lin's design.' Furthermore, Lin's partners on the project, Edwina von Gal and Nick Benson, the well-regarded local engraver, disappeared from the debate. It was Lin's design, and her design only.[25]

Such use and non-use of titles revealed how people really felt about both of the women and, by extension, their work. Duke was portrayed as a do-gooder who was trying to nurture and heal the city of Newport at a time when it really needed help. Duke's embodiment of this role was consistent with how women had traditionally been involved in urban design in the United States. Historic preservation movements had been initiated and led by women, and were often considered an extension of their traditional role as custodians of the family hearth and educators of children, as in the saving of George Washington's home of Mount Vernon. Park planning had also long been a purview of women interested in improving urban conditions, again often with children in mind.[26] Importantly, Duke was not a professional architect, and her role was not described as such. In the public's imagination, she did fashion a city park, but that park's creation was essentially a domestic embellishment of an urban setting: the siting of trees and the planting of flowers within a city park were used to enhance the city's Colonial identity, provide a protective buffer for a historic church, and establish an open space for Newport's citizens to enjoy. Duke's design was not seen as artistic and functional, but rather as nurturing, sentimental, deferential, and affectionate, to be received and cherished accordingly. Phrases like 'Let's keep it that way' and 'Why mess with a wonderful place?' were commonly heard throughout the debate, even as they completely ignored the real issues faced by the square.[27]

Lin, in contrast, is a professional architect and therefore came to Queen Anne Square not as a concerned citizen and homemaker but as a designer. In this role, Lin operated as a woman in a professional field that has remained stubbornly male-dominated and male-oriented since its mid-nineteenth century founding. While a trailblazer in architectural circles, relative to Duke, Lin was an outsider who lacked community standing. Furthermore, her design included sculptural enclosures evoking buildings that, while intended as art, read better as architecture: her design consisted of masculine-associated hardscape features while Duke's consisted of softer, more feminine landscape elements. As a result, as both sides vetted Lin's background and her design portfolio, they evaluated her previous successes relative to other male designers, in very significant contrast to Duke, whose flowery design was never vetted in any way.[28]

Lin, herself, was no stranger to controversy, nor to controversy with a gendered component. Her first major project, the Vietnam Veterans Memorial, was widely criticized on several levels. In arguments that prefigure those presented in the Queen Anne Square debate, some argued that the Vietnam Veterans Memorial should not be built; the war was immoral, a loss for the US, and should not be commemorated at all. Others felt that the design itself was too ambiguous and was a 'disservice to history and to the memory of those who died.'[29] Many veterans felt that as a female and Asian-American designer who was only nine years old when the Tet Offensive took place, Lin was not an appropriate designer for this memorial. However, while these criticisms presented Lin's gender as insufficient, the attacks themselves were not gendered. Queen Anne Square would be the first instance where Lin encountered gender-biased criticism as well as criticism of her gender.

Proponents of Lin's Queen Anne Square plan tried to leverage her impressive portfolio and credentials as a reason to move forward with the design. As Ross Cann noted in several letters, Lin was an excellent, highly reputed, and well-trained designer, and therefore her design for Queen Anne Square merited approval.[30] At the same time, opponents used the same details to argue that Lin did not measure up. For example, an editorial in *The Providence Journal* published on May 24, 2011, described having 'a Maya Lin' in Newport as being 'almost as good as having "a Frank Gehry."'[31] In another comparison, however, local critic David Brussat pointed out that 'a work by Maya Lin is not quite at the level of "a Gehry."'[32] In both cases, Lin was measured against a prestigious male designer and found inferior, despite the fact that her Vietnam Veterans Memorial design had almost instantly become a national icon and was praised by leading historian and critic Vincent Scully as 'the single most significant work of architecture to be constructed in the United States during the second half of [the 20th] century.'[33]

Curiously, opponents ignored the Vietnam Veterans Memorial, Lin's best known and most famous work, and instead compared her Queen Anne Square design to one of her lesser-known projects, Bicentennial Park in Athens, Ohio. Mary Shepard was the first to reference this project, claiming that it 'has lots of rectangles and is apparently quite dysfunctional,' while acknowledging that she had never seen it.[34] Later on, Laurence Cutler claimed that Lin was recycling the Bicentennial Park design at Queen Anne Square, arguing that this 'failed … park installation at Ohio University' was evidence of the fact that 'her heart is no longer interested in designing monuments.'[35] Cutler's words implied that Lin's design successes did not come from the rigor of a trained mind but from the sentimental faculties of her heart, which could become exhausted without her even knowing it. Furthermore, Shepard's and Cutler's designation of Bicentennial Park as 'dysfunctional' and a 'failure' was suspect. On December 17, 2011, *The Newport Daily News* published a glowing letter from Vernon R. Alden, former president of Ohio University, who spoke ardently of how successful Lin's design for Bicentennial Park had been and how the community loved the space.[36]

As Duke was praised for providing a warm, simple, passive stage for the appreciation of Newport, Lin was damned for her ambitious sculptural program that sought to program the square with an identity and sense of place. Mary Shepard complained that 'Lin's plan calls for removing beautiful, established trees and replacing them with new ones that may create too much shade in an area where openness, views to the church and getting the sun are paramount.'[37] Herb Armstrong felt that 'The stone pit proposed for the square are evocative of nothing and will be intrusive to the park's focal point – Trinity Church.'[38] Ed Paul argued that the design represented 'some "foo foo" [sic] sculptural representation of foundations of the many derelict buildings Doris Duke had the great foresight to demolish.'[39] The phrase 'foo foo' inevitably evokes the irrational preening of a vain, childish woman.

Seeking allies with unquestionable authority, opponents raised two men from the dead. Anita Rafael wondered,

> What would a great mind like [Frederick Law] Olmsted have envisioned in relandscaping this particular space, now or at the time when Duke was recreating her then-controversial version of colonial history there? (Had he been alive in the 1970s, Duke certainly would have hired him …)[40]

In a letter to the Newport City Council in advance of their December 14, 2011, meeting on the issue, Lynne Bryer wrote,

> I don't believe Carter Brown, the deceased National Gallery Director – and arts professional formerly on the Doris Duke Foundation Board – active on the advisory council for buildings in Washington, DC – who grew up in Newport, would have approved of this proposal by Maya Lin.[41]

Voices like Olmsted and Brown, even raised in speculation, conveyed male establishment authority, trumping Lin, and even diminishing the agency of Duke herself. Whether Duke would have hired Olmsted is moot; she had every landscape designer, male or female, at her disposal but chose to design the space herself anyway.

Most women working in design are compelled by the forces of history and demographics to face the male establishment. Lin, however, is not known for taking a feminist stance against the inequalities of the architecture profession. In fact, her work tends to avoid controversy altogether. Reflecting later upon the Queen Anne Square debate, she commented:

> I don't think anything I've done has been as controversial as [Queen Anne Square]. And to be honest, there have really only been two projects of mine that have been controversial: my first project [the Vietnam Veterans Memorial] and Queen Anne Square. So, yes, it took me by surprise.[42]

It was not only the gendered nature of the debate, but the fact that the debate was even happening that astounded many. Throughout the debate, however, Lin remained quiet.

While the Queen Anne Square controversy raged on, outside events provided an interesting counterpoint. In October, 2011, Zaha Hadid (1950–2016) received the 2011 Stirling Prize, the United Kingdom's most prestigious architecture award, for her design for the Evelyn Grace Academy in London, England.[43] After becoming the first woman to win the Pritzker Prize in 2004, she had stated,

> I used to not like being called a woman architect: I'm an architect, not just a woman architect … But I see the incredible amount of need from

> other women for reassurance that it could be done, so I don't mind that at all.[44]

Yet, criticism of Hadid's designs were routinely mixed with discussions of her behavior and dress, both of which countered traditional gender stereotypes of women. For example, in addition to having a reputation as a diva with a temper, both qualities that would have gone unremarked upon in a male architect, her physical appearance was often discussed in the media.[45] Furthermore, unmarried and with no children, Hadid was portrayed as someone who had 'sacrificed' an inherent part of being a woman for her career, and she was constantly pressured to discuss whether she had a 'man in her life.'[46] While Hadid structured her career in the model of male architects who had come before, she was still called out for choices that did not align with expected gender norms.

Not long thereafter, as Lin's Queen Anne Square design inched towards completion, another famous woman architect fell into the spotlight. In April, 2013, Denise Scott Brown (1931–) was thrust into the headlines when two students at Harvard's Graduate School of Design started a petition to have the administrators of the Pritzker Prize retroactively give her the 1991 award that had been given to partner and husband Robert Venturi for work the two had done together. Sponsored by Arielle Assouline-Lichten and Caroline James, the petition argued that 'for women's equality to become a reality today, we need to rectify the mistakes of the past.'[47] The pair noted that Scott Brown's 'role as "wife" seemed to have trumped her role as an equal partner when the Pritzker jury chose to only honor her husband, Venturi.' Ultimately, the Pritzker Prize jury rejected the petition, but not before the effort sparked a timely and comprehensive discussion over the role of women in the field of architecture and the gender bias most faced as practitioners in the field.[48]

Echoing Scott Brown's and Hadid's experiences, Lin was compared unfairly and unfavorably to male predecessors and peers. In Newport, however, Lin was also compared to another woman, giving rise to a unique wave of gender-biased criticism that pitted women against each other. This dynamic set the Queen Anne Square debate apart from other conversations about gender and urban design, and signaled the opening of a new front in architecture's gender wars. As opponents of Lin's design used gender-loaded terms to venerate Duke and denigrate Lin, the familiar virgin–whore dichotomy emerged. Duke was the good, simple girl from a bygone age of purity and honesty, with a good, simple design that provided a passive, flowery stage for the adoration of surrounding male accomplishments. Lin was the ambitious, assertive, interloping outsider and 'park'-wrecker. Complicating the matter was the opposition of Duke's lack of training, which implied that her design had sprung naturally from an innate woman-ness, with Lin's well-educated and credentialed background. These characterizations were ironic: of the two, Duke had the more scandalous past, now forgotten and buried under the mythology of Duke as preservationist. Ultimately, the comparison robbed Duke of her status as a genuine, if imperfect, urban designer, even as it dismissed the established professional and creative accomplishments of Lin.

In the end, most Newporters were unconvinced by the debate's gendered rhetoric. On December 14, 2011, with passions still smoldering, the Newport City Council voted five to one to approve the Lin plan for Queen Anne Square (Figures 7.7–7.9). Per the NRF's original plans, $3.5 million in privately raised funds were used for the construction and at least $500,000 was designated for a park maintenance fund. As Mayor Stephen C. Waluk commented, 'A year from now, on Dec. 14, 2012, Queen Anne Square will be a place people won't just walk through, but a place people will walk to. People will ask what all the fuss was about.'[49]

The council meeting ended with two key observations. The first was an acknowledgment that Lin had not been treated well throughout the process. Councilman Harry Winthrop spoke out against people who had tried to discredit Lin personally: 'That is just wrong.'[50] The other was to note that debate had gotten the city talking about architecture in a way it never had done before. Despite the uproar's negative tone, each side was invested in their arguments, a fact acknowledged by the press throughout.[51] The intensity of discourse would be missed by the city, although the acrimony would not. A year and a half later, the Lin park was opened with celebrations and fanfare. Today, it lives up to its promise as a beautiful and active park adding life to Newport's urban fabric. It is difficult to guess what Olmsted would think of it (and who cares, anyway), but Doris Duke would undoubtedly have been proud.

FIGURE 7.7 Queen Anne Square, Maya Lin, 2013

Source: Photograph by the author

FIGURE 7.8 Queen Anne Square, Maya Lin, 2013. Photograph by the author

FIGURE 7.9 Queen Anne Square, Maya Lin, 2013. Photograph by the author

Notes

1 'History: The Navy and Narragansett Bay,' the Official US Navy Website, accessed February 11, 2019: www.cnic.navy.mil/regions/cnrma/installations/ns_newport/about/history.html
2 Many Newport citizens remember this period acutely and 'pulling out' is the term they universally use.
3 Robert Foley, A. Bruce MacLeish, and Pieter N. Roos, *Extraordinary Vision: Doris Duke and the Newport Restoration Foundation* (East Greenwich, Rhode Island: Meridian Printing, 2010), p. 14.
4 *Ibid.*, 14.
5 Holly Collins, 'The Preservation Society of Newport County, The Founding Years 1945–1965,' (manuscript written for the Preservation Society of Newport County, 2006), p. 11, accessed February 11, 2019, www.newportmansions.org/documents/the_preservation_society_of_newport_county_1945.pdf
6 Foley, MacLeish, and Roos, *Extraordinary Vision*, pp. 18–19.
7 *Ibid.*, pp. 16–17.
8 'Doris Duke Kills Friend in Crash,' *Newport Daily News*, October 7, 1966.
9 Joe Baker, 'Then & Now: Walsh Brother/Queen Anne Square,' *Newport Daily News*, August 18, 2011; 'A History of Queen Anne Square' (undated paper in the collections of the Newport Restoration Foundation, possibly dating to about May 7, 2011).
10 Personal communication between the author and Robert Foley, October 7, 2015.
11 William M. Kutik, 'Elizabeth II, Philip Arrive on Saturday,' *Newport Daily News*, July 6, 1976. The event was covered extensively in the Newport and Providence press.
12 Foley, MacLeish, and Roos, *Extraordinary Vision*, 30.
13 *Ibid.*, 30.
14 Elizabeth Abbott, 'In Newport, the Many-Faceted Legacy of Doris Duke,' *New York Times*, September 7, 1997.
15 Press release, undated but released on May 5, 2011, Collections of the Newport Restoration Foundation.
16 Nick Benson is Esther Fisher Benson's grandson, see Kristen G. Congdon and Kara Kelley Hallmark, *American Folk Art: A Regional Reference*, vol. 1 (Santa Barbara: ABC-CLIO, LLC, 2010), pp. 29–32.
17 Docket, City Council Meeting for May 25, 2011, City Clerk's Office, Newport City Hall.
18 Timothy McGuinness, 'Newporters Should Say No to "Pieter's Ruse,"' *Newport Daily News*, September 13, 2011.
19 Laurence S. Cutler, 'In Opposition to Maya Lin's Queen Anne Square Proposal,' *Newport This Week*, October 13, 2011.
20 Ross Cann, 'Queen Anne Square Plan is True to Duke's Vision,' *Newport Daily News*, August 13, 2011.
21 'Doris Duke would not be happy with the Dwarves,' *Newport This Week*, November 13, 2011. Ross Cann, 'Cartoon Went Too Far,' *Newport This Week*, November 10, 2011.
22 Personal communication between the author and Pieter Roos, September 23, 2015. Roos mentioned that when the park was under construction, he had performed a cleansing ritual in which he wrote the names of the top opponents on a small piece of paper, crumpled them up one by one, and threw into the base of the house foundations as the concrete was being poured.
23 'Not as Old as She Looks,' *Newport This Week*, May 19, 2011.
24 Edward Morris, *Rogues and Heroes of Newport's Gilded Age* (Mt. Pleasant: The History Press, 2012), p. 68.
25 On the role of speech in creating identity, see Judith Butler, *Gender Trouble* (New York: Routledge, 1990), pp. 156–160.

26 Daphne Spain, *How Women Shaped the City* (Minneapolis: University of Minnesota Press, 2001).
27 Mary Weston, 'Queen Anne Square Should Stay Way it is,' *The Newport Daily News*, June 29, 2011. Beth R. Graham, 'Leave Garden Alone,' *Newport This Week*, September 15, 2011.
28 Bill Van Siclen, 'Noted Designer Takes on City's Heart,' *The Providence Journal*, May 19, 2011.
29 Patrick Hagopian, *The Vietnam War in American Memory* (Amherst: The University of Massachusetts Press, 2009), pp. 101–02.
30 Ross Cann, 'Maya Lin and the Challenge of Creating Public Art,' *Newport This Week*, June 9, 2011. Ross Cann, 'Four Sides to Queen Anne Square Debate,' *Newport This Week*, August 11, 2011.
31 'Leave Queen Anne Square Alone,' *The Providence Journal*, May 24, 2011.
32 David Brussat, 'Let's Honor Doris Duke, not Maya Lin,' *The Providence Journal*, November 3, 2011.
33 Donald Langmead, *Maya Lin: A Biography* (Santa Barbara: Greenwood, 2011), p. 113.
34 Mary Shepard, 'Block Maya Lin's Cold Design in Newport,' *The Providence Journal*, May 1, 2011.
35 Laurence Cutler, 'Tribute created by "Memorialist,"' *Newport This Week*, August 23, 2012.
36 Vernon R. Alden, 'Ohioans are Proud of Lin's Park', *The Newport Daily News*, December 17, 2011.
37 Mary Shepard, 'Block Maya Lin's Cold Design in Newport,' *The Providence Journal*, June 1, 2011.
38 Herb Armstrong, 'Please Make Better Use of NRF Gift,' *Newport This Week*, September 8, 2011.
39 Ed Paul, '"Foo Foo" Queen Anne Square Plan Goes Against Duke's Mission,' *Newport Daily News*, August 9, 2011.
40 Anita Rafael, 'No Faux Needed, Thanks,' *Newport This Week*, September 1, 2011.
41 Lynne Bryer, letter to the Newport City Council dated December 12, 2011, contained in the docket files of the December 14, 2011, City Council Meeting, City Clerk's office, Newport City Hall.
42 Bill Van Siclen, 'How Maya Lin Remade Newport's Queen Anne Square,' *The Providence Journal*, May 24, 2013.
43 'Evelyn Grace Academy Wins 2011 Stirling Prize', Zaha Hadid Architects, accessed November 25, 2018: www.zaha-hadid.com/2011/10/03/evelyn-grace-academy-wins-2011-stirling-prize/
44 Randy Kennedy and Robin Pogrebin, 'Female Architects on the Significance of Zaha Hadid,' *New York Times*, April 1, 2016.
45 Carolina A. Miranda, 'Why we Talk about Zaha Hadid's Gender and Ethnicity Even Though her Architecture Transcended Both,' *Lost Angeles Times*, April 4, 2016.
46 Troiani, Igea, 'Zaha: An Image of "The Woman Architect,"' *Architectural Theory Review*, pp. 352–354.
47 The petition can be found online, accessed February 11, 2019: www.change.org/p/the-pritzker-architecture-prize-committee-recognize-denise-scott-brown-for-her-work-in-robert-venturi-s-1991-prize
48 Media articles on the topic include: Robin Pogrebin, 'Partner Without the Prize,' *New York Times*, April 17, 2013; Gareth Cook, 'What About Denise?', *The New Yorker*, April 15, 2013; Catriona Davies, 'Denise Scott Brown: Architecture Favors "Lone Male Genius" Over Women,' May 29, 2013, accessed February 11, 2019: www.cnn.com/2013/05/01/business/denise-scott-brown-pritzker-prize/index.html
49 Sean Flynn, 'Council OKs New Look,' *Newport Daily News*, December 15, 2011.
50 *Ibid.*
51 Jim Gillis, 'Spare Change: Redesign was No Walk in the Park,' *Newport Daily News*, December 16, 2011.

8

BEYOND THE BIND

Architecture, gendered agency and South African urban struggle

Sharóne L. Tomer

Lauretta Ngcobo's novel, *And They Didn't Die*, opens with a white, male, apartheid official, Mr. Pienaar, bemoaning civil disobedience by the rural, black women he was tasked with governing. Despite his threats, the women had yet again emptied the 'dipping tanks.'[1] The dipping tanks were ostensibly used to treat cattle for insect-borne illness, and the (apartheid) state required women to maintain them without payment. This was just one of a litany of unreasonable demands put upon rural women consigned to living in ethnic *Bantustans*, or homelands, during apartheid. Maintaining the tanks symbolized women's deep, vast, socio-economic struggles.[2] The tanks represented a system in which women were bound to poor-quality rural land, denied access to better resources or opportunities, and then made to financially support exactly the mechanisms that denied them freedom and livelihood. The tanks were part of an entrapping life and landscape, which consigned women to laborious 'waiting': sitting 'in the dust, eyeing the road that might bring a husband, a parcel of children's clothes, a pay-check.'[3] Thus, to empty the tanks was a small act of rebellion, intended to speak far beyond cattle and domestic labor. Tanks were emptied to resist the stripping of lives and livelihoods, and the state's system of gendered and racialized inequality. Not understanding the interconnectedness of space, race, gender, governance and economy, Mr. Pienaar asks himself, 'What do dipping tanks have to do with clinics and doctors and starving children; what do they have to do with schools and beer halls?'[4] As the women in Ngcobo's novel go on to illustrate, they have *everything* to do with each other.

The same argument has been made by living, breathing women across South Africa, through numerous space-based urban struggles. In Durban, in 1929 and again in 1959, women led the resistance against state-run, male-only beer halls. These protests sought to close the beer halls, but also stood in for a larger set of concerns around healthcare and housing. In Cape Town in the 1980s and 1990s, women living in migrant labor hostels organized childcare and training centers, ablution blocks and a market. These sought to redress the space and social services available to them, but also subvert the gendered hierarchy of traditional, tribally based ordering systems. In both cases, black women, many originally from rural areas, resisted domination by the white state, by black men and by an economic system that structurally marginalized them.

Ngcobo's characters answered Mr. Pienaar's question by illustrating, painfully, the interconnectedness of the politics of female identity and the deprivation of rural space and the political economy of apartheid.[5] They, like the women in Durban and Cape Town, experienced – and transcended – *the bind*, which is to say, a multi-faceted network of oppressive restrictions that permeated nearly every dimension of life, including intangible socio-political systems and tangible fabrics of rural space and the built environment. They found themselves bound by their race: their blackness in a state premised upon whiteness and subjugation of that which was racially 'other.'[6] They were bound by their gender: their status as females excluded them from participation in the economy and governance that was afforded to men, and valued them solely for their labor, both manual and reproductive. They were bound by their economic class: as rural migrants, they were members of the urban subaltern, structurally excluded from the wealth of the South African nation. Yet, all of these women also transcended the bind. They found ways to exercise agency and make their voices heard. Significantly, in the Durban and Cape Town cases, women did so through space and architecture.

Architecture, in these cases, includes but also exceeds built form. It even goes beyond the immersive fabric of urbanism. It serves as a terrain of action and a symbolic feature through which to strategically and politically operate. Architecture is both a design(ed) object and a site for making claims for social equality and recognition. Henri Lefebvre has argued that space is not an empty, Cartesian vessel; rather, it is socially produced and productive.[7] Space is the site of all social relations, but it is not a blank, silent site.[8] For Lefebvre, space and society are inextricably linked, and intimately co-productive. It is a small leap to similarly assert that architecture is about much more than its physical form; like space, it is never neutral and its political productivity is always at play. Architecture operates as 'an object of and for negotiation.'[9] While architecture is very much about design – it is about creatively conceptualizing how to bring together space and materials to serve a function and context – the design imagination never operates completely free or independent of societal influences, particularly when working at the scale of a community. In Durban and Cape Town, architecture – and urbanism – have been claimed by women as vehicles for agency. It has been put to use to push against the constraints of the bind.

Space, alcohol, repression and resistance

On June 17, 1959, black women in Cato Manor, Durban, entered the area beer hall, 'scattered the utensils and had chased the men folk out of the Beerhall.'[10] (Figure 8.1) On the surface, the protests concerned the role of alcohol in racialized

FIGURE 8.1 Armed women performing war dances to taunt and challenge the police at Cato Manor. 18th June, 1959

Source: The collection of SB Bourquin, Native Affairs Commissioner. Courtesy of Local History Museums' Collection, Durban

control: the beer halls siphoned money away from black men – and thus their families – as well as suppressed competition from black women, who themselves produced alcoholic beverages. The intensity of the riots spoke to the traditional significance of alcoholic beverage production and consumption in South Africa.[11] The riots were also, however, as much about the urban provision of clinics and housing as they were the regulation of indigenous traditions. They were ultimately connected to deep struggles around gender, space, labor and the rural–urban divide being produced in industrial South Africa, particularly under apartheid.

Beer halls were established in South African cities early in the twentieth century. These were state monopolies, which admitted only adult, black African men.[12] The beer halls were the only places legally allowed to sell beer to Africans, and the only places in which Africans were allowed to purchase and consume beer. The beer halls were visible spaces of difference in their spare, industrial architecture. Urban beer halls fit into the Victorian streetscape with corrugated tin roofs, simple colonnades at the sidewalk and open, factory-like interiors and courtyards, furnished only with rows of wooden benches. In peripheral township areas, such as Cato Manor, beer halls were specially built structures of concrete block interiors and enclosed courtyards. In both the architecture and accoutrements of drinking, the aesthetic was functionalist: men lined up to purchase beer, which they received in metal pails, and drank from tin cups (Figure 8.2).[13] Rather than being architecturally similar to pubs, spaces of white alcohol consumption, the beer halls helped produce urban and peripheral landscapes of racialized division and inequality.

FIGURE 8.2 Umgeni Beer Hall, a functionalist architecture of difference

Source: The collection of SB Bourquin, Native Affairs Commissioner. Courtesy of Local History Museums' Collection, Durban

In both their architecture and regulatory function, the beer halls were integral to South African urban–rural relations and divides. The making and consuming of fermented beverages had been a long-standing cultural tradition in southern Africa, related to ritual as well as relaxation. Within indigenous traditions, beer is brewed and consumed within the community, most often by women, and any payment exchanged remains within the community. The state's appropriation of beer operated as part of a larger network of regulations and spatial practices which sought to control the native population and maximize profit from their labor.[14] South African industrialization, which began with the nineteenth-century discoveries of gold and diamonds, led to widespread migrant labor, in which black men left their rural homes for long stretches of time to work in mines or cities. The dislocation of men from their homes and communities opened space for activities such as beer brewing and consumption to be captured by the state. Beer halls were a venue for the state to regulate who had access to liquor and generate revenue. They served as a double financial burden on black South Africans, as already fractured social and economic structures became more fractured still under the weight of this opportunistic exploitation.

The fact that the revenue extraction most intensely punished black South African women rendered beer making and consuming a site of both racial and gendered contestation. While black South African women traditionally brewed and sold beer, white South African women had been lobbying for temperance since the turn of the twentieth century.[15] In fact, ambitions to see temperance legislated propelled the South African women's suffrage movement.[16] Although I am not aware of scholarship that argues that the white women's temperance movement influenced the state's regulation of traditional beer brewing, it remains that temperance, and by extension white women's suffrage, were sites of racial opposition rather than gendered solidarity.

For black South African women, the beer halls stood in for the ways in which the migrant labor system served as a particularly stark illustration of modernity's gendered assignations: men literally left the home, leaving women to remain as the home's 'guardians.'[17] Materially, the beer halls threatened their livelihoods, and constricted their opportunity to make and sell beer when living in urban environments.[18] The beer halls served as both symbol and enabling device in a larger system that constricted the possibilities for constructing fulfilling – or even basic – livelihoods. Whereas beer making and consuming traditionally took place in central community gathering spaces, now they were removed from the space and the societal and economic infrastructures of pre-colonized life (Figure 8.3). This was a burden that women particularly recognized, arguably more than men.[19]

Thus, in 1929, when the state announced severe restrictions on the brewing and consumption of 'kaffir beer' – African-brewed beer – an intense wave of women-led protests broke out in Durban.[20] These were violent and impactful, leading to mass arrests of women and injuries on both racial sides. The protests spread across the Natal province to smaller towns and rural areas, galvanizing women to undertake political action and 'agitation.' While calm eventually

FIGURE 8.3 Domestic brewing of Bantu beer

Source: The collection of SB Bourquin, Native Affairs Commissioner. Courtesy of Local History Museums' Collection, Durban

returned, thirty years later beer hall protests again erupted, in the Cato Manor area of Durban. On the surface, the protests began after the state initiated another wave of beer-making restrictions, as had occurred in 1929. The protests were so intense that three days after they began, the state ordered all beer halls in the Durban area to be closed for ten days, so calm could be restored.[21] However, three weeks later, eight out of Durban's nine beer halls remained closed because of lack of business.[22] Many would remain permanently closed.

While opposition to the beer halls always included concerns regarding the state's capture of income and controlling behavior, the 1959 riots point to an even more complex, intertwined set of concerns, that reached far beyond beer making and selling. Women contested the larger apartheid economic system, which included but also exceeded the beer trade:

> Women have a serious grievance. They are not permitted to trade. They may not open a business. They cannot get stalls or trading facilities. They are permitted to do nothing legally to provide for themselves and their children. Then the Europeans [white South Africans] accuse us of not wanting to help ourselves.[23]

Beer halls were also part of a larger government system in which spatial mobility was restricted: Africans were expected to only be temporary urban dwellers, and were only allowed in cities for the purpose of work. Yet, subsistence farming in the rural homelands to which they were assigned to live was increasingly untenable. As Anne McClintock described, 'the ruined land is burdened with too many people, too many cattle and goats and can no longer support the basic needs of life.'[24] Just as rural land was becoming progressively unproductive, the apartheid state simultaneously constricted the movement of black people, and particularly women, making travel passes very difficult to obtain. Apartheid and preceding colonial policies used influx controls to limit 'African' or black population in cities, as the state sought to secure cities as 'white spaces;' doing so required barring black women in particular from living in cities, as they were seen as the 'primary cause of African urban population growth.'[25] Traditional rural life was becoming unbearable, but urban dwelling was temporary and forbidden to most women. The beer halls symbolized the impossibility of black South African lives under apartheid.

As Mr. Pienaar questioned in Ngcobo's novel, the beer halls were also related to clinics. In 1957, a typhoid epidemic had swept through Durban's informal settlements. Women spent the following two years agitating for improved living conditions and health facilities, to no avail.[26] Far deeper lay complicated issues concerning housing and gender: at this time the municipal council was deeply mired in developing housing policies for Durban's growing 'Native' population. The options they proposed would make women's married status and their access to income generation and urban housing increasingly precarious.[27] Again, Ngcobo eloquently and heartbreakingly expresses this as her book's protagonist,

Jezile, is forced by apartheid laws to live at her rural homestead instead of in Durban with her husband. When she fails to become pregnant during his brief, annual visits, her mother-in-law, with whom she shares the homestead, accuses her of not fulfilling her reproductive duty to the family. Worn down by her mother-in-law's taunts, and noting her vulnerable position in her husband's family, she asks the Bantu Affairs Department for a temporary pass to visit her husband, to try to become pregnant. Once in Durban, however, she sees the horrific conditions Africans are forced endure in the city, and how forgettable women back home become to the migratory men. Outside of the novel, in Cato Manor, women faced similar realizations and struggles (Figure 8.4). Frustration over the state's lack of clinic construction and detrimental housing policy had primed women to strike out, even before the 1959 rounds of beer-making restrictions. Their protests therefore physically attacked the beer halls but implicitly critiqued the larger system of governance imposed in Durban, and particularly the gendered precariousness it produced.

Ngcobo illustrates that rural women such as Jezile are bound by not only the state, but also by their communities' customary expectations of women's roles and responsibilities. Women are to silently bear the burden of reproductive labor; if and when they resist such assignations – as Jezile did when she engaged

FIGURE 8.4 While Bantu family is awaiting transport to take them and their belongings to Kwa Mashu Township, shacks are being demolished in the background

Source: Cato Manor, June 1959. Courtesy of Local History Museums' Collection, Durban

in the type of resistive acts bemoaned by Mr. Pienaar – they face rebuke from both the state and community. When Jezile participated in rural protest, the state literally imprisoned her, while her community rejected her. In the beer hall protests, women drew criticism from both the white-controlled state and black men. Neither group could fathom nor accept the women's leadership in struggle. Black men were embarrassed that women had taken on the state instead of them. Such lack of male activism was a site of redress being expressed by women. In essence, the battle to close the beer halls was a struggle against the state and its abuses, and a strategy to address the missteps of 'husbands and sons.'[28] It was a double struggle against a double bind.

Historians argue that the successful closure of the beer halls, which were located in urban areas, led to the spread of resistance to the rural countryside; by mid-August 1959, women were conducting widespread, destructive attacks on dipping tanks.[29] Ngcobo, answering Mr. Pienaar, illustrates that dipping tank sabotage was clearly deeply connected to clinics and beer halls. In the case of the beer hall protests and their subsequent closure, protest was an architectural act, in that they were productive *of* urban life, not just taking place *in* urban life. The closure of beer halls was government reaction to gendered demands for participation in economic systems and cultural traditions. However, the closure also exceeded being merely a work of policy and state relations. The 'hall' part of the beer hall renders the protests spatially productive.[30] The protesters' site of attack was the site in which beer halls architecturally displaced traditional community gathering. Where there had been beer halls were now boarded-up buildings, chipping away at the industrial infrastructure and functionalist architecture of the divided apartheid city. Until housing and clinics were satisfyingly produced, spatially and administratively, beer halls would remain vacant reminders of the refusal of women to accept their subjugation by both the state and their male partners.

Building gendered agency

Thirty years later in Cape Town, women again drew out connections between housing, healthcare, childcare and income generation. Actions in the two cities differed in that women in Durban deployed architecture through its attack, denying the beer halls their inhabitation; in Cape Town women undertook action through the design and construction of architecture.

The Cape Town site of redress was the city's migrant labor hostels. The hostel residents traveled to Cape Town in search of work, predominantly from rural areas similar to those inhabited in Ngcobo's novel. They were considered temporary residents in the city, subject to 'influx controls:' apartheid's notorious 'Pass Laws,' which, as experienced by Jezile, typically only granted passes for verified employment, and otherwise restricted black men and women to their assigned ethnic homelands. Their residency in the city was thus transitory and precarious.

Once in the city, hostel dwellers were marginalized through numerous conditions. As both laborers and residents, they were assigned the lowest status in the city. Similar to the beer halls, the hostels they were assigned to live in were spatially and visually distinct from the remainder of the city. They were located on the periphery of the city, in single-race 'townships,' but distinguished as the residences of outsiders even by other township dwellers. A typical hostel unit consisted of six bedrooms – each with two to four 'beds,' which were no more than hard sleeping platforms – a kitchen meagerly appointed with a counter and sink, a single bathroom with toilet and cold-water taps, and a storage room. Two to four hostels were clustered into single- or double-story buildings, which were arranged in a sprawling fashion. All of the hostels were single-sex, with spouses forced to reside elsewhere, most often back in the rural homelands. The spatial condition of the hostels was deplorable, and life opportunities for their residents were severely constricted.

In the mid-1980s hostel dwellers undertook efforts to upgrade their meager shelters, initiating an effort that eventually began converting the hostels into family accommodations. The process has been widely celebrated by architects and activists for transforming deplorable examples of South Africa's migrant labor system into modest permanent housing.[31] However, the male hostel dwellers marginalized and excluded their spouses and female counterparts from the upgrading process. In response, the women focused their attention on non-housing realms that were central to the domestic and reproductive labor they performed: crèches, clinics and a market space. These filled out the spatial and social infrastructure of the hostel areas, while claiming a role in spatial production for women and illustrating the gendered marginalization reproduced by black men.

While there were a small number of women's hostels in Cape Town, men's hostels were the subject of the upgrading efforts. The project to improve the hostels' condition began in 1985, as a way of agitating against apartheid without participating in labor-related strikes or protests.[32] At this time, the apartheid Pass Laws were still in effect, not allowing men's wives and children to join them in the city. The hostel dwellers' demands linked these prohibitions on domestic life to the precariousness of their employment and urban life. It was only one year later, in 1986, that the Pass Laws were repealed, and whole families were allowed to live together in the hostels. This legalized the illicit temporary urban migration that was already taking place, as women frequently came to cities, with their children, to join their spouses and find employment. However, until the hostels were 'upgraded,' the conditions transformed from 'one man per bed' to 'one family per bed.'

The repeal of the Pass Laws brought an opportunity to make the hostel upgrading effort a vehicle for gendered cooperation. When I first began researching the hostel upgrades, I expected that there would be an intriguing gender component to a political action that took place at the site of the domestic. I found that there was, but in the opposite way I expected. The upgrading project was gendered in that it was the perpetuation of male sublimation of female agency. Men dominated the entire process.

The gendered nature of the internal governance of the hostels was not unique to the upgrading process. Hostels were long self-governed through hierarchies and processes that reproduced the traditional authority structures used in rural areas, from which most hostel dwellers hailed. Dwellers elected representatives, who were typically elderly men, to adjudicate any conflict between hostel dwellers.[33] Gendered difference was marked under this *izibonda*, or 'headman,' system: women were recognized only as 'non-persons.' If they had any concerns, these had to be represented by a man. They were literally silenced in the eyes of the local law.[34]

In the upgrading process, a dynamic, mutually respectful relationship developed between the male hostel dwellers and the predominantly white professionals that came in to assist in the process.[35] The architects and planners became close colleagues with the hostel dwellers, in ways that disturbed the racialized and class-based divisions fabricated through apartheid.[36] Yet, such disturbances stopped short of destabilizing traditional gendered hierarchies. Women were essentially excluded from the hostel upgrading process, and it took much effort to achieve any sort of female representation in the Hostel Dwellers Association, which was established to manage the upgrading process.[37]

In response, women turned to other sites of action: sites which were equally architectural but worked outside of housing provision. South African townships such as Langa, Nyanga and Gugulethu – where the hostels in question were located – were conceived as residential dormitories, with little-to-no industry or services. The women in this story were marginalized not only by their racial status in the city and gender status in the hostels, but also their precarious economic condition. In the face of these conditions, they contributed to a larger story of resisting the control and monotony of the township landscape.[38] They did so by addressing that which is 'reproductive,' meaning they sought to provide spaces and services outside of housing, but integral to the maintenance of daily life.[39] They attended to three realms complimentary to the housing upgrades: care for others, which included childcare centers and training for different types of care providers; bodily care, in the form of bathhouses and a (relatively short-lived) mobile clinic; and informal trading.[40] The action undertaken by women brought together social action with spatial engagement, at times simply working spatially and at others working with architects. In both conditions, the women sought to produce the facilities necessary to enable the activities they saw as crucial to their daily lives.

The initiatives were urban in scale and nature, but differed in the degree to which they were architectural. Some, such as mobile health clinics, had a spatial presence but not a related architectural artifact. The childcare projects were not architect-designed, but were the first moves to create a system of collaborative childcare, which freed women from full-time child rearing so they could engage in paid work. The first crèches were too crowded to be developmentally beneficial for children, but they led to a practice of establishing crèches in the upgraded hostel areas (Figure 8.5).[41]

The women's efforts most closely aligned with 'architecture,' in the sense of being designed by a trained professional, in a set of projects that commissioned architect Carin Smuts and her firm, CS Studio. Smuts is a white Cape Town-based architect, who has established an architectural firm rooted in participatory practices and devoted to work for marginalized black communities.[42] Smuts worked with female hostel dwellers and township residents to produce a number of projects, including the Ulwazi Youth Center and Langa Bathhouses in Langa, the Zolani Multipurpose Center in Nyanga, and the Gugulethu Central Meat Market. The projects represent gendered spatial action, through both the programs being supported and the ways in which the architectural designs, developed in collaboration with the female users, manifested a gendered perspective on the ideal spatiality needed to support daily life.

The Langa bathhouses, for example, were situated in the public space between upgrading hostels. Women organized to have the bathhouses constructed to serve the residents whose hostel units had not yet been updated. Through a participatory process, the facilities were designed to meet the needs of those often marginalized: the elderly, disabled and children. To do so, they broke away from conventional spatial arrangements; in addition to private showering stalls, each bathhouse (male and female) included larger rooms with a large tub in the center. These eased access to bathing for the elderly, and

FIGURE 8.5 Crèche in upgraded hostel area in Nyanga

Source: Photograph by the author, June 2012

enabled multiple children to be washed simultaneously, facilitating childcare labor.[43] By permanently locating bathhouses in public space, in the transitioning hostel upgrade area, the project was imagined as both the backdrop for un-programmed public space between hostel building, and as a programmed public resource for collectively accomplishing a typically private, domestic act (Figure 8.6).

An even more public project was the Gugulethu Central Meat Market. The project was initiated by a set of female hostel dwellers to provide needed infrastructure for their informal trading activities. Women were already engaged in selling meat to area residents, especially passersby traveling to and from the nearby train station. The market would support their activities; electricity and lighting in particular would enable them to extend the hours they traded, and thus their economic efficiency. As Smuts tells the story, she initially proposed 'a little European model' for the meat market, at which the women 'laughed' because of its unsuitability to their needs.[44] Using models and drawings, they were able to communicate their desire for a plan of an L-shaped bar that provided the infrastructure for the market's varied traders and sheltered the market from prevailing winds.[45] The women also instead on a 'petrol station roof,' and this became the market's most significant architectural feature. The undulating corrugated metal form provides protection for the agglomeration of cooking areas and vendor tables below. It also ensures that the market stands out amongst the low-slung township landscape: although only single story,

FIGURE 8.6 Papu Bathhouse, Langa. In each of the Langa bathhouses, an undulating enclosing wall creates open-air public spaces that residents can use for waiting, gathering and laundry

Source: Photograph by the author, May 2018

the roof gives the building a striking presence amongst the surrounding hostels and informal dwellings. The completed design is a joining of rethinking the spatial scale of the township landscape, and an address of the informal trading that provides one of the few sources of income on the historically impoverished Cape Flats.

Both the meat market and bathhouses represent an architectural approach of material modesty, enlivened by community pride and aspiration. The buildings' programs and architectural language speak to the quotidian, while their presence on the landscape slowly builds up the township scale and the presence of formally designed architecture (Figure 8.7). The introduction of an architecture that serve's the community's self-identified needs is radical in a terrain in which historically all formal architecture was functionalist and imposed upon the community by outside authorities, while all else was informally constructed. The insistence by women to break from convention, and claim an architecture that serves their specific, lived realities, broadens an often-unconsidered aspect of modernism's history. Alice Friedman has illustrated that the 'modern house,' as an architectural type for privileged classes, has long been a product of the female client and her willingness – or insistence – to rethink the norms of domestic space. Friedman argues that 'individual women clients proved to be such effective catalysts for creativity in modern domestic architecture' because of 'the conviction shared by modern architects and their women clients that the essence of modernity was the complete alteration of the home: its construction, materials, and interior spaces.' She goes on to state that 'not only did women commission avant-garde architects to provide them with houses in

FIGURE 8.7 Zone Eight Bath House, Langa.

Source: Photograph by the author, May 2018

which to live out their visions of a new life, but these visions rested on a redefinition of domesticity that was fundamentally *spatial* and *physical*.'[46] Friedman, as well as Gwendolyn Wright and Dolores Hayden, focus on the power exercised by middle- and upper middle-class women: 'many women recognized that by taking control of the domestic realm – and by claiming expertise in all matters relating to it – they could gain a measure of independence in their own lives.'[47] Yet, the female hostel dwellers were far from the middle class; they lacked the economic means to surpass gendered assignations that were available to the wealthy patrons who Friedman studies. The hostel dwellers' spouses excluded them even from control over the transformation of their homes. They were marginalized by class, race and gender.

In spite of such constraints, they managed to give shape to their demands, their needs and their imaginaries. Theirs was a project of voice, taking place in a larger context of struggle. While marginalized by numerous arenas, the female hostel dwellers were operating in a culture of politicized resistance. Similar to the ways in which the male hostel dwellers turned to upgrading as a means of resisting apartheid when labor-based struggles were impractical for them, female hostel dwellers turned to the reproductive when denied participation in the upgrading process. Their work characterizes them as what Dolores Hayden refers to as 'material feminists:' women who 'dared' to (re)define women's material conditions.[48]

Disturbing architectural boundaries

Material feminist practices work to destabilize traditional social relations and architectural typologies. The significance of such practices rests in how social relations and architecture are re-framed in relation to each other. Doing so highlights the limitations of the normative ways architecture is framed as a discipline, which typically is confined to study of its artefacts and their authors. Material feminist practices help illustrate that architecture is much more than buildings and designs.

Architecture can instead be understood as both a built product and a site of the processes that produce it. Architecture works as *action* – as types of labor and agency – which operates in dialectic relationship with architecture as object. In the cases of the women working to transcend their binds, the protests they staged transformed the beer halls and migrant labor hostels. Both came to exceed their building program, to serve additionally as sites and loci of gendered political action. This understanding diverges from conservative definitions of 'architecture,' which, as Lesley Lokko argues, typically fixate purely on the built object and its design features:

> Discussions of architecture ... are often limited to traditional formal qualities, supposedly intrinsic to architectural form, such as quality of light, space, organization, materials, axialities, orders and so on. This reduction supports the classification of architecture as an object-driven exercise – the building, validated through reproduction of those same qualities, is, in the end, *everything*.[49]

The beer hall protests and Cape Town constructions illustrate how much more there is, beyond the form of the object – and perhaps architects' imaginations – to architecture and to an architectural history. To ignore the conditions that inform the production of a design is to impose a normativity that silences important histories of the production of difference. It is to imply a false and impossible political neutrality to architecture. It is not an unreasonable stretch to connect silencing the role of production to traditions of ignoring certain bodies of architecture in the writing of architectural history. Bannister Fletcher almost completely omitted 'African' – and even more broadly 'non-Western' – architecture from his schematic 'Tree of Architecture.'[50] The histories discussed here illustrate the crucial importance of background events, even those that take place far from building sites, and the larger contexts of urbanism and, still larger, landscape, and the richness they add to our understanding of the built environment at all scales. To read architecture and architectural histories beyond the confines of the designed object is to include actions such as the beer hall closures within the frame of architectural history, and thus to include the women protesting the beer halls within architectural narratives.

Expanding the sphere of architectural history and discourse also destabilizes the privileging of wealth and power in the content of architectural and urban history. One of the labors performed by architecture is the work of representing ambitions. Because architecture so often is used to reproduce wealth, it is frequently associated with the trappings of global modernity. In South Africa and much of the Global South, the images that architects and planners produce imagine 'high-rise buildings, sweeping boulevards, tarred roads, motor vehicles,' which tell of an 'already-existing modernity and … ambition to be part of the global world.'[51] In these imaginations, the future of the South African city reflects certain sets of aspirations, which most often come from 'above.' The women in Durban and Cape Town represent a quite different set of ambitions, which reject the pressures exerted through architectural imagery and imaginary for a uniform level of modernity to be achieved globally.[52] They illustrate that architecture can also serve to represent alternative aspirations, which operate within the pressures of globalization and modernity, but resist the ways women are often marginalized under such regimes. The resultant architecture, in these cases, operates spatially and conceptually at the scale of the human, as opposed to that of global capital.[53] This shift in scale reflects not only the reduced means available to construct such architecture, but even more significantly, it reveals a resistive set of priorities, which focus on elements of care for community members. The architecture represents sets of values about the city and society that strive for more just and equitable conditions, and broader participation in making the city. Sometimes such ambitions require the demolition of architecture, in the case of the beer halls. Other times they call for creation of new architectural forms and new configurations of participation in the creation of architecture such as bathhouses and meat markets.

Such calls have localized significance that builds upon the re-framing of the disciplines of architecture and architectural history. To expand the agreed-upon valid aspects of the disciplines is historically revisionist, in a politically progressive manner. Space and architecture held central roles within South Africa's fraught political history of apartheid and colonial regimes. It is therefore important to the production of both history and the future of cities to integrate protest and other forms of social action into our understanding of space and architecture. This has already been illustrated in *Blank: Architecture, Apartheid and After*, a collection of textual and visual essays that is based upon an exhibit mounted by the Netherlands Architecture Institute.[54] Compiled only a few short years after apartheid's ending, the book very creatively brings together a host of historical and contemporary perspectives on the built landscape of apartheid and its 'after.' The book seeks not to assemble an overarching argument, but rather to give voice to sites and methods that diverge from traditional architectural or urban histories. It includes revisionist histories of colonial and apartheid architecture, planning, monument design and governance, which sit alongside photographic essays and drawings. Each essay, whether visual or textual or hybrid, is treated as a valid method of architectural and urban story-telling. The array of subjects and methods that are presented as 'architecture' in the book diverges widely from the perspective that the 'building is everything.' In short, *Blank* offers a map for taking the lessons taught by the women of Durban and Cape Town and implementing them in future design, construction and rehabilitation processes and projects.

Conclusion

It is in this spirit, in which the building is *not* everything, and the built environment is so much more than buildings, that the significance of the gendered protests begins to enter into the realm of architectural discourse. The women written about in this chapter have sought to claim a place, which brings together their spatial environment with their economic livelihoods, their health and their families. Some of their struggles produced 'architecture' as it is traditionally framed. Some, however, produced changes to space, in ways that question the limits of the concepts of 'design' and 'construction.'

Both sets of women discussed in the chapter, in Durban and Cape Town, were precarious urban dwellers under repressive racialized legislation. In the South African migrant labor system, women who were forced to remain at home, rather than to travel to cities, were placed outside of modernity. This is because, as Heidegger and Adorno have pointed out, to leave home is to be modern.[55] Even for women who do dislocate themselves from the rural home, such as Ngcobo's Jezile or the women of the Cape Town hostels, their role is still to protect the home. Their ambitions to venture out and 'conquer the unknown' remained an illegitimate choice for women.[56] This is seen in the stories of beer hall protests and hostel upgrades, where women faced a second round of refusals: from men of their own race. These stories illustrate the range of binaries which attempt to force black women to the periphery: masculinity vs. femininity, urban vs. rural, white vs. black, modern vs. traditional. Yet, what also connects both stories are the ways in which architecture and urban space were used to articulate demands for fair treatment, and the opportunity to create a life, where and how one wants. These are clearly stories of ambitions: for voice, for agency, for meaningful participation in the nation's economy. Architecture, whether as artefact or action, serves as a site and vehicle for the intertwined practices of protest and aspiration.

This chapter's settings are temporally and geographically disparate; they stretch across the time and space of the South African nation. The city in both becomes a site of speculative, aspirational imaginings: a place where alternative gendered and racialized realities are set into motion. Together the stories make explicit connections that are otherwise unseen – illustrating how instances of gendered, racialized struggle in South Africa have been productive of space and architecture. These connections not only answer Mr. Pienaar's question, but also show how attention to gendered racial struggle can help us identify, and ideally transcend, the binds and boundaries of the architectural discipline, making it less complicit with systems of exclusion and oppression.

Notes

1 Lauretta G. Ngcobo, *And They Didn't Die* (London: Virago Press, 1990).
2 Nicholas Reed, 'Women's Revolts in Natal: 1959,' *South African History Online* (blog), June 15, 2015, www.sahistory.org.za/article/women%E2%80%99s-revolts-natal-1959-nicholas-reed (accessed March 12, 2019).
3 Anne McClintock, *Imperial Leather: Race, Gender, and Sexuality in the Colonial Contest* (New York: Routledge, 1995), 387.
4 Ngcobo, *And They Didn't Die*, 1.
5 McClintock, *Imperial Leather: Race, Gender, and Sexuality in the Colonial Contest*, 386–87 points out Ngcobo's unprecedented attention to issues of female sexuality in apartheid/post-apartheid South Africa.
6 I am using contemporary commonly used terms such as 'white' and black' to describe racial identity. However, for much of the twentieth century, including the earlier period discussed in the chapter, the terms used were 'European' and 'African.'
7 Henri Lefebvre, *The Production of Space*, trans. Donald Nicholson-Smith (Oxford: Blackwell, 1991).
8 In a very similar argument, Doreen Massey defines space as 'social relations stretched out.' See Doreen B. Massey, *Space, Place and Gender* (Cambridge, UK: Polity Press, 1994).
9 Florian Kossak et al., eds., *Agency: Working with Uncertain Architectures, Critiques*, vol. 5 (London; New York: Routledge, 2010), 9.
10 Notes taken at an informal meeting of the combined Native Location Advisory Boards, the Cato Manor Welfare and Development Board and the Ibandla Lenkosi (Trans: meeting of important men, in this case chiefs) held in No. 3 Committee Room on Sunday June 21, 1959, at 10:20 am, quoted in Katherine D. Sadler, '"Trouble Was Brewing": South African Women, Gender Identity, and Beer Hall Protests, 1929 and 1959' (PhD diss, University of California, Los Angeles, 2002), 107.
11 J. S. Crush and Charles H. Ambler, *Liquor and Labor in Southern Africa* (Athens: Ohio University Press, 1992).
12 Helen Bradford, '"We Women Will Show Them": Beer Protests in the Natal Countryside, 1929,' in *Liquor and Labor in Southern Africa*, eds. Jonathan Crush and Charles Ambler (Athens; Pietermaritzburg: Ohio University Press; University of Natal Press, 1992), 211.

13 The description of the beer halls is garnered from photographs in the collections of the Old Court House Museum, Durban.
14 Paul la Hausse, 'Drink and Culture Innovations in Durban: The Origins of the Beerhall in South Africa, 1902–1916,' in *Liquor and Labor in Southern Africa*, ed. Jonathan Crush and Charles Ambler (Athens; Pietermaritzburg: Ohio University Press; University of Natal Press, 1992), 78–114.
15 The Women's Christian Temperance Union was founded in 1899. See 'White women achieve suffrage in South Africa,' in South African History Online (March 16, 2011), www.sahistory.org.za/dated-event/white-women-achieve-suffrage-south-africa (accessed November 9, 2018).
16 'White women achieve suffrage in South Africa.'
17 The gendered dimension of modernity and the home is discussed by Hilde Heynen, 'Modernity and Domesticity: Tensions and Contradictions,' in eds. Hilde Heynen and Gülsüm Baydar, *Negotiating Domesticity: Spatial Productions of Gender in Modern Architecture* (London: Routledge, 2005), 1–29.
18 Bradford, '"We Women Will Show Them": Beer Protests in the Natal Countryside, 1929,' 211.
19 Sadler, 'Trouble Was Brewing,' 34.
20 The protests were not spontaneous events, but rather the climax of tensions and resistances mounted since the passage of the 1928 Liquor Act. See Bradford, '"We Women Will Show Them": Beer Protests in the Natal Countryside, 1929'; Sadler, 'Trouble Was Brewing,' 1–2.
21 'Durban Beer Halls Closed After Riots,' *New York Times*, June 21, 1959.
22 Sadler, 'Trouble Was Brewing,' 112.
23 Testimony of Ruth Shabane at Round Table Sports Ground, Cato Manner, July 18, 1959, quoted in Sadler, 'Trouble Was Brewing,' 104.
24 McClintock, *Imperial Leather: Race, Gender, and Sexuality in the Colonial Contest*, 386.
25 Sarah Thurman, 'Umzamo: Improving Hostel Dwellers' Accommodation in South Africa,' *Environment and Urbanization* 9, no. 2 (October 1, 1997): 59.
26 Iain Edwards, 'Cato Manor: Cruel Past, Pivotal Future,' *Review of African Political Economy* 21, no. 61 (1994): 420–421; Sadler, 'Trouble Was Brewing,' 104.
27 Iain Edwards, 'Dr. Iain Edwards on Cato Manor,' n.d., 47991/2 Cato Manor General (Info), Old Court House Museum (Durban).
28 Sadler, 'Trouble Was Brewing,' 49.
29 Reed, 'Women's Revolts in Natal: 1959.'
30 Lefebvre, *The Production of Space*.
31 A partial bibliography of the hostel upgrading includes Julian Cooke, 'Lessons from an Upgrade Project in Migrant Labour Hostels,' *Architecture South Africa*, September/October (1993): 24–27; Julian Cooke, 'Housing,' *SA Architect*, November/December (1999): 18–25; Julian Cooke, 'High-Density Low-Cost Housing: Cape Town Cape Flats,' *Architecture South Africa*, November/December (2005): 20–25; Thurman, 'Umzamo.'
32 During the 1980s, factories were intense sites of anti-apartheid action. However, the hostel dwellers' right to live in the city was precariously tied to their employment: if they lost their job, they lost their pass. Making claims around the living conditions of the hostels was a 'safe' way of resisting apartheid. This was explained by Susan Liebermann in an interview on June 27, 2012. The likelihood that those inclined to participate in trade union activities would participate in the Hostel Dwellers Association is also explained in Mamphela Ramphele, *A Bed Called Home: Life in the Migrant Labour Hostels of Cape Town* (Cape Town: David Philip, 1993), 90–91.
33 Ramphele, *A Bed Called Home*, 60–62.
34 Thurman, 'Umzamo.'
35 The claim that the upgrading was male-dominated reflects the gendered nature of the resident participants. While the architects were majority male, the professionals

involved were conscious of and tried to mediate gender disparities. Additionally, the architects' attention to the domestic realm fits in with traditions of the Modern Movement, as argued by Heynen, 'Modernity and Domesticity: Tensions and Contradictions,' 15.

36 Sharone Tomer, '"After" Modernism: Architectural Articulations of Apartheid's End in Cape Town' (PhD dissertation, University of California, Berkeley, 2016).

37 Ramphele, *A Bed Called Home*, 92; Thurman, 'Umzamo,' 59–60.

38 Owen Crankshaw and Susan Parnell, 'Interpreting the 1994 African Township Landscape,' in *Blank: Architecture, Apartheid and After*, eds. Hilton Judin and Ivan Vladislavic (Rotterdam: NAi Publishers, 1998), 438–443.

39 Reproductive labor is a Marxian term, distinguishing economic labor – that work which generates income through the production of goods or services – from the labor which quite literally reproduces society. Reproductive labor is typically thought to include domestic work such as cooking, cleaning and caring for children and family members, and as such was commonly historically assigned to women. For an example of the spatiality of reproductive labor, see Silvia Federici, *Revolution at Point Zero: Housework, Reproduction, and Feminist Struggle* (Oakland: PM Press, 2012).

40 For discussion of topics related to care, see Nancy Chodorow, 'Excerpts from "Why Women Mother,"' in *Gender Space Architecture : An Interdisciplinary Introduction*, ed. Jane Rendell, Barbara Penner, and Iain Borden (London: Routledge, 2000), 56–59.

41 Carin Smuts, Interview, July 6, 2012.

42 Pierre Frey and François Hauter, *CS Studio Architects: Carin Smuts, Urs Schmid: Anatomy of a Dream* (Arles: Actes sud, 2016).

43 Carin Smuts, 'An African Approach: A Market and Some Bathhouses,' *Architecture SA*, March (1998): 44–49.

44 Smuts, Interview.

45 'Gugulethu Central Market,' *Digest of South African Architecture* 3 (1999): 42–47.

46 Alice T. Friedman, *Women and the Making of the Modern House: A Social and Architectural History* (New Haven: Yale University Press, 2006), 16, emphasis added.

47 Friedman, *Women and the Making of the Modern House*, 16.

48 Dolores Hayden, *The Grand Domestic Revolution: A History of Feminist Designs for American Homes, Neighborhoods, and Cities* (Cambridge, MA: The MIT Press, 1981), 3.

49 Lesley Naa Norle Lokko, *White Papers, Black Marks: Architecture, Race, Culture* (London: Athlone Press, 2000), 15–16 (emphasis added).

50 Lokko, *White Papers, Black Marks*, 14–16; Gülsüm Baydar Nalbantoğlu, 'Toward Postcolonial Openings: Rereading Sir Banister Fletcher's "History of Architecture,"' *Assemblage* April, no. 35 (1998): 6–17.

51 Lindsay Bremner, *Writing the City into Being: Essays on Johannesburg 1998-2008* (Johannesburg: Fourthwall Books, 2010), 25. For discussions of the ambitions of cities of the Global South, see Susan Parnell and Sophie Oldfield, eds., *The Routledge Handbook on Cities of the Global South* (London: Routledge, 2014); Saskia Sassen, *The Global City: New York, London, Tokyo* (Princeton: Princeton University Press, 1991).

52 This rejection aligns with the framework of 'ordinary cities' as opposed to 'global cities' as seen in Jennifer Robinson, *Ordinary Cities: Between Modernity and Development* (London: Routledge, 2006).

53 South African cities' 'world class' ambitions are discussed by David A. McDonald, *World City Syndrome : Neoliberalism and Inequality in Cape Town*, Routledge Studies in Human Geography 18 (New York: Routledge, 2008); Martin J. Murray, *Taming the Disorderly City : The Spatial Landscape of Johannesburg after Apartheid* (Ithaca: Cornell University Press, 2008).

54 Hilton Judin and Ivan Vladislavic, *Blank: Architecture, Apartheid and after* (Rotterdam: NAi Publishers, 1998).

55 Heynen, 'Modernity and Domesticity.'

56 Heynen, 'Modernity and Domesticity,' 2.

9

INROADS FOR THE OUTSOURCED

Call-center graveyard shifts and women's impact on the nocturnal streets of Mumbai, India

Aparna Parikh

'I'm just here. I'm smoking. How is that everyone's business?' – Anushi[1]

Anushi is a young woman working night shifts in an outsourced call center in Mumbai, India. The quotation above was a remark she made early in our conversation on the street outside a call center in Mumbai, India, in October 2015. Anushi was smoking during a break in her shift, and I was explaining my dissertation research to her, hoping she was willing to be interviewed for the same. Starting from Anushi's bewilderment, in this chapter I examine the political implications of decisions for leisure made by young women working graveyard shifts in outsourced call centers. I consider these decisions in tandem with strategies adopted by ongoing social movements in South Asia which counter patriarchal norms regulating women's access to urban public space. In doing this analysis, Anushi's presence and decisions become my 'business,' and the business of readers interested in her life and her world.

Women working night shifts in call centers conduct activities of leisure in Mumbai's urban public space during breaks and after their shifts. They do so while navigating societal concerns of safety, respectability and continued household responsibility.[2] Individually and in groups, numerous women and men engage in smoking while socializing outside call centers. These activities occur within a landscape that witnesses a vibrant informal economy supporting those working at night. Through these everyday acts, women appropriate the public realm, illustrating one aspect of Lefebvre's conception of the 'right to the city.' The other arm of the 'right to the city' is constituted by demands for a right to social and political participation. Such are the aims of ongoing social movements in South Asia, involved in asserting women's presence in public space. Placing everyday acts in conversation with these social movements, I show continuities in strategies across these realms, and highlight the entanglements between these differential approaches to paint a broader picture on gendered reclamations of urban public space.

This chapter is based on ten months of qualitative field-based research and document analysis. Part of a broader project, it includes data collected from participant observation on Mumbai's streets around call centers, primarily at night, and semi-structured interviews with forty women and twelve men who worked in call centers. These interviews occurred primarily on streets surrounding call centers during their break periods, as well as after shifts, and focused on interviewees' experiences of the city and decisions for leisure and commute. Additionally, I conducted a document analysis of social movements' websites, focusing on their stated goals, strategies for achieving them, and instances of success that they showcase.

The rest of this chapter begins with an overview of the scholarship that interweaves to guide this research, which includes insights on the 'right to the city' and appropriation of public space. Following this is an account of how women use and produce Mumbai's public space at night, through a focus on smoking as an individual and group activity. This is compared to the goals and strategies adopted by ongoing social movements in South Asia that aim to increase women's access to urban public space. Similarities in tactics across these spheres are analyzed, while differences in political motivations are highlighted. Through this analysis, I show the importance of considering everyday acts of urban appropriation in tandem with larger social movements, arguing that such consideration facilitates a broader understanding of gendered rights to the city.

Women's rights to the city

In French philosopher Henri Lefebvre's critique of everyday life, he has made important connections between social and spatial aspects that constitute the everyday, with important repercussions for understanding the urban built environment[3] and one's place within it. Regarding the latter, Lefebvre provocatively defined the right to the city as both 'a cry and a demand'[4] for spatializing the claim to political rights and re-scaling political belonging from the abstract, distant nation-state to the tangible, local urban polity. Such re-scaling is crucial given the growing importance the state accords to the urban in various global contexts under a neoliberal political economy, including in contemporary India.[5] In this realm, the urban becomes an important site to consider oppositional interventions of state-supported neoliberal growth and claims for public space under the aegis of rights to the city. In the case of Mumbai, as is the focus of this chapter, such tensions arise, among other places, in public spaces surrounding booming service industries. This sector forms an important facet of the neoliberal economy and, as such, is seen as a beacon for both Mumbai's and India's modernization.

Lefebvre's cry for rights to the city has been taken up across a spectrum of initiatives in places across the globe, from informal attempts at appropriation to institutional goals to instill 'urban policies that promote justice, sustainability, and inclusion in cities.'[6] In numerous cities, including Istanbul, Barcelona, and

New York, social movements, too, have been organized under the rallying cry of rights to the city.[7] Additionally, the right to the city has featured extensively in urban geographic and other critical scholarship.[8] Thus, this notion is taken up in numerous ways across academic, policy, and activist spheres.

The right to the city is conceived to include possibilities for participating in governance and transforming city-space. As critical geographer David Harvey has put it, the right to participation means 'to claim some kind of shaping power over the processes of urbanization, over the ways in which our cities are made and re-made and to do so in a fundamental and radical way.'[9] In India, discourses on participation are intertwined with larger urban social movements in South Asia. Some of these movements list among their stated goals the defiance of patriarchal norms for gendered mobility, the increase of women's presence in urban areas, and the improvement of women's ability to participate in urban governance.

The second, and more everyday focus in the right to the city canon is the physical appropriation of urban space. A central tenet in Lefebvre's conception of right to the city is the importance of 'use value of urban space over and above its exchange value.'[10] Through such a focus, Lefebvre prioritizes the experience of those inhabiting the city over capitalist valuations of urban fabric which emphasize real-estate and the exchange value of city-space, which in Mumbai is evidenced in growing property values near concentrations of the service sector. Building on Lefebvre's notion of right to the city, urban geographer Purcell[11] argues that appropriation can potentially provide a tactic to democratically reorient the city away from its status as an object and site of capitalist accumulation to a living urban fabric that serves as the stage for social and political life. A focus on inhabitation as physical appropriation helps move the right to the city beyond an oppositional claim to one that asserts its reality and viability through tangible presence.[12] This includes the rights of inhabitants to 'full and complete use of urban space in their everyday lives,'[13] encompassing their daily lives, and including aspects of production, social reproduction, and leisure. Fenster argues that the right to use and the right to belong are interweaved, and that

> belonging and attachment are built … on the base of accumulated knowledge, memory and intimate corporal experiences of everyday use, mainly by walking. Use of public space creates informal claims, which take place as part of the casual daily encounters between people or groups. It usually takes place when individuals wish to appropriate sections of public settings for various reasons, sometimes to achieve intimacy or anonymity or for social gatherings, mostly temporary.[14]

Within the paradigm of the 'right to the city,' certain scholars have brought to attention the need to consider experiences from a position of difference.[15] As Fenster has argued, 'the identification of the right to the city lacks sufficient attention to patriarchal power relations, which are ethnic, cultural and gender-related and as such it doesn't produce a practical standpoint.'[16] Addressing these gaps can help articulate uneven claims to city-space with an emphasis on populations who face systemic oppression. As groups who are least likely to have access, their experiences can help assess the effectiveness of claims-making efforts.

Gender is an important aspect of difference. Women have historically been systematically marginalized from public space in many different nations, including India.[17] In fact, historically, women have been symbolically aligned with the private realm, making their very presence antithetical to the public realm.[18] The idealized absence of women from public space is contested in numerous locations with differential outcomes and have become important avenues of exploring rights to the city. Feminist geographers have examined gendered power dynamics in myriad ways and focused on the 'relationship between gendered identities and constructed space.'[19]

For women working in India's call centers, the patriarchal norms that constrain their urban mobility are closely linked with their symbolic yet contradictory positioning within the modernizing nation-state. Historically, women's symbolic relation with the Indian nation-state manifested in two ways[20]: first, it entailed the feminization of the nation-state as a space that needs protection, and second, it placed the burden of upholding tradition and the reputation of the nation-state on the shoulders of women, particularly those belonging to the upper caste and middle class.[21] A failure to undertake such responsibility is often met with admonishment and even violence by men.

Women's movements in India have long sought to address this violence while also challenging imbued patriarchal expectations. Feminist scholar Shilpa Phadke[22] has provided a cogent overview of these movements. While feminist resistance was part of anti-colonial struggles as well, Phadke roots the contemporary iteration in a national report on the status of women in India published in 1974. This report displayed gender disparities and women's lack of representation in various sectors, which gave important backing to women's movements in the following years. These groups raised a range of issues, with a particular focus on violence against women – marked by a campaign against rape in the late 1970s, and against dowry[23] in the 1980s. These two decades marked an important shift in the perception of women from victims to enablers of change. Akin to other issues impacting women in India, numerous strategies were deployed to resist dowry and rape. Radha Kumar,[24] in her seminal work on women's social movements in India, has captured some epochal moments in these struggles and its manifestation in urban public space. In the case of dowry, these have included – amongst others – the 1979 demonstrations in New Delhi against the death of Tarvinder Kaur and of Kanchan Chopra. In both cases, the organizers claimed that their deaths were murders that occurred because of their parents' inability to meet her in-laws' dowry demands. In response to the latter case, a street play titled 'Om Swaha,' aimed at communicating issues surrounding dowry, was enacted at numerous locations. These demonstrations helped the issue gain political currency, even as legislative change occurred slowly. An important protest against rape took place in 1980 in response to judicial mishandling of what is known as the Mathura rape case. This protest was organized by Bombay's[25] feminist group entitled Forum Against Rape.[26] The group proposed a nationwide protest on International Women's Day to demand a retrial,[27] marking the first time feminist groups across the country were coordinating campaign efforts, even while fissures appeared fairly soon. While feminist groups – akin to their counterparts in various contexts – were contending against external patriarchal forces, they had internal fissures along the lines of class, religion, and caste.

While earlier issues continue to persist, women's movements in India since the 1990s also contend with the global forces of neoliberalism, whose advent has been marked with increasing market pressures and the rise of the political right. Within this milieu, upper-middle class populations – particularly women – gain symbolic visibility in the representation of the nation-state.[28] These women experience a paradoxical legitimacy in public life unmatched by their access to public space, which remains incomplete.[29] As such, women's role within a modernizing nation and its associated urbanism demonstrates a persistence of traditional patriarchal norms.[30] As I detail later on in the chapter, contemporary women's movements in India at various scales have attempted to counter these tendencies. Women's experiences of leisure and activism in public space are useful in articulating how a historically marginalized group sets the terms of their belonging and access to urban areas. Such a focus also helps articulate and challenge their symbolic and patriarchal association with the Indian nation-state.

Everyday appropriation of urban public space

As an outcome of neoliberal economic policies facilitating foreign investment, India has hosted numerous outsourced call centers since the 1990s. These are outsourced from the U.S. and other Western nations. India was favored as a destination because of low wages and a large population base with fluency in spoken English. The primary operating hours in call centers outsourced to India are at night, or during the graveyard shift, to suit daytime hours in the U.S. A large number of these call centers are concentrated in Mumbai. During interviews, call center managers used familiar stereotypes to explain their preferences for hiring women based on women's 'natural docility' and 'natural nurturing qualities' that make them well-suited for this kind of work. Women constitute 45 percent of the workforce in call centers, a higher gender ratio than any other jobs in the information technology (IT) sector in India, and they dominate the entry level positions while men dominate supervisory roles.[31]

This research focused on Malad, an area which houses a concentration of call centers in Mumbai and a surrounding network of eateries that are open all hours. This portion of the city has historically been peripheral to Mumbai's urban core. It was characterized by fishing villages and middle-class housing prior to the 1990s, but with the entry of outsourced call centers and associated real-estate transformations, the area came to symbolize the current phase of neoliberal investment in the city. The business park and IT hub of Mindspace Malad is an iconic representation of this new kind of Mumbai urbanism, characterized by glass and steel buildings edged with green lawns, with a security guard up front (Figure 9.1). These anonymous buildings are synonymous with the area and are indicative of the globalized architectural character of the city's modernization in the last two decades. In Mumbai, such architecture is not limited to Mindspace, and nor is Malad the first documented instance for such a built environment. Rather, the proliferation of this built environment marks its ascendance – its growing and pervasive presence in the city at large. Further, it is important to note that while individually fenced in, buildings in Mindspace Malad are not encased within a wider privatized development scheme. Instead, public streets intersect office buildings in Mindspace Malad, with call centers directly looking onto dense urban activity.

These streets have a high concentration of informal night-time activity (Figure 9.2). Such informal activity consists primarily of vendors selling food, beverages, and cigarettes. The vendors have a tenuous legal status, which prevents them from leaving their stalls and wares in place on public streets.

FIGURE 9.1 The built environment of Mindspace Malad, Mumbai

Source: Photograph by the author

FIGURE 9.2 Food stalls near call centers in Mumbai
Source: Photograph by the author

Instead, they set up their stalls anew each evening, otherwise storing their materials in nearby restaurants. Some vendors also have mobile carts or baskets that they carry atop their head, allowing them to circumvent legal spatial challenges. Food vendors set up shop on sidewalks closely adjoining compound walls of office buildings or on the street itself in the absence of a sidewalk. Their legal and spatial uncertainty contrasts with their pivotal role in providing affordable sustenance to call center employees. These eateries were also pivotal for conducting fieldwork, as they provided me with the opportunity to loiter without feeling awkward or seeming too conspicuous. Vendors at these eateries also served as informants providing valuable information about the functioning of the call center industry, and occasionally introduced me to the employees they were most familiar with, and whom they thought would be willing to be interviewed. Some of these vendors and employees had known each other for several years.

Women's leisure activities on the streets surrounding Mindspace Malad involved buying food and beverages from informal food vendors, socializing individually and in groups around these food stalls, and smoking and disposing of cigarettes. Smoking typically involved buying cigarettes from one of numerous *paanwalas*, or tobacco vendors, followed by borrowing a lighter from a *paanwala* or a colleague, or else availing of one hanging from a nearby tree (Figure 9.3).[32] The *paanwalas*, the employees who had lighters and the suspended lighters all became ephemeral focal points for a concentration of night-time social activity.

After lighting their cigarettes, some women and men socialized with strangers around the *paanwala*, while others stood in small clusters on the sidewalk and street adjacent to call centers (Figure 9.4). Thus, these women and men formed a temporary social group based on their shared activity of smoking. Others stood off by themselves, either busy on their smartphones or simply smoking. They used smoking as a way to have a private moment on an otherwise public street. These individual or 'private' acts of smoking typically occurred at some distance from the food vendors, often against compound walls and aluminum sheets that barricaded sites with ongoing construction activities.

The end of a smoking session was marked by a movement towards ashtrays. While some women and men disposed their cigarettes on the sidewalk or street, others utilized ashtrays located in crevices on the outside of compound walls. Similar to lighters, these mysteriously present ashtrays appeared to be a small insertion by people who subtly shaped the street in a manner that was conducive to their everyday activities. In the absence of an ashtray, some utilized for ashtrays glass mugs usually used for *chai* – an Indian drink made of tea leaves boiled with milk and sugar, and often containing a range of spices. The assistant of the *chaiwala*, or tea vendor, often a young child or an adolescent boy, would deliver *chai* ordered at the stall to employees on the sidewalk or street, in order to prevent an overcrowding at the stall itself. This *chai* was delivered in small glass mugs. On completion of their *chai*, the employees used this mug to dispose cigarette butts, and it was subsequently collected by the young delivery boy. These *chai* mugs were often lined up adjacent to the compound wall on the sidewalks, or in niches within compound walls. Similar to the suspended lighter, the glass mugs and ashtrays were innocuous urban elements that formed a part of employees' everyday routine as they came out for a smoke during breaks or after their shift. This description of individual and group activities of smoking is not aimed at suggesting its uniqueness in affording potential for socializing, but rather helps sketch the nightscape of leisure activities occurring around Mumbai's call centers.

FIGURE 9.3 Cigarette lighters suspended from a tree adjoining a call center in Mumbai
Source: Photograph by the author

The presence of young women smoking in urban public space at night is a political act on some levels and has symbolic value. The act of smoking, correlations between night work and smoking, and socializing through smoking came up at various points during interviews with research participants. Smoking was used as a shorthand to describe someone employed in a call center, particularly those working night shifts. This stereotype was presented in various ways. Call center employees deployed this stereotype to justify smoking. They argued that night-time work induced a unique type of stress that was relieved by

FIGURE 9.4 Women and men socializing in areas around call centers in Mumbai

Source: Photograph by the author

smoking. This stereotype was also used to identify call center employees. This was illustrated in a conversation with Piyush, with whom I was chatting outside a call center in Mindspace Malad:

Piyush: 'Look around you! Everyone you can see works in a call center.'

Me: 'I see. Is that because all the buildings around here are call centers?'

Piyush (impatiently): 'Ya ya. But *look* – you need to just look. Call center people will have IDs during breaks, and they will be smoking. If they come after [their] shifts, they may remove IDs, but they will still be smoking. Those women are always smoking – because they work in call centers.'

While Piyush pointed out both men and women to me, he focused on identifying women who worked in call centers through their act of smoking. Further, as Tirth, another research participant, remarked:

> Women – smoking – call center – night. That's all the same. If you see those ladies smoking, then they must be working at night in call centers. That's why I say, they should not work only in call centers. It's unhygienic. They don't have option. It's all peer pressure, and stress.

Oftentimes, within the same interview, I found both male and female research participants tussling in the direction of causality they made between call center work and smoking.

The relation between women smoking and working night shifts was inflected with morality. Morality became the linchpin to explain the role of the industry in 'spoiling young women,' as suggested in another remark by Tirth, who said: 'See what call centers have done to our girls.'[33] The state views outsourced call centers, along with various other multinational offices involved in service sector work, as ushering in an era of modernization in India. While such development is largely positively viewed, the negative effects of such modernization are suggested through the role of this industry in spoiling or corrupting the youth, especially young women. Such corruption occurs because modernization is purported to bring in vices that run counter to traditional Indian values, which women are to uphold through appropriate behavior.[34] In her work examining responses to beauty pageants in India, feminist scholar Rupal Oza similarly finds that women's act of smoking (or drinking) is associated with 'transgressive sexuality and the contamination by Western cultural influences made possible through globalization.'[35]

Women's act of smoking is seen as a deviation from appropriate behavior, a sign of being corrupt and making immoral decisions. While some of my research participants made disparaging comments about the presence of women in public space, they often pivoted or coalesced their criticism around women's activities of smoking to make broader claims about their morality. As such, research participants used smoking, made worse through its brazen display in urban public space, as a shorthand to describe broader trends of women's corruption brought about through their association with call centers.

By contrast, I also found a converse relation drawn between women smoking and the reputation of the industry, where seven of my twelve male research participants considered that young women tainted the reputation of the call center sector through acts of smoking in urban public space. This notion was suggested by a research participant who said: 'You know, 95 percent of women working in call centers smoke. No wonder the industry is so *badnaam* [infamous].' Irrespective of the direction of causality, urban women and their decisions for public leisure were intertwined with the process of modernization itself.

This chapter opened with a statement made by Anushi at the start of our interview. As our conversation unfolded, Anushi explained that she was not merely expressing her annoyance at me, but her question about smoking pointed to the broader context in which her presence in public space and role in the industry were constantly placed under scrutiny. While I point to instances where women socialize individually and in groups in Mumbai's urban public spaces, it is important to recognize the significance of these decisions within constraints posed by the symbolic weight attached to their presence. Whether as an outcome of call center work, or as resulting in the ill reputation of the call center industry, women's act of smoking continued to be stigmatized. Within this realm, the stigma against women smoking is indelibly tied to patriarchal concerns about their independence from the protective moral boundaries of the home and contaminating presence in urban public space, a domain traditionally assumed to be male. The presence of women smoking and pursuing other activities of leisure in urban public space thus challenge patriarchal notions restricting women's spatial access. Through these acts, women are asserting their rights to occupy city-space and to do so not merely as transients moving in between other places, but as independent social agents who claim the space as their own, loitering, chatting, and entertaining themselves, on their time and on their terms.

Social movements in South Asia

Young women who work night shifts in call centers contribute to shaping urban spaces in the Global South. These decisions involve struggle, and lead to a 'broad range of gendered practices and subjectivities.'[36] Such struggles are mirrored in ongoing social movements, which uphold women's ability to reclaim urban public space. These social movements are spurred by and aim to counter patriarchal norms that curtail women's mobility. An influential contemporary movement engaging with women's mobility in South Asia is entitled 'Why Loiter', grounded in conceptions proposed by feminist urbanists Shilpa Phadke, Sameera Khan, and Shilpa Ranade. They argue that loitering, as 'a suspicious performance of non-productivity,'[37] holds potential to disrupt discourses that forbid women from urban public space and provide ways for them to gain visibility through presence in such space. Why Loiter started as an academic research project and has since translated into a social movement. This social movement occurs through coordinated efforts between women on social media to deliberately 'loiter' in public spaces in an effort to temporarily claim them. I have followed this movement primarily through their blog for a duration of three years from 2014–17. Here, they post descriptions and photos of their activities, and reflect on the same.[38] For the past three years, their weekly loitering activities have occurred at night, with each event located in a different area within Mumbai. On a few occasions, they invited men for these walks. For these events, men were expected to cross-dress and 'walk like a woman,' as an act of solidarity with women and their experiences in the city.[39] While Why Loiter is coordinated and constituted mainly by middle-class women, its implementation has seen an occasional extension across class.

Similar movements have also occurred in New Delhi and Karachi. Pinjra Tod (break the hostel locks) was established in New Delhi about two years ago. This movement challenges curfews in women's hostels, arguing that these serve to curtail women's personal freedom in the name of their safety. Pinjra Tod aims to address restrictions on women, moral policing, creation of affordable housing, and implementation of anti-sexual harassment laws. Devangana Kalita, one of the founding members of Pinjra Tod, explains their motivation for the movement as follows:

> For far too long, women's personal freedom has been curtailed in the name of safety. State institutions and universities need to understand that they cannot protect women by undermining their autonomy. The campaign's name resonates with the situation women hostelers in different colleges and universities find themselves in today – 'big walls, huge metal gates, locking of gates at night, numerous security guards, constant checking of Id-cards, a plethora of arbitrary and regressive restrictions.' The idea is to raise our voices against it.[40]

Pinja Tod has held numerous protests to give visibility to their cause. Members of this movement have also prepared a report outlining concerns of women living in hostels. This report was taken up by the Delhi Commission for Women, who issued a notice to all universities in Delhi to

> answer several questions including the number of students in hostel disaggregated by gender, a separate similar list of students with disabilities, the entry and exit time restrictions in the hostel (with reasons if there are differences in timings based in gender and the penalties on violating these times) and the annual hostel fees charged disaggregated by gender.[41]

As such, the Pinjra Tod movement has raised awareness and successfully taken steps to make universities answerable for gender bias. Pinjra Tod's cause is underpinned by an argument seeking greater freedom for women and improving their access to urban public space.

Girls at Dhabas took off in Karachi in 2015. This movement is constituted by feminists and women in Pakistan who wish to reclaim public space. It involves women going to *dhabas*, street- and highway-side restaurants, and posting a selfie or photo of this event on social media using the hashtag #GirlsatDhabas. This movement was started by a group of young women who were motivated to see women occupy spaces they were traditionally thought not to occupy. Like my research participants in Malad, this collective found that women often do not occupy spaces where they are unlikely to see other women. Shafi, one of the organizers of Girls at Dhabas, explains that:

> We [women] don't even allow ourselves to consider the possibility of going out alone, let alone sitting at a *dhaba* alone. It isn't like *dhabas* and

> other public sites specifically say 'Women not allowed' and it isn't like once a woman is there (usually with her family or husband or male chaperon) she is made to feel uncomfortable, but the way men outnumber women in public spaces says a lot. The disproportion is outrageous, even disturbing. It is also equally important how a space is occupied, and you will see that men in Karachi's public spaces (parks, *dhabas*, bus stops) behave very differently from women. They will linger, smoke, talk to each other, move around the space comfortably. Women will stand on edge, constantly adjust their *dupattas*, try to get out of the open space into a confined 'safe' interior (like a bus or car) as soon as possible.[42]

While these movements have emerged independently, they have since engaged in social media conversations and exchanged strategies for claiming access to urban public space. For example, Phadke reached out to Girls At Dhabas on Facebook, following which one of the organizers read *Why Loiter?*, the book co-written by Phadke, Khan, and Ranade.

A primary goal of the social movements described above is to highlight restrictions women face in public space and increase their access to urban areas. These movements aim to create conditions where women can make decisions for their bodies and mobility in urban areas. While sharing concerns about women's mobility, such movements differ from social movements exclusively seeking women's safety in urban areas. A call for safety was emphatically voiced in a large-scale movement that took place on January 21, 2017 across thirty Indian cities. This social movement was in solidarity with the U.S. Women's March but emerged independently in response to mass violence against women in Bangalore on December 31, 2016. The protests were titled #IWillGoOut and their momentum derived largely from social media conversations, which translated into women and some men taking to public space with signs and demands.[43] These signs were in numerous languages, including some which said, 'The day is ours, so is the night,' and 'Reclaim the night.'[44] The movement also included a petition which demanded safety, the ability to exist in public space, and greater accountability for men who threaten the wellbeing of women.[45] Organizers of some of the aforementioned social movements focusing on freedom also participated in the #IWillGoOut movement. It is important to note that women's safety and freedom are not dichotomous concerns. The state and society often respond to calls for safety through increased supervision of women in public space.[46] Such supervision can in fact curtail women's mobility and autonomy. Hence, movements for safety have often resulted in outcomes contradictory with its aims, even as they bring greater visibility to concerns around women's right to the city.

Between appropriation and participation

> Therein lies the problem: one moment leads to other moments, and a politics of encounter explodes when moments collide, collide on the

> street. Yet how to sustain the intensity of the encounter, how to harmonize it with a contentious political evolution, with an authentic politics of transformation? How to ensure that this moment in everyday life – this spontaneous lived moment – assumes a mutation of world historical significance? Nobody can answer the question in advance; nor are there any preconceived formulas for success. What's evident, though, is how any moment of encounter will likely be a kind of process without a subject, spreading rapidly like wildfire … [p]articipants will congeal not only as a singularity sharing their passion and affirming their hopes, but as a force that creates its own historical space.[47]

As the quotation above suggests, it is difficult to provide a formulaic predictor to sustain the intensity of the encounter or its translation into something that holds lasting significance. Despite such uncertainty, the encounter is considered important and holds potential to form a historically transformative space. Transposing this conception of the encounter to my case, I similarly recognize the challenges of considering the long-term transformative potential of women's everyday appropriation of urban public space through their leisure activities. Despite this note of caution, I contend that these activities and their consideration in tandem with ongoing social movements hold potential to challenge patriarchal tendencies that constrain women's mobility and ability to participate in urban life.

The various facets involved in smoking help to explain women's use and production of public space in the city. These activities, and their roles in transforming urban areas, should be understood in light of stigma faced by women. Such stigmatization is shaped by patriarchal discourses that ascribe a conforming symbolic place for women within the modernizing nation-state. This expected conformity circumscribes their behavior, and in some instances, extends to their absence from the public domain.[48] The women whose activities I document counter an expected adherence to such patriarchal symbolism. These women benefit from social movements that seek to challenge patriarchal constraints. While efforts of such movements are incremental, they aim to shift societal discourse, which I posit can serve to normalize the presence of various women in the city, including those working night shifts in call centers.

There are multiple ongoing social movements in South Asia that aim to increase women's visibility in public space and foster their role as political actors who can participate in conversations about their autonomy and their safety. As I show, such movements straddle between appropriation and participation, as is construed within the 'right to the city' canon. Within these movements, some are incremental and long-term, such as Pinjra Tod, Why Loiter and Girls at Dhabas, while others are intensely energetic but short-lived, such as #IWillGoOut. The former set of movements called for women's *azaadi*, or freedom, while the refrain in the latter was focused primarily on safety. These are distinct calls, and while they can serve to reinforce one another in improving women's visibility, they can also, as noted above, compete with one another.[49] The apparent playfulness of the former set of movements serves to conceal their importance in attempting to improve women's sense of comfort and belonging in accessing public space for purposes of leisure. I argue that such social movements serve to validate women's decision-making for leisure while working night shifts in call centers. These women further the use value of urban space, even while they contribute to the city as a site of capitalist accumulation, which harnesses the exchange value of city-space. A focus on these women explicates the struggle between exchange and use value as it plays through the spatialization of their everyday activities, even while being attentive to the contradictions inherent in their presence. For this reason, when Anushi smokes a cigarette, it is truly everybody's business.

Notes

1 All names throughout this chapter are pseudonyms.
2 Aparna Parikh, 'Politics of Presence: Women's Safety and Respectability at Night in Mumbai, India,' *Gender, Place & Culture* 25(5) (2018): 695–710; Aparna Parikh, 'Gendered Household Expectations: Neoliberal Policies, Graveyard Shifts, and Women's Responsibilities in Mumbai, India,' in Alexandra Staub (ed.) *The Routledge Companion to Modernity, Space and Gender* (New York: Routledge, 2018), 367–379.
3 Nathaniel Coleman, *Lefebvre for Architects* (London and New York: Routledge, 2014), https://doi.org/10.4324/9781315736549
4 Henri Lefebvre, 'The Right to the City,' in E. Kofman and E. Lebas (eds) Writings on Cities, (London: Blackwell, 1996), 63–184.
1967, 58 cited in Neil Brenner et al., Cities for People, Not for Profit: Critical Urban Theory and the Right to the City (Routledge, 2012), 29.
5 Leela Fernandes, 'The Politics of Forgetting: Class Politics, State Power and the Restructuring of Urban Space in India,' *Urban Studies* 41, no. 12 (November 1, 2004): 2415–2430, https://doi.org/10.1080/00420980412331297609
6 Mark Purcell, 'Possible Worlds: Henri Lefebvre and the Right to the City,' *Journal of Urban Affairs* 36, no. 1 (2014): 141.
7 Francesca Perry, 'Right to the City: Can This Growing Social Movement Win over City Officials?,' *The Guardian*, April 19, 2016, www.theguardian.com/cities/2016/apr/19/right-city-social-movement-transforming-urban-space
8 Mark Purcell, 'Excavating Lefebvre: The Right to the City and Its Urban Politics of the Inhabitant,' *GeoJournal* 58, no. 2–3 (2002): 99–108; Don Mitchell, *The Right to the City: Social Justice and the Fight for Public Space* (New York: Guilford Press, 2003); David Harvey, 'The Right to the City,' *The City Reader* 6 (2008): 23–40; Kafui A. Attoh, 'What Kind of Right Is the Right to the City?,' *Progress in Human Geography* 35, no. 5 (2011): 669–685; Margit Mayer, 'The 'Right to the City' in the Context of Shifting Mottos of Urban Social Movements,' *City* 13, no. 2–3 (2009): 362–374; Tovi Fenster, 'The Right to the Gendered City: Different Formations of Belonging in Everyday Life,' *Journal of Gender Studies* 14, no. 3 (2005): 217–231.
9 Harvey, 'The Right to the City,' 2.
10 Purcell, 'Possible Worlds,' 142.
11 Purcell, 'Possible Worlds,' 149.
12 Attoh, 'What Kind of Right Is the Right to the City?'
13 Fenster, 'The Right to the Gendered City,' 219.
14 Fenster, 'The Right to the Gendered City,' 222–223.
15 Fenster, 'The Right to the Gendered City'; Tony Roshan Samara, Shenjing He, and Guo Chen, *Locating Right to the City in the Global South*, vol. 43 (London and New York: Routledge, 2013); Gautam Bhan, '"This Is No Longer the City I Once

Knew". Evictions, the Urban Poor and the Right to the City in Millennial Delhi,' *Environment and Urbanization* 21, no. 1 (2009): 127–142.

16 Fenster, 'The Right to the Gendered City,' 217.

17 Lynn A. Staeheli, 'Publicity, Privacy, and Women's Political Action,' *Environment and Planning D: Society and Space* 14, no. 5 (1996): 601–619, https://doi.org/10.1068/d140601

18 Melissa Wright, *Disposable Women and Other Myths of Globalization* (London: Taylor and Francis, 2006).

19 Nancy Fraser, "Rethinking the Public Sphere: A Contribution to the Critique of Actually Existing Democracy," Social Text 25/26: 56–80., cited in Nazgol Bagheri, 'Mapping Women in Tehran's Public Spaces: A Geo-Visualization Perspective,' *Gender, Place & Culture* 21, no. 10 (2014): 1286.

20 Mrinalini Sinha, 'Refashioning Mother India: Feminism and Nationalism in Late-Colonial India,' *Feminist Studies* 26, no. 3 (2000): 623–644, https://doi.org/10.2307/3178643

21 Lower-class and caste women and men are rendered invisible in the narratives of the nation-state and urban, and occupy a position of difference that warrants discussion, but this is not within the scope of this chapter.

22 Shilpa Phadke, 'Thirty Years On: Women's Studies Reflects on the Women's Movement,' *Economic and Political Weekly* 38, no. 43 (2003): 4567–4576.

23 Dowry is a patriarchal practice where a bride's family pays a 'wedding gift' to the groom's family to consolidate the marriage. A bride's family often goes into intergenerational debts trying to raise a dowry. When brides' families are unable to procure the dowry, or the price is deemed unsatisfactory, women face harassment from their husband and in-laws. Such harassment has often resulted in murder of or suicides by women. Banned by the Indian state in 1961, this practice continues to prevail and has had some resurgence under contemporary modernization.

24 Radha Kumar, *The History of Doing: An Illustrated Account of Movements for Women's Rights and Feminism in India 1800–1990* (New Delhi: Zubaan, 1997).

25 Now Mumbai.

26 Now Forum Against Oppression of Women.

27 It is important to note that it was only after preparations were well under way that the members from the Bombay-based feminist group conferred with Mathura to find out her views on the protest and confirm her assent of the same. She provided her assent, but the organizers were ashamed that they had not asked for her consent or views earlier on.

28 Leela Fernandes, 'Nationalizing 'the Global': Media Images, Cultural Politics and the Middle Class in India,' *Media, Culture & Society* 22, no. 5 (September 1, 2000): 611–628, https://doi.org/10.1177/016344300022005005

29 Shilpa Phadke, 'Dangerous Liaisons: Women and Men: Risk and Reputation in Mumbai,' *Economic and Political Weekly*, 2007, 1510–1518.

30 Parikh, 'Politics of Presence.'

31 Dipa Dube et al., 'Women in BPO Sector in India: A Study of Individual Aspirations and Environmental Challenges,' *Asian Social Science* 8, no. 7 (2012): 157; Randeep Sudan, *The Global Opportunity in IT-Based Services: Assessing and Enhancing Country Competitiveness* (Washington, DC: World Bank Publications, 2010).

32 Literally defined, a *paanwala* is a betel leaf seller. Most *paanwalas* in India operate a small stall or push cart, and sell betel leaf with areca nuts, as well as cigarettes, mints, and occasionally small packaged snacks as well; I noticed lighters suspended from some tree branches on streets around call centers. I asked numerous people who had put up the lighters, and no one knew for sure. Some speculated that it was either a *paanwala* who wished to prevent overwhelming crowd at his stall during every break, while others thought it was an employee who did not want their families to find out that they smoked, and potentially considered that the best way to

store their lighters was to suspend them from a tree branch outside their office. This allowed them to access the lighters on an everyday basis while letting other people use them as well.

33 '*Dekho yeh* call centers *ne kya kiya hai hamaari ladkiyon ko*.' Translation by the author.

34 Smitha Radhakrishnan, 'Professional Women, Good Families: Respectable Femininity and the Cultural Politics of a "New" India,' *Qualitative Sociology* 32, no. 2 (2009): 195–212.

35 Rupal Oza, 'Showcasing India: Gender, Geography, and Globalization,' *Signs: Journal of Women in Culture and Society* 26, no. 4 (2001): 1085.

36 Linda Peake and Martina Rieker, 'Rethinking Feminist Interventions Into the Urban,' in *idem, Interrogating Feminist Understandings of the Urban* (London and new York: Routledge, 2013), 6.

37 Shilpa Phadke, Sameera Khan, and Shilpa Ranade, *Why Loiter?: Women and Risk on Mumbai Streets* (Nee Delhi: Penguin Books India, 2011), 192.

38 Devina Kapoor, 'Why Loiter Exactly?' *Why Loiter* (blog), August 4, 2014, http://whyloiter.blogspot.com/2014/08/why-loiter-exactly.html

39 Japleen Pasricha, 'Walk Like A Woman! Men Wear Women's Clothes to Support Why Loiter,' *Feminism in India* (blog), April 6, 2015, https://feminisminindia.com/2015/04/06/walk-like-a-woman-men-wear-womens-clothes-to-support-why-loiter/

40 Shikha Sharma, 'Pinjra Tod: Student Campaign Exhorts Women to Oppose "Sexist" Hostel Rules,' *The Indian Express*, September 22, 2015, http://indianexpress.com/article/cities/delhi/pinjra-tod-student-campaign-exhorts-women-to-oppose-sexist-hostel-rules/

41 Jahnavi Sen, 'The Pinjra Tod Movement: DCW Issues Notice to Universities on Gender Biased Hostel Rules,' *The Wire* (blog), May 9, 2016, https://thewire.in/34782/the-pinjra-tod-movement-dcw-issues-notice-to-universities-on-gender-biased-hostel-rules/

42 Afshan Shafi, 'Spotlight: Girls at Dhabas,' *The Missing Slate*, March 24, 2016, http://themissingslate.com/2016/03/24/girls-at-dhabas/

43 Maanvi, '#IWillGoOut Because I Can and I Want To: Women Storm Delhi Streets,' *The Quint*, January 21, 2017, www.thequint.com/women/2017/01/21/iwillgoout-because-i-can-and-i-want-to-women-storm-delhi-streets-march-solidarity-feminism-jantar-mantar; Shilpa Phadke, 'Freedom: Without Binaries, without Borders,' *Live-Mint*, February 3, 2017, www.livemint.com/Politics/F1X2jekyLSMHLAwbgf9FLL/Freedom-without-binaries-without-borders.html; Huizhong Wu, 'Furious Women in India Fight Back,' *CNN*, January 27, 2017, www.cnn.com/2017/01/26/asia/india-march-i-will-go-out/index.html

44 Scroll Staff, 'From Bengaluru to Silchar: Women across India Join "I Will Go Out" Marches,' *Scroll.In*, January 22, 2017, https://scroll.in/article/827352/from-bengaluru-to-silchar-women-across-india-join-i-will-go-out-marches

45 Swasti Chatterjee, '#IWillGoOut, Say Pune Women – Times of India,' *The Times of India*, February 3, 2017, http://timesofindia.indiatimes.com/city/pune/iwillgoout-say-pune-women/articleshow/56956483.cms

46 Parikh, 'Politics of Presence.'

47 Andy Merrifield, 'The Right to the City and beyond: Notes on a Lefebvrian Re-Conceptualization,' *City* 15, no. 3–4 (2011): 480.

48 Parikh, 'Politics of Presence.'

49 Parikh, 'Politics of Presence.'

INDEX